Myrna Rosen and Lesley Loon's

SOUTH AFRICAN GOURMET FOOD AND WINE

DORRANCE PUBLISHING CO., INC.
PITTSBURGH, PENNSYLVANIA 15222

The following companies provided props for the photo shoots in South Africa:
Block & Chisel, Cape Town, South Africa
Indaba Curios, Cape Town, South Africa
Martha's Vineyard, Cape Town, South Africa
Stuttafords, Cape Town, South Africa
The Yellow Door, Cape Town, South Africa

ISBN # 0-8059-4187-8
Printed in the United States of America

Third Printing

For information or to order additional books, please write:
Dorrance Publishing Co., Inc.
643 Smithfield Street
Pittsburgh, Pennsylvania 15222
U.S.A.
Fax (412) 288-1786

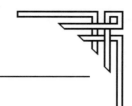

DEDICATION

I dedicate this book to the memory of my beloved parents, Mercia and Maurice Fine.

Myrna

I dedicate this book to my mother, Ethel Grayce, who nurtured my love for cooking and is always there to encourage and support me and to the memory of my beloved father, Jack Grayce.

Lesley

ACKNOWLEDGMENTS

It is mainly because of her extreme capability, her love of cooking, the encouragement, devotion and inspiration that my friend and partner, Lesley Loon, has given to me that this third book has materialized. Thanks, Les, I think we have done a great job and above all, so enjoyed working together!

Myrna

To be asked by Myrna Rosen, a gourmet cook of international repute to co-author this book, is both flattering and exciting. Myrna brings to the table (excuse the pun) such a marvelous reputation and delicate talent that I am sure all who read this book will not only enjoy this adventure, but will provide their guests a culinary experience second to none. Thank you Myrna, for giving me the opportunity of a lifetime—to cook with you!

Lesley

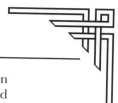

ACKNOWLEDGMENTS

A very special thanks goes to KWV, and Janette Wiehahn, S.A.; Mr. Ken Onish, U.S.A. and Sainsbury & Co., Canada, for their contribution and commitment.

Myrna and Lesley

As always, my most sincere thanks to my South African friends and loyal supporters, scattered all over the USA and Australia, whose praise and adulation have always given me the inspiration and determination to do yet another book.

I never do anything without feeling in my heart how proud my parents, Mercia and Maurice Fine would have been; they were such special people who have filled my life with wonderful memories and an appreciation of their great sense of compassion and generosity as well as the inspiration to fulfill my goals. They will always be shining examples for me; and in honor of their memory, we intend to donate a portion of the proceeds of this book to cancer research.

Myrna

Sincere thanks to our very special friends and family who have been so willing to share their recipes with us and especially Ethel Grayce who helped us in the preparation of the desserts for the photographs.

Myrna and Lesley

A very special thanks to our husbands, Ron Rosen and Martin Loon, and our children Desiree, Dean, and Samantha Rosen and Toni, Carla, Anton, and Cindy Loon for their love, support, and encouragement.

Myrna and Lesley

A special thanks to Cindy Loon for so kindly sharing her talents and creating the graphics in this book.

Myrna and Lesley

CONTENTS

This is a book of not only traditional South African foods, but also international cuisine prepared with South African flair and presented in the style and manner that you would experience in South African homes of every description. From traditional family favorites to modern easy techniques to sophisticated entertaining, you will find a range of foods to suit every occasion and also experience something new and different.

SOUTH AFRICAN CUISINE

South Africa is a melting pot of different ethnic groups, just as is America. There is a wide selection of foods available such as Italian, Russian, Jewish, Greek, Portuguese, Dutch, German, English, African, Indian, and Malay, each of these contributing to South African traditional cuisine, which makes it so interesting and different. Recipes which the Dutch settlers, the Malay slaves, and the French Huguenots brought with them have all influenced the style and tradition of South African cuisine.

Whatever your taste in food, you are due to find bountiful fare in South Africa. Highlights are the fish at the coastal regions; the game meats; the good old South African steak houses, where their meats are marinated and chargrilled; the traditional South African "Braai" (barbecue) where one can sample Boerewors (Farmers' Sausage), Stywepap (a cornmeal mixture) served with gravy, Sosaties (Dutch Kebabs), Soutribbetjies (Lamb Ribs), any grilled fish or vegetables, or even Potjiekos (food cooked in a cast iron pot).

Generally speaking, South Africans are a nation of extremely accomplished chefs and cooks who have the skill, imagination, and availability of ingredients and fresh produce to provide a gastronomic experience to anyone who visits this land of sunshine and beauty.

The climate in South Africa, glorious as it is, dictates the lifestyle of the people, and entertaining outdoors in the form of a Braai (barbecue) is an art that South African men have perfected. The meat is usually marinated and then chargrilled. Steaks, rump, top sirloin, and T-bone are the most popular. Chicken, fish, and a bounteous selection of salads are served to complete the meal.

Venison, ostrich, and other game meats are also available at various locations throughout the country, especially at the game reserves. South African wines and beers accompany the Braai. A selection of fresh fruits conclude the meal.

FOREWORD FROM KWV INTERNATIONAL

On the first Saturday of every February the who's who of the South African wine industry gather in KWV's Cathedral Cellar to commemorate the pressing of the first grapes at the Cape in 1657; or rather, to celebrate the vision of Jan van Riebeeck, first commander of the Dutch East India refreshment station, to introduce European grapes to Africa long before vineyards were established in other parts of the New World.

Riebeeck must have realised that the Cape offered a Mediterranean climate—cold, wet winters, but without severe frost, while the summers were long and hot, with a steady temperature. What varieties were used is still a matter of speculation, but it is generally believed that Muscadel, Chenin blanc (also referred to as Steen), and Muscat d'Alexandrie were among them. The Dutch, alas, had little knowledge of viticulture and an indifferent attitude to hygiene in the cellar. As could be expected the first grapes pressed in the shadow of Table Mountain yielded wine of dubious quality and as the passing ships provided a guaranteed (albeit captured) market, there was little reason to improve.

Twenty-five years later the altogether more sophisticated and cultured Simon van der Stel was given command of the Cape and on arrival acquired for himself the land and other symbols of wealth which he deemed suitable for his position. This included a fertile, cool valley about twelve miles from the Cape Town Castle and here he started applying principles like allowing pressing only when the grapes were fully ripe, dusting the bunches and destalking the berries to reduce some of the harsh tannins present in most Cape wines at the time. He also stressed the general importance of orderliness and cleanliness in the cellar and during transportation. These ultimately led to the production of the premium sweet wine, probably from Muscat d'Frontignac and Pontac, on which his farm Groot Constantia later established its worldwide reputation. The graceful Cape-Dutch homestead and surrounding farmland—regarded as the Cradle of the South African wine industry—is a national monument and has become one of Cape Town's premier tourist attractions.

Van der Stel, a curious mixture of self-interest and altruism, ensured though that the main object for settling at the Cape was not forgotten; he decreed that for every morgen of grapes planted, six morgen of other crops should be planted. But it was clear from the start that wine-farming had an attraction that no other crop was able to provide. As former company officials were settled well outside the environs of the Cape, the preference was for making wine which could be sold to the Dutch East India Company. During Van der Stel's time Stellenbosch (a colonists' settlement conceived and nurtured by himself) and subsequently also Paarl, Drakenstein, and Franschhoek became major viticultural and cultural areas. By the mid-1680s 75 percent of the vines at the Cape were owned by Free Burghers and the new affluence became evident in the splendid homesteads which have become a feature of the winelands.

Of great assistance to the newly established colony—and of special importance for the quality of its wines—was the arrival of 200 French Huguenots who emigrated through Holland to the Cape with the assistance of the Dutch East India Company. They were settled at Franschhoek and as they were hard-working and skilled in many trades, including wine-making, France's loss became the Cape's gain. Huguenot names like De Villiers, Du Toit, Malherbe, Le Roux, and Hugo have become intertwined with Cape wine. Today, Franschhoek is an important tourist destination, bristling with restaurants still quaintly French and with an active circle of chefs.

The British occupation in 1814—partly a prophylactic measure against the effects of the revolution in France and its consequences on a Dutch colony, and finally because of Napoleon's escapades and the capitulation of the Dutch—also played a substantial part in the improvement of agriculture. English consumers attached to the squadron at the Cape—and later also the British export market—were much more meticulous in their demands, and this led to a gradual improvement in vineyard and cellar conditions. Trellising became common and a smaller percentage of the leaves and stalks were crushed with the grapes. The market for wine was also vastly increased; by 1825 production at the Cape reached an apex of 13.6 million liters, more than 30 million vines had been planted, and some 30,00 people were directly involved in the wine industry.

Vivid accounts of daily life on a Cape wine farm came from Lady Anne Barnard, wife of the Secretary to the British Governor, who was a great friend of Hendrik Cloete of Groot Constantia.

"Mynheer Cloete took us to the wine press hall," she wrote, "where the whole of our party made wry faces at the idea of drinking wine that had been pressed by three pairs of black feet; but the certainty that the fermentation would carry off every polluted article settled that object with me."

The wines had a rich, almost syrupy quality, as Cloete's practices included twisting the branches of the vines to stem the flow of nutrients to the clusters, thus concentrating the flavor and sugar content of the grapes. These unfortified dessert-type Constantia wines pleased the palates of emperors, kings, and aristocrats all over the world and were acclaimed as the best ever made from any of the New World vineyards.

However, by this time the descent of peace over Europe was slowly starting to affect the fortunes of Cape wine farmers. Trafalgar broke the French sea power, Russia broke the army, Waterloo broke Napoleon. As trading relations between Britain and France were resumed, so were French wine exports to Britain. The supply of British revenue to the Cape dried up and the wine lands became an industry without an overseas market. By the middle of the nineteenth century the decline in export business was so significant that a general feeling of despondency prevailed throughout the industry.

The discovery of diamonds and gold and the influx of fortune hunters, with the high consumption accompanying such enterprises, came as a windfall of sorts. "Exports" to the wild interior provided an adequate market for Cape wines and especially for the rough Cape brandy of the time, called Cape Smoke.

Then nature struck. Up to then the Cape wine farmers' concerns were mainly about politics and the state of commerce. Apart from oïdium, a rustlike fungus which was relatively easy to control, nature played along until phylloxera, the parasitic insect that feeds off the roots of the vines and devastates them within a few weeks, reached the Cape via Europe.

But the local industry recovered relatively easily, as by the time the disease took to reach the Cape, it had already been discovered that vines could be rendered phylloxera-free by grafting them onto resistant American rootstock. An ironic twist was that the recovery was maybe too rapid and the recurring problem of overproduction was compounded by the collapse of the ostrich-feather market which brought many farmers back into the wine industry.

In 1916 farmers gathered in Paarl to try to save their industry from ruin. It led to the formation of a single representative organization—the KWV—which was to regulate the price of brandy and wine and to bring some order to the haphazardness.

A sophisticated system of origin was introduced in 1972. This certifies that the origin and contents of a bottle correlate to claims on the label and, in the case of South Africa's 70 some wine estates, wine has to be grown and made on the estate.

KWV

In the 75 years of its existence the KWV (acronym for the Dutch title) played a key role in the organized growth of the South African wine industry. Apart from directives on market-related pricing, it provides expert advice to wine farmers and runs extensive cellar facilities at its headquarters in Paarl, about 50 kilometers east of Cape Town. Selected yeasts, a variety of sophisticated presses, gleaming stainless steel tanks for fermentation at controlled temperatures, an enviable array of several thousand French oak maturation barrels, five lines for the swiftest bottling possible, and state-of-the-art quality control has been keeping the fine products of the Cape winelands at the center of the world arena.

Owing to the Mediterranean climate, French quality cultivars have taken to the Western Cape with ease. Bordeaux type blends from Cabernet Sauvignon, Merlot, and Cabernet franc are normally the flagships of their range, while excellent Shirazes, Cinsauts, or blends of these have become a Cape hallmark. There is a wide choice from quality white wines made from Chardonnay, Sauvignon blanc, Chenin blanc (also known as Steen), Cape Riesling, and Colombard. The KWV's luscious Noble Late Harvest botrytis wines never fail to astonish visitors.

KWV has won many international awards for its smooth, potstilled 5-, 10-, and even 20-year-old brandies and for its famous ports (fortified with pure brandy spirits), luscious heart-warming, full-sweet muscadels, and fine sherries. The dry sherries undergo flor treatment and then age in a solera; a complicated, triangularly stacked set of wooden barrels which can contain portions of sherry up to 80 years old. Roodeberg, a dry red wine made from Caberbet Sauvignon, Shiraz, Cinsaut, and Pinotage, has become a legend; the award winning, tangerine-based Van der Hum liqueur is unique. It is an amber colored blend of matured brandy, cloves, pimento, cinnamon, and the distillate of tangerine rind and sugar syrup. The flavor is distinctively tangerine, and there's an intriguing spicy aftertaste.

Climate

KWV's wines are mostly sourced from the hauntingly beautiful Western Cape, the undulating stretch of indigenous shrubbery, streaks of pine forest, and oak-lined vineyards between the sea and the first big mountains. It includes the famous Constantia valley, Durbanville on the cool and mist-shrouded west coast, the Berg River valley running along the Drakenstein Mountains, with Paarl as the pivotal town; and historical Stellenbosch with its Cape-Dutch architecture, oak-lined streets and bustling student pubs, and the western slopes of the Helderberg, the South African Côte d'Or, but for red wines.

The area's Mediterranean climate—cold, rain-soaked, wind-whipped winters and warm, dry summers moderated by breezes from the Atlantic and Indian Oceans—is ideal for quality production, as most vineyards can be grown without irrigation. Other wine-producing regions include the drier northern and eastern regions: the semi-desert Klein Karoo, arid, sun drenched cornucopia of sweet wines; the fertile Breede River valley with its wide stream languidly snaking through the towns of Worcester and Robertson; and the Olifants River region along the west coast and the Orange River valley skirting the Kalahari Desert which straddles the border with Namibia. These areas have larger differences between summer and winter temperatures and although some rain falls in summer, irrigation is still necessary and viticultural practices differ. But each region proudly boasts an individual style.

KWV Products

KWV International—a full subsidiary of KWV—markets high-quality wine and spirit products in more than 50 countries. The internationally known KWV brand and associated products are:

Wines
Cathedral Cellar Range
KWV Range
Springbok Range
Paarl Range (only available in Canada)
Cape Country Range

Brandies and Liqueurs
Paarl VSOP Brandy (Canada only)
KWV VSOP and 10-Year-Old Brandy
KWV Van der Hum Liqueur

KWV Ports and Sherries
Paarl Ports and Sherries
KWV Muscadel

LIST OF SUPPLIERS IN THE UNITED STATES AND CANADA OF SOUTH AFRICAN PRODUCTS

KWV Products available in the US from:

Cape Ventures Company
73 Tyler Drive
Stamford, CT 06903
Tel: 203-329-6623
Fax: 203-329-6663
http://www.capeventures.com

KWV Products available in Canada from:

Sainsbury & Co., Ltd.,
Suite 703, 2345 Yonge Street
Toronto, Ontario
Canada M4P2E5
Tel: 416-485-3000
Fax: 416-485-3633

Vintage Consultants Ltd.
#401 611 Alexander Street
Vancouver, B.C.
Canada V6A 1E1
Tel: 604-251-3366
Fax: 604-255-3841

Maison Remy et Associes
999 Boulevard de Maisonneuve Ouest
Bureau 560
Montreal, Quebec
Canada H3A 3L4
Tel: 514-285-8910
Fax: 514-285-8913

South African Products available from:

Protea Imports
PO Box 82069
420 Highway #7 East
Richmond Hill
Ontario L4B 3X2
Tel: 905-889-0993
Fax: 905-886-8597

The African Hut
1277 S. Coast Highway
Laguna Beach, CA 92651
Tel: 1-888-323-3889
Fax: 714-831-2974

African Traditions
Clive Botha
1-888-898-9463

KWV's Special Recipes

KWV 10-YEAR-OLD TRUFFLES

Yield: 25-30 truffles

5 Tbs (75 ml) cream
2 Tbs (30 ml) KWV 10-Year-Old Brandy
8 oz (250 g) dark chocolate
4 Tbs (60 ml) butter at room temperature
cocoa powder, sifted

Boil cream in a small saucepan until only 1½ Tbs (25 ml) remains. Remove from stove and stir in brandy and chocolate; return to stove and stir over low heat until chocolate has melted. Beat in butter. Transfer mixture to a shallow dish and refrigerate until set (about 30 minutes). Scoop out teaspoonfuls of mixture and roll into balls. Roll in sifted cocoa powder and refrigerate until needed.

Truffles can also be served after the dessert, with coffee.

KWV VAN DER HUM BANANA FLAMBÉ

Serves 6-8

3 cups (750 ml) orange juice (or peach juice)
12 bananas (or canned peaches)
2½ Tbs (35 ml) butter
½ cup (125 ml) KWV Van der Hum Liqueur
2½ Tbs (35 ml) Paarl or KWV VSOP or 10-Year-Old Brandy

Pour orange juice or peach juice into a flambé saucepan. Halve the bananas or peaches horizontally and add them to the orange (peach) juice. Heat to boiling point, remove from heat and add the butter and liqueur. Warm the brandy in a spoon over a flame and as it catches alight pour it over the fruit and serve it immediately as is, with whipped cream, or with ice cream.

KWV VAN DER HUM AND BRANDY MOUSSE

Serves 6

5 extra large eggs, separated
5 oz (125 g) castor sugar
1 Tbs (15 ml) KWV Van der Hum Liqueur
1½ Tbs (25 ml) KWV or Paarl VSOP brandy
1 Tbs (15 ml) gelatin
3½ Tbs (50 ml) cold water
2 cups (400 ml) crème Fraîche or fresh cream
extra fresh cream
cocoa powder

Beat egg yolks and castor sugar over steam until thick and creamy. Beat in KWV Van der Hum and brandy. Remove from heat.

Sprinkle gelatin over cold water, clarify over steam, allow to cool slightly, and beat into brandy mixture. Leave until cold. Beat crème Fraîche until stiff; whisk egg whites until stiff and carefully fold into the brandy mixture. Spoon into long-stemmed glasses and chill in refrigerator. Spoon a little fresh cream on top and sift cocoa powder over.

KWV VAN DER HUM MERINGUES

Yield: 2-3 dozen

4 egg whites
9 oz (225 g) castor sugar
2½ Tbs (40 ml) KWV Van der Hum Liqueur
¾ tsp (2½ ml) salt

Beat the egg whites and salt until stiff. Add the castor sugar gradually. Stir in the liqueur. Line a baking tray with greaseproof paper and spray with cooking spray to prevent the meringues from sticking.

Either spoon onto baking sheet or make use of piping bag. Bake in cool oven 250°F (120°C) for at least 5 hours.

HOT HONEY AND KWV VAN DER HUM SAUCE FOR ICE CREAM

2 Tbs (30 ml) honey
¼ cup (60 ml) KWV Van der Hum Liqueur
9 cherries and 4 walnuts finely chopped

Heat the above in a double-boiler until very hot. Serve over ice cream.

Plain Van der Hum can also be served over ice cream.

GLAZED ORANGES WITH KWV VAN DER HUM

Serves 6

6 whole oranges
¾ cup (200 ml) sugar
⅓ cup (100 ml) water
2 Tbs (30 ml) KWV Van der Hum Liqueur
1½ Tbs (25 ml) KWV 10-Year-Old Brandy

Peel oranges thinly, cut peels into strips, and simmer for 10 minutes in water. Drain well. Using a sharp knife, remove pith and center of oranges.

Dissolve sugar in water and boil for 5 minutes. Add rind and boil for 10 more minutes. Stir in liqueur and brandy.

Pour glaze over oranges and allow to cool before serving with chopped walnuts and whipped cream.

KWV VAN DER HUM SOUFFLÉ

Serves 6

4 eggs separated
1 cup (250 ml) castor sugar
grated rind of 1 orange
¾ cup (200 ml) orange juice
2 Tbs (30 ml) KWV Van der Hum Liqueur
1 Tbs (15 ml) gelatin
4 tsp (20 ml) 10-Year-Old Brandy
3½ Tbs (50 ml) cold water
1 cup (250 ml) cream, whipped
⅓ cup (100 g) dessicated coconut, toasted
whipping cream for garnishing

Beat egg yolks, sugar, orange rind and juice, Van der Hum, and brandy until light and creamy.

Soak gelatin in cold water and heat to dissolve. Stir into orange mixture and allow to set until the texture of egg white.

Whisk egg whites and carefully fold into orange mixture. Fold in whipped cream and pour into a prepared soufflé dish. Chill until set.

Garnish with coconut, cream, and fresh orange segments or canned mandarin oranges.

KWV VAN DER HUM CREAM DELIGHT

Yield: 2 drinks

crushed ice
fresh cream
castor sugar
2 tots (shots) KWV Van der Hum Liqueur

Frost the glasses in refrigerator. Put crushed ice in glasses. Fill with Van der Hum and top with cream which has been whipped with castor sugar. Sip through straws which have been cut in half.

KWV VAN DER HUM CHOCOLATE CHARLOTTE

Serves 6-8

½ lb (225 g) slab bitter chocolate
¼ (60 ml) cup milk
3 eggs, separated
pinch of salt
packet of sponge finger biscuits (cookies)
KWV Van der Hum Liqueur

Grate chocolate and melt in double-boiler with milk. When cool add well-beaten egg yolks. Fold in stiffly beaten whites of eggs and a pinch of salt. Steep the biscuits in a mixture of Van der Hum Liqueur and a little water. Arrange layers of biscuits each covered with chocolate mixture in a glass dish. Garnish with whipped cream, cherries, and chopped walnuts. Chill.

DON SIMON

A marvelous summer drink, or dessert, ideal with any meal. The dessert got its name because it was created as a tribute to Simon van der Stel.

Yield: 2 drinks

1⅓ cups (300 ml) vanilla ice cream, softened
3½ Tbs (50 ml) KWV 10-Year-Old Brandy or KWV Van der Hum Liqueur
a few drops coffee extract or 1 tsp (5 ml) instant coffee granules

Thoroughly mix all the ingredients. The texture should be firm, but fluid. Decorate with shaved chocolate (optional). Serve in a long-stemmed white wineglass, with a straw.

COFFEE ROYALE

Yield: 1 drink

¾ cup (200 ml) strong black coffee
sugar to taste
1 tsp (5 ml) KWV 10-Year-Old Brandy

Cream:
2 Tbs (25 ml) cream
1 tsp (5 ml) brandy

Mix coffee and sugar until dissolved. Pour into a glass or cup. Add brandy (do not stir). Whip cream and brandy together and pour onto coffee, over back of a spoon. Decorate with ground cinnamon or instant coffee granules and cinnamon stick.

KWV 10-YEAR-OLD BRANDY COFFEE

Yield: 2 cups

½ stick cinnamon
6 whole cloves
rind of 1 orange and 1 lemon, thinly sliced and cut into slivers
1½ Tbs (15-20 ml) sugar
½ cup (125 ml) brandy (or ¼ cup brandy and ¼ cup Van der Hum liqueur)
2 cups (500 ml) strong black coffee
cream, lightly whipped (optional)

Mix cinnamon, cloves, rind, sugar, and brandy. Cover and set aside for 2-3 hours. Heat through over low heat. Ignite and add hot coffee once the flames die down. Pour into cups through a small strainer and serve with or without whipped cream.

CHILLED SUMMER PUNCH

Yield: 8-10 drinks

½ cup (125 ml) brandy
½ cup (125 ml) KWV Van der Hum Liqueur
1 cup (250 ml) fresh fruit, cleaned, peeled, and cubed
3 cups (750 ml) white wine or sparkling wine
1½ cups (375 ml) soda water
ice cubes made from fresh fruit juice

Chill all ingredients, then combine brandy, liqueur, and fruit. Cover and chill for a few hours to allow flavors to mingle and fruit to absorb alcohol. Just before serving, add wine and soda water and plenty of fruit juice ice cubes. Garnish with fruit or herbs. Serve in chilled wineglasses.

BRANDY COCKTAIL

Yield: 10-12 drinks

2 cups (500 ml) KWV or Paarl VSOP brandy
1 cup (250 ml) KWV Van der Hum Liqueur
2 cups (500 ml) soda water
1 cup (250 ml) orange juice
2 cups (500 ml) dry wine (KWV, Paarl, or Springbok Sauvignon Blanc)
2 tsp (10 ml) Angostura bitters

Chill all ingredients and equipment before use.

Meanwhile, decorate glasses as follows: dip rims first in water, then in castor sugar and lightly shake off excess sugar.

Mix all ingredients in a large glass jug with plenty of ice cubes. Taste and add more soda water, if desired.

Pour into decorated glasses, decorate with lemon curls and serve.

South African Traditional Recipes

CHICKEN LIVERS PERI-PERI

Serves 10-12

1 lb (500 g) chicken livers
1 cup (250 ml) peri-peri oil or hot fire oil (available with Chinese ingredients) or chili oil
3 tomatoes
3 onions
1 pkg (25 g) onion soup

Fry livers in a few tablespoons of hot oil until browned. Chop tomatoes and onions. Fry in remaining hot oil. Add onion soup and browned livers. Add salt to taste.

Serve with hot French bread.

Ros Shuster
Johannesburg, South Africa

KWV Late Harvest or Paarl Golden Vintage or Groot Constantia Estate Weisser Riesling

CRAYFISH COCKTAIL

When you order a crayfish or shrimp cocktail in a restaurant in South Africa, this is the sauce with which the diced seafood is combined.

Serves 4

4 crayfish tails or lobster tails
(you may substitute imitation crab, poached grouper, cod loin, monkfish, or snapper)*

Boil tails in salted water for 25 minutes. Shell and cut into bite-sized chunks. Chill until ready to use.

Sauce:

1 cup (250 ml) mayonnaise
½ cup (125 ml) ketchup (tomato sauce)
1 tsp (5 ml) lemon juice
few drops Tobasco

2 Tbs (30 ml) cream
1 Tbs (15 ml) KWV VSOP Brandy
dash salt

Combine all ingredients. Combine with crayfish and serve in cocktail glasses on a bed of lettuce.

*Poach grouper, cod loin, monkfish, or snapper in 1 cup (250 ml) white wine and 1 cup (250 ml) water, a few bay leaves and peppercorns and half an onion. Cover with grease-proof paper (wax paper) which has been greased and placed directly onto fish and tucked into dish. Bake in a 350°F (180°C) oven for 7-10 minutes. Cool, skin, and flake.

KWV Steen or Paarl Cape Riesling

CURRY TUNA

Serves 4

3 Tbs (45 ml) margarine
1 onion, finely diced
¼ tsp (1 ml) ginger
¼ tsp (1 ml) onion salt
1 Tbs (15 ml) curry powder
¼ cup (60 ml) flour

1⅓ cups (325 ml) milk
1 cup (250 ml) green peas
1 small can mushrooms, drained
2 cans tuna, 7.5 oz (213 g) drained and flaked
⅓ cup (80 ml) sour cream

Sauté onion in margarine until brown. Add ginger, onion salt, curry powder and flour and stir over low heat. Gradually add milk and stir constantly until sauce thickens. Add peas, mushrooms, tuna and sour cream. Serve over pasta or rice.

KWV Late Harvest, Paarl Golden Vintage, or Boschendal Estate Petit Pavillon

DANISH HERRING

This is a delicious traditional South African Jewish dish with which Americans are not familiar. It is almost always served during any Jewish holiday.

Serves 12

2x32 oz (900 g) jars herring, drained, reserving vinegar and onions
little less than 1 cup (230 ml) sugar
¼ cup (60 ml) oil
1 cup (250 ml) vinegar reserved from jar
1 cup (250 ml) tomato puree (tomato sauce)
1 cup (250 ml) diced apple
1 tsp (5 ml) mustard powder
a little pepper

Combine sugar and oil very well. Add reserved vinegar, tomato puree, diced apple, mustard powder and pepper.

Place herring in jar with reserved onions and pour over above mixture. Refrigerate at least 24 hours.

Barbara Wolfson
Atlanta, Georgia

Cathedral Cellar Chardonnay, Backsberg Estate Chardonnay

SAMOOSAS

Indigenous Cape cooking results from the Dutch, Old Cape, and Eastern influences. The Malay population who were imported as laborers from Malaysia toward the end of the eighteenth century are responsible for spicy foods such as samoosas.

Yield: 32

Dough:
3½ cups (420 g) all-purpose flour
1 tsp (5 ml) salt
1 tsp (5 ml) baking powder
⅓ cup (80 ml) oil
1¼ cups (300 ml) warm water

You may substitute halved tortillas for homemade dough.

Filling:
1 Tbs (15 ml) oil
1 tsp (5 ml) finely grated gingerroot
1 onion, diced
2 green or red chilies, diced
1 carrot, peeled and grated
2 cloves garlic, crushed
½ cup (125 ml) peas
2 potatoes, boiled and diced
½ tsp (3 ml) salt
¼ tsp (1 ml) pepper
½ tsp (3 ml) cumin
1 tsp (5 ml) curry powder
½ tsp (3 ml) ground coriander
½ cup (125 ml) water

To prepare dough, combine flour, salt, and baking powder. Stir in oil and water and mix well. Turn out onto a smooth surface and knead very well. Cover and allow to "rest" for ½ hour.

Divide dough in half. Roll out paper thin. Cut into strips 3" (7.5 cm) wide and 10" (25 cm) long.

If using tortillas fold rounded sides over filling to form triangle and then fold bottom up and fry seam side down first.

Heat oil in frying pan. Add ginger, onion, chilies, carrots, and garlic. Sauté for a few minutes, then add peas, potatoes, seasonings, and spices. Finally, add water and simmer 10 minutes. Allow to cool thoroughly. Place a spoonful of filling at the top of each strip and fold into a triangle four times, until filling is enclosed. Place samoosas, a few at a time into deep, hot oil. Fry until golden brown and drain.

KWV Late Harvest, Paarl Golden Vintage, or Groot Constantia Estate Gewürztramiaer

SAUSAGE ROLLS

Yield: 60

2 lbs (1 kg) puff pastry
1½ lbs (750 g) ground beef
1½ tsp (7 ml) salt
½ cup (125 ml) fresh bread crumbs
1 small onion, peeled and grated
1 small tomato, peeled and chopped
½ cup (125 ml) cold water
1 tsp (5 ml) coarsely ground black pepper
½ tsp (3 ml) garlic powder
½ tsp (3 ml) ground ginger
½ crushed chicken bouillon cube dissolved in 1/4 cup (60 ml) boiling water, cooled

Glaze: 1 egg, beaten

Roll out the pastry into a rectangle on a lightly floured board.

Combine the meat with all remaining ingredients and mix well.

Using wet hands, shape mixture into a sausage approximately 1" (2.5 cm) thick and place along width of the pastry. Wet edge of pastry, roll up, and cut off this filled strip. Cut strip into 2" (5 cm) pieces. Continue in this manner, using all the meat mixture and pastry.

Brush with beaten egg, place on greased baking sheet, and bake in 400°F (200°C) oven for approximately 25 minutes or until golden brown.

KWV Steen, Paarl Chenin Blanc, or Groot Constantia Estate Blanc De Blanc.

SNOEK PATE

Serves 12

1 lb (500 g) smoked snoek or smoked whitefish, deboned and flaked
1 onion, diced
2 oz (60 g) butter
2 Tbs (30 ml) mayonnaise
1 Tbs (15 ml) lemon juice
½ cup (125 ml) cream
few drops Tabasco
pepper to taste

Sauté onion in butter until lightly browned. Place in food processor with snoek and blend together. Combine with remaining ingredients and mix well. Adjust seasoning. Press into a small bowl that has been lined with plastic wrap, allowing ends to hang over. Cover over the pate with excess plastic and refrigerate until needed. Unmold by lifting out of bowl with plastic and invert onto serving platter. Remove plastic and decorate with lemon twists and capers. Serve with whole wheat toast points, crackers, or melba toast.

Paarl, KWV or Springbok Chardonnay or De Wetshof Estate Chardonnay

SNOEK SALAD

Serves 6-8

1 lb (500 g) smoked snoek or smoked whitefish, deboned and flaked
2 hard-boiled eggs, chopped
½ English cucumber, chopped
4 spring onions (green onions), chopped
1-2 fresh tomatoes, chopped
dash lemon juice
mayonnaise
chopped parsley and paprika for garnish

Combine ingredients and bind lightly with mayonnaise.

Decorate with chopped parsley and sprinkle with paprika.

Variation: Add diced pickled cucumber and diced fresh pineapple.

KWV, Paarl or Springbok Sauvignon Blanc or Boschendal Estate Sauvignon Blanc

STEPH'S SWEETCORN FRITTERS

Yield: 12-16

1 cup (250 ml) flour
1 tsp (5 ml) baking powder
1 egg white
⅔ cup (160 ml) milk
7 oz (200 g) can sweet corn, drained
oil (for frying)
salt
black pepper

Place the flour, baking powder egg white, and milk in a food processor with half the sweet corn. Process until smooth. Season well with the salt and pepper. Add the remaining corn.

Put a small amount of oil in a pan and heat. Drop tablespoons of the batter into the pan and cook until golden. Turn over and cook other side of fritter.

Serve hot.

Stephanie Gilinsky
Cincinnati, Ohio

CAPE PICKLED FISH

A very popular dish amongst all South Africans and those who taste it.

Serves 12

3-4 lbs (1½-2 kg) cod loin fillets, halibut, snapper, grouper, kingklip, or hake
salt and pepper
fish spice or Old Bay seasoning
flour
3 eggs, beaten
1½-2 cups (375-500 ml) oil for frying

Pickling solution:
2 cups (500 ml) red wine vinegar
2 cups (500 ml) water
3-4 onions, halved and then sliced
1½ tsp (7 ml) salt
½ tsp (2 ml) ground ginger
2 Tbs (30 ml) apricot jam or preserves
3 Tbs (45 ml) brown sugar
2-3 Tbs (30 ml) sugar
2-3 bay leaves
6-8 peppercorns
3 Tbs (45 ml) curry powder (best purchased from Indian store)
2 Tbs (25 g) sultanas (golden raisins)
8-10 gingersnaps, broken into pieces

Rinse fish and pat dry thoroughly. Season lightly with salt, pepper, and fish spice or Old Bay seasoning. Coat with flour, dip into beaten egg, allowing the excess to drip off, then fry in hot oil over medium heat until deep golden brown on both sides.

Remove and drain on absorbent paper. Cool.

To prepare pickling solution, combine vinegar and water in saucepan. Add sliced onion and boil together for 10-15 minutes. Reduce heat, add remaining ingredients and cook until thickened, stirring constantly until gingersnaps have dissolved.

Pour over cooled fish and refrigerate 24 hours before serving.

This fish keeps beautifully if stored in Tupperware in the refrigerator for about a week, or maybe even more.

Paarl Chenin Blanc or KWV Steen or Groot Constantia Estate Weisser Riesling.

CURRIED SHRIMP

For kosher households, substitute chicken, halibut, or swordfish.

Serves 4

1 to 1¼ lbs (½ to ¾ kg) shrimp, peeled and deveined
1 Tbs (15 ml) butter or margarine
1 medium onion, chopped
¼ cup (60 ml) raisins
2 cloves garlic, crushed
1 jalapeno chili, seeded and minced
1 Tbs (15 ml) grated ginger
½ crushed chicken bouillon cube
2 tsp (10 ml) curry powder, or to taste
½ tsp (3 ml) salt or to taste
1 cup (250 ml) coconut milk
2-3 chopped green onions

Melt margarine over medium high heat. Add onions and cook, stirring occasionally, until light brown, approximately 10 minutes. Add raisins, garlic, ginger, chili, crushed chicken cube, curry, and salt and stir until fragrant. Add coconut milk and allow to simmer. *Cream may be added, if desired. You may find it necessary to thicken sauce with a mixture of 1-2 tsp (5-10 ml) cornstarch (corn flour) and cold water.* Add shrimp, cover and simmer gently, stirring occasionally, until shrimp are pink outside and white in center (approximately 5 minutes). Stir in green onions.

Serve over hot rice with bananas, peanuts, coconut, chopped mango, and chutney.

KWV Paarl Springboic Chardonnay Backsberg Estate Chardonnay

FISH BALLS

Serves 8-10

1 medium potato, quartered
1 carrot, sliced
¼ medium onion
salt and pepper, tabasco and peri-peri powder or chili powder
2 eggs, separated
2 lbs (1 kg) hake, cod, or orange roughy
1 Tbs (25 g) butter

Boil potato, carrot, and onion with enough water to cover allowing potato to soften. If necessary, add more water. When potato is soft, add ½-1 tsp (3-5 ml) salt and a dash pepper. Add fish and continue to cook gently for about 10 minutes. Strain and reserve stock.

Place fish and potato mixture in bowl. Add 1 Tbs (25 g) butter and a little stock. Mix together and cool.

Grind fish mixture with onion and carrot and, if necessary, add more stock. Mixture must be fairly soft. Add egg yolks and season with salt, pepper, and tabasco and a dash of peri-peri powder or chili powder to taste.

Beat 2 egg whites stiffly and fold into mixture. Shape into balls with wet hands and place on floured waxed paper. Roll in flour (not too much) and fry in hot oil until golden. Drain on absorbent paper.

Eve Berger
Johannesburg, South Africa

Note: Eve says it does not have to fry too long as fish is already cooked.

KWV, Paarl Springbok Sauvignon Blanc, or Saxenburg Sauvignon Blanc.

FISH BOBOTIE

A recipe from the Cape Malays

*Generous
Serving for 6*

2 lbs (1 kg) white fish, such as cod loin or stock fish (hake)
2x1" (2.5 cm) slices white bread, soaked in cold water
2 onions, chopped
2-3 Tbs (30-45 ml) butter or margarine
2 tsp (10 ml) curry powder
2 tsp (10 ml) sugar
1 tsp (5 ml) turmeric (borrie)
handful of raisins
1½ Tbs (20 ml) lemon juice
1 tsp (5 ml) salt
1 tsp (5 ml) seafood spice or Old Bay Seasoning
dash of pepper
1 egg
1 cup (250 ml) water
handful of shredded almonds
lemon leaves (optional) or bay leaves

Custard:
2 cups (500 ml) milk
2 eggs

Mince fish. Press excess water out of bread, crumble, and add to fish. Brown onions in butter or margarine. Add curry, sugar, turmeric, and raisins and fry a minute longer. Add lemon juice, salt, seafood spice, and pepper to fish and fold in lightly. Beat egg and water together and add to fish.

Pack mixture into well greased ovenproof dish, 13" x 8" x 2" (33 x 20 x 5 cm). Press almonds onto surface and intersperse with lemon leaves. Prepare the custard by whisking milk and eggs together just until blended. Pour gently over bobotie taking care not to disturb almonds and lemon leaves. Bake in a bain marie filled with water at least halfway up the sides of the dish. Bake in a 350°F (180°C) oven until set, approximately 1 hour.

Serve with steamed rice, chutney, sambals, and pappadums.*

*Sambals are side dishes traditionally served with all curry dishes and can be a mixture of diced onion, green pepper and tomato, or sliced banana, sliced mango and papaya, shredded coconut and raita (a combination of sliced cucumber and yogurt). Pappadums are available at Indian grocery stores. When deep fried in oil, they puff up and become crisp on cooling. They can be crushed with fingers and sprinkled over bobotie or broken off and eaten in pieces.

KWV Late Harvest Paarl Golden Vintage or Boschendal Estate Petit Pavillon

"GESMOORDE" SNOEK

Snoek is a Cape fish which we have never found anywhere else in the world; although there are many preparations for it, we really only love it smoked. It is also loaded with long, thin bones, and so one must be careful when eating it. It is easily available in Hout Bay, that quaint little fishing village which comes into view as you round one of the many curves of scenic Chapman's Peak Drive. The hustle and bustle and friendly banter of the fishermen can be seen as they unloaded their catch of pilchards, mackerel, and anchovies onto the pier—not to forget the delicious smoked snoek that has become a trademark of the Cape.

Serves 6-8

2 lbs (1 kg) snoek (smoked whitefish)
4 potatoes
4 onions
6 tomatoes
1 bay leaf
1 tsp (5 ml) sugar
pepper and garlic powder to taste
butter or half butter and half oil for frying

Dice potatoes and boil. Skin, bone, and flake the fish. Strain the potatoes, reserving the liquid. Dice the onions and skin the tomatoes. Fry onions, add tomatoes, bay leaf and sugar. Stir in flaked fish, potatoes, and small amount of liquid from potatoes. Cook for a few minutes until well combined. Add pepper and garlic powder, to taste.

Serve with rice.

Stephanie Gilinsky
Cincinnati, Ohio

KWV Paarl, Springbok Sauvignon Blanc, or Weltevrede Estate Prive du Bois

GRILLED PRAWNS PORTUGUESE STYLE

The most common ingredients in Portuguese cooking include olive oil, lemons (leaves and juice), bay leaves, peri-peri, and lots and lots of garlic. The Portuguese are expert cooks but reign supreme in their preparation of fish. South African cuisine has been strongly influenced by the Portuguese and this is evident, particularly in Johannesburg, by the number of Portuguese-owned restaurants and their subsequent popularity. In South Africa, shrimp are referred to as prawns.

Serves 4

24 prawns or shrimps
1½ tsp (7 ml) salt
4 to 5 whole peri-peri (North African chili) or any red hot chili
4 cloves of garlic
juice of 1 lemon
4 Tbs (60 ml) olive oil
1 tsp (5 ml) mixed herbs (optional)

Butterfly each prawn, remove vein but do not remove shells. (The shells keep them moist and succulent.) Combine salt, peri-peri or chili, garlic, lemon juice, olive oil, and herbs in food processor and then rub over flesh of prawns and allow to marinate for 2-3 hours. Place prawns, flesh side down onto foil-lined baking sheet and place directly under broiler until golden brown. Turn over and cook an additional few minutes. If necessary, baste with 2 oz (50 ml) butter, melted with 1 clove crushed garlic.

These prawns may also be grilled on barbeque using a fish basket.

KWV, Paarl or Springbok Sauvignon Blanc or Neil Ellis Sauvignon Blanc

GRILLED SARDINES A LA PORTUGAISE

The Portuguese do not gut the sardines for themselves, but they do for most other people.

4-6 sardines per person
coarse salt

Rinse sardines well under cold running water. Pat dry and place in a large flat dish. Sprinkle with salt and leave for an hour or so. Grill on Braai (barbecue) until crisp and brown.

Serve with baked potatoes and roasted red and green peppers which have been dressed with a combination of olive oil, vinegar, and garlic. Sprinkle with finely chopped coriander (dunia).

KWV Steen Paarl Cape Riesling or Groot Constantia Blanc

PORTUGUESE GRILLED CALAMARI

Serves 6-8

**2 lbs (1 kg) squid steaks or rings (if using steaks, score lightly in a diamond pattern
   with a sharp knife)**
½ cup (125 ml) olive oil
juice of 1 lemon
2 cloves garlic, crushed
1 bay leaf

Combine oil, lemon juice, garlic, and bay leaf. Marinate squid for a few hours or
overnight. Grill on hot pan or under broiler on a foil-lined pan, very briefly until flesh
begins to curl and becomes opaque.

Overcooking will make squid tough.

Cathedral Cellar, Sauvignon Blanc or Neil Ellis Sauvignon Blanc

SABI SABI VENISON SOUP

*By courtesy of Jacqui and Hilton Loon of Sabi Sabi Game Reserve. A visit to Sabi Sabi
Game Reserve is a truly memorable experience...*

1 kg (2½ lbs) Impala bones (neck and shoulder)
2-3 beef bouillion cubes
2 large onions, roughly chopped
12 cups (3 litres) boiling water
bouquet garni of celery leaves and bay leaves
6 celery sticks, chopped
2 large onions, chopped
2-3 tomatoes, skinned and diced
2-3 leeks, sliced
6 Tbs (90 ml) cooking oil, divided
2 Tbs (30 ml) flour

Heat oil in a large saucepan. Add onions and bones and braise slowly over gentle heat
until slightly brown.

Add boiling water, beef bouillion cubes, bouquet garni and allow to simmer for 3
hours. Strain.

In a separate saucepan, heat remaining oil and saute the onions, celery, tomatoes and
leeks for 5-10 minutes. Add flour and stir to form a roux. Add impala stock slowly,
stirring constantly as you do so. Heat to boiling. Season with salt and pepper. Garnish
with fresh garden peas.

SOUTH AFRICAN FRIED FISH

Use cod loin, orange roughy, grouper, kingklip, sole or hake.
Rinse fish and pat dry with absorbent paper.

Lemon juice
salt and pepper, fish spice (Old Bay Seasoning)
all-purpose flour
beaten eggs
oil for frying

Sprinkle fish with a little lemon juice. Season with salt, pepper, and fish spice on both sides. Roll the portions in flour and then dip in beaten egg.

Heat oil in a shallow heavy-based frying pan and place portions in it. Lower the temperature and fry the fish on each side, turning only once, until nicely browned.

Drain on absorbent paper. Serve with lemon wedges and garnish with sprigs of parsley.

Serve fish with vetkoek:

1 lb (500 g) commercially prepared frozen bread dough

Allow bread to rise according to package directions.

Pinch small balls of risen bread dough and roll into elongated shape and press flat to ½" (10 mm). Allow to rise 5 to 10 minutes. Drop into hot oil and fry on both sides until brown. Drain on absorbent paper.

Alternatively, you may make vetkoek from the leftover flour and egg which you used to coat fish, as follows:

Blend egg, flour, water to form consistency of thick cream and add 1 tsp (5 ml) baking powder. Drop by spoonful in boiling oil. When it puffs up, turn over and cook until golden on both sides. Drain on absorbent paper.

KWV, Paarl or Springbok Sauvignon Blanc or Groot Constantia Estate Sauvignon Blanc

BAKED CHICKEN PERI-PERI

Serves 10-12

2 chickens, cut into portions
peri-peri or cayenne pepper
salt and garlic powder
flour
½ cup (125 ml) chili oil or peri-peri oil
2-3 onions
2 large tomatoes, skinned and diced
1 tsp (5 ml) dried or fresh rosemary
2 bay leaves
2-3 cloves garlic, crushed
1 pkt onion soup
1 lb (450 g) well rinsed chicken livers (optional)

Season chicken with peri-peri (or cayenne pepper), garlic powder and salt. Sprinkle with flour. Place chicken portions in pan or casserole. Sprinkle with half the peri-peri oil (or chili oil) and place in a 500°F (250°C) oven to brown on both sides. In skillet, brown onions in remaining peri-peri or chili oil. Add tomatoes, rosemary, bay leaves, garlic, onion soup and chicken livers. Add ½-1 tsp (3-5ml) peri-peri or cayenne pepper if a stronger flavor is required. Pour over chicken. Cover with foil and bake at 400°F (200°C) for 45 minutes. Uncover and cook for further 15-20 minutes.

Sprinkle with chopped parsley and serve over rice.

KWV Steen, KWV Paarl, Springbok Chardonnay, or Backsberg Estate Chardonnay

CHICKEN ALGARVE

By slow roasting this chicken, it remains very juicy inside and the skin becomes real crisp.

Serves 4

1 whole chicken	1 tsp (5 ml) paprika
2 bay leaves, coarsely crushed	5-6 whole peri-peri or dry red chili
6 cloves garlic	juice of 1 lemon
2 tsp (10 ml) salt	2 Tbs (30 ml) olive oil

Process all ingredients (except chicken and bay leaves) and rub into chicken, place in plastic bag and marinate overnight in refrigerator.

Split chickens down back. Place on rack over roasting pan which has been lined with foil for easy cleaning.

Preheat oven to 450°F (220°C). Bake 15 minutes. Turn oven down to 300°F (150°C) and bake another 2-3 hours. Reserve juices that drip onto foil, skim off fat and spoon over chicken.

This chicken may also be barbequed or roasted in the traditional way in a 375°F (190°C) oven for 1¼ to 1½ hours.

Cathedral Chardonnay, De Wetshof Estate, Lesca Chardonnay

SPICY INDIAN-STYLE GRILLED CHICKEN

Serves 4

3 lbs (1½ kg) chicken portions	juice of 1 lemon
2 Tbs (30 ml) oil	1 Tbs (15 ml) red dried chilies, crushed
1½ tsp (7 ml) tumeric	2 green (jalapeño) chilies
4 cloves garlic, crushed	1½ tsp (7 ml) salt
2 tsp (10 ml) grated fresh ginger	melted margarine or oil

Wash chicken portions and pat dry. Blend remaining ingredients in food processor or blender. Rub over chicken and allow to marinate at least 3 hours in refrigerator. Place on rack over shallow roasting pan and bake in a 350°F (180°C) oven for 1½ hours, basting occasionally with melted margarine or oil.

Serve with lemon wedges, tossed salad, and hot rolls.

This chicken is great grilled on the barbeque "braai" and basted with melted margarine or oil, occasionally.

KWV, Paarl or Springbok Sauvignon Blanc, Neil Ellis Sauvignon Blanc

BOBOTIE

A traditional dish of the Cape Malays

Serves 6-8

1½ lbs (750 g) ground beef
2-3 Tbs (30-45 ml) oil
1 large onion, finely chopped
2 cloves garlic, crushed
2 x 1" (2.5 cm) thick slices of white bread, soaked in milk and squeezed dry
1 Tbs (15 ml) curry powder
1 tsp (5 ml) tumeric
1 tsp (5 ml) salt to taste
½ tsp (3 ml) ground ginger
dash pepper
1 handful chopped blanched almonds (optional)
1 tart apple, peeled and grated
1 Tbs (15 ml) raisins
1 Tbs (15 ml) apricot jam(preserves)
2 Tbs (30 ml) fruit chutney

Heat oil in large frying pan. Add onions and garlic and sauté until golden brown over low heat. Add meat and cook until nicely browned and no longer pink. Remove from heat and add remaining ingredients, including soaked bread. Place mixture in a greased 9" x 13" (22 x 32 cms) ovenware dish.

Custard:
2 cups (500 ml) milk or 1 cup (250 ml) milk and 1 cup (250 ml) cream
½ tsp (3 ml) salt
¼ tsp (1½ ml) ground nutmeg
3 large eggs
1 Tbs (15 ml) brandy
½ tsp (3 ml) pepper
1-2 bay leaves

Whisk all ingredients together except bay leaves. Strain custard on top of beef mixture. Top with bay leaves. Bake in a 350°F (180°C) oven until custard sets, approximately 50 minutes. Serve immediately.

Serve with rice and condiments—chutney, peanuts, mango, toasted coconut, chopped green onions, and raisins.

KWV Steen or Paarl Chenin Blanc or Groot Constantia Weisser Riesling

BOEREWORS

If you don't want to go to the trouble of making sausages, you can mix all the seasonings with ground beef plus 2 cups (500 ml) water and 4 slices of finely crumbled brown bread, shape into patties and cook as you would hamburgers.

Serves 8

4 lbs (2 kg) fatty beef—chuck is a good choice—it must be fatty in order to be moist
6 Tbs (90 ml) whole coriander, scorch, grind, and sift (the coriander can be scorched in microwave for 2-3 mins)
2 Tbs (30 ml) salt
4 oz (100 g) casings
2 tsp (10 ml) freshly ground black pepper
1 Tbs (15 ml) coriander, finely ground
½ tsp (3 ml) ground cloves
½ tsp (3 ml) grated nutmeg
1 tsp (5 ml) brown sugar
½ cup (125 ml) grape vinegar or sherry

Cut meat into cubes and combine with all ingredients except vinegar. Grind meat coarsely. Toss with vinegar until thoroughly mixed. Stuff into casings.

KWV Paarl, Springbok Pinotage or Backsberg Chardonnay

COTTAGE PIE

An English tradition which has become a popular household meal amongst South Africans.

Serves 4-6

1½ lbs (½ kg) ground beef or turkey
1 large onion, diced
1 tsp (5 ml) chopped garlic
2 Tbs (30 ml) oil
1 lb (500 g) sliced mushrooms (optional)
1 tsp (5 ml) freshly ground black pepper
¾-1 tsp (3-5 ml) salt
few drops tabasco
½ tsp (2 ml) garlic powder
½ cup (125 ml) ketchup
2 Tbs (30 ml) Worcestershire sauce
chicken or beef bouillon cube
½ cup (125 ml) water
1 Tbs (15 ml) sugar

Brown onions and garlic in oil. Add mushrooms and meat and cook until meat is brown. Add remaining ingredients and allow to simmer gently for 15-20 minutes. Pour into prepared 9" x 13" x 2" (22 x 32 x 5 cms) casserole dish.

Topping:
4 large potatoes, peeled and quartered
1-2 Tbs (15-20 ml) butter or margarine

Boil potatoes until tender, drain and reserve liquid. Press through ricer. Add butter, some of the reserved water, salt and pepper to taste. Spread potatoes evenly on top of meat. Make lines with fork, dot with additional butter and bake at 400°F (200°C) until potatoes are crisp and golden.

KWV Paarl, Roodeberg, or Groot Constantia Rood

CURRIED MEAT BALLS

Serves 8

2 lbs (1 kg) ground beef
3 slices bread, finely crumbled
1 ripe tomato, grated
1 medium onion, grated
1 medium potato, grated
½ cup (125 ml) water

dash garlic powder
½ chicken bouillon cube, crushed finely
½ tsp (3 ml) pepper
2 tsp (10 ml) salt
½ tsp (3 ml) ground ginger
oil for browning

Combine meat, bread, tomato, onion, and potato. Add water and spices. Mix well with fork. Roll mixture into balls and brown in oil. Remove from pan and set aside.

Sauce:
1 onion, chopped
2-3 Tbs (30-45 ml) oil
1 tomato, chopped
½ Granny Smith apple, chopped
1 cup (250 ml) coconut milk or water
2 Tbs (30 ml) vinegar

1 Tbs (15 ml) apricot preserves
1 tsp (5 ml) freshly grated ginger
2 cloves garlic, crushed
1 tsp (5 ml) salt
1½ Tbs (20 ml) curry powder (or to taste)
1 Tbs (15 ml) cornstarch (corn flour)

Fry onions in oil until glossy. Add tomato, apple, and coconut milk or water and simmer 10 minutes. Add meat balls and allow to simmer 1½ hours. Add vinegar, apricot jam (apricot preserves), ginger, garlic, and salt. Combine curry powder and cornstarch and mix to a paste with cold water. Add to sauce and simmer until thickened. Serve over rice or spaghetti.

Serve with the following sambals (six variations):

1. **2 tomatoes, chopped**
   1 small onion, chopped
   ½ tsp (3 ml) salt
   dash pepper
   1 green pepper, chopped
   ½ cup (125 ml) vinegar
   1 tsp (5 ml) sugar
   Mix all ingredients well.

2. **2-3 bananas**   **juice of 1 lemon**
   Slice bananas. Pour over lemon juice.

3. Sliced **mango** and **papaya**, when in season.

4. **Cucumber, sliced**   **dillweed**
   1 cup (250 ml) yogurt
   Sprinkle cucumber with dill and pour over yogurt.

5. **Chutney**

6. Dessicated coconut

KWV, Paarl, or Springbok Sauvignon Blanc or Saxenburg Sauvignon Blanc

LAMB CURRY

Because India and South Africa were British Colonies, it was the British who brought the Indians into South Africa to work in the sugar cane fields in Kwazulu, Natal. The Indians are masters of their spices and curries and even today at the Indian market in Durban, Natal, and the Oriental Plaza in Johannesburg, Gouteng (formerly the Transvaal), they will blend a mixture to suit every individual.

Serves 8

4 lbs (2 kg) lamb. Can use knuckle of lamb, shank, ribs, chops, shoulder chops, and neck or a combination of the above.
oil for cooking
2 medium chopped onions
1½ inch piece of ginger root, grated
4-5 cloves garlic, chopped
2-3 green chilies, seeded and chopped
1-2 skinned, seeded, and chopped tomatoes
½ chicken bouillon cube
1 tsp (5 ml) salt
coconut milk prepared as described on Page 164
1-2 Tbs (15-30 ml) curry powder mixed to a paste with cold water
1 Tbs (15 ml) sugar

Brown meat in hot oil. Remove and set aside.

Adding more oil to pot, brown onions. Add ginger, garlic, chilies, and tomatoes and simmer for 5-6 minutes. Return meat and their juices to pot with chicken cube, salt, coconut milk, and sugar. Simmer gently until meat is tender.

Add curry powder paste. Adjust seasonings with salt and sugar. If the sauce still needs thickening, add 1 Tbs (15 ml) cornstarch mixed to a paste with cold water, and stir continuously until thickened.

Serve over rice or pasta with sliced mango, chutney, salsa, and sliced bananas and/or cucumbers in yogurt (raita).

Absolutely Delicious!

KWV, Paarl, Springbok Pinotage, or Beyerskloof Pinotage

LEKKER BOBOTIE

Serves 4-6

2-3 Tbs (30-45 ml) olive oil
1½ lbs (¾ kg) ground beef
2 large onions, chopped
2 large tomatoes, skinned and diced
1 tsp (5 ml) brown sugar
1 tsp (5 ml) tumeric
1 tsp (5 ml) salt
¾ tsp (3 ml) pepper
2 Tbs (30-45 ml) chutney
1 Tbs (15 ml) lemon juice or vinegar
1 Tbs (15 ml) apricot jam or preserves
1 Tbs (15 ml) Worcestershire sauce
1½ bananas, sliced
1 Tbs (15 ml) curry powder
1 x 3" (7.5 cm) thick slice of brown bread, soaked in water, then squeezed out
1 egg
¾ cup (180 ml) milk
2 bay leaves
margarine to dot on top (optional)

Heat oil in large saucepan and brown meat. Remove from saucepan and set aside. Pour off excess fat from meat but leave a little in the saucepan and brown onions in that. Return meat to the saucepan with the diced tomatoes and simmer until mushy. Add brown sugar, tumeric, salt, pepper, chutney, lemon juice, apricot jam, Worcestershire sauce and bananas. Allow to simmer over low heat 15-20 minutes. Add curry and bread and continue to cook and stir until well blended and thickened. Spoon mixture into a 8" x 11½" x 2" (20 x 29 x 5 cms) ovenware dish which has either been greased or sprayed with non-stick spray. Beat egg and milk together and pour over bobotie. Insert bay leaves and dot with margarine. Bake in a 350°F (180°C) oven for approximately 30 minutes.

Note:
We made this bobotie using ground turkey and skim milk and half of a 4 oz (113 gms) container of Egg Beaters. We omitted the margarine dotted on top and it was absolutely outstanding and low fat too.

For Kosher requirements, substitute chicken stock for the milk in the topping. The original recipe that Etta gave us was double this quantity. Etta also stated that it reheats extremely deliciously!

Etta Lurie
Johannesburg, South Africa

KWV Steen, Paarl Chenin Blanc, or Groot Constantia Estate Weisser Riesling

MONKEY GLAND STEAK

We have no idea where this name came from but it is a very popular barbeque sauce in South Africa.

Serves 4

Use 4 rump steaks, New York strips, or rib eye steaks, 1½" (7 cm) thick. Season steaks with salt and pepper and spread mustard on both sides. Brown meat quickly in hot oil.

Place meat in ovenware dish.

Prepare the following sauce:
1 Tbs (25 ml) oil
1 onion, finely chopped
1 lb (500 g) sliced mushrooms
½ cup (125 ml) ketchup (tomato sauce)
1½ Tbs (25 ml) Worcestershire sauce
½ cup (125 ml) chutney

Fry onions and mushrooms in oil for five minutes.

Combine ketchup (tomato sauce), Worcestershire sauce and chutney.

Add to onions and mushrooms and allow to boil.

Pour sauce over meat and cover with foil; place in a 375°F (190°C) oven until meat is tender—approximately 30 to 45 minutes.

KWV Paarl, Shringbok Cabernet Sauvignon, or Rust en Vrede Estate Cabernet Sauvignon

OXTAIL WITH BAKED BEANS

South Africans love oxtail, although, here in America, it does not seem to be too popular. It is a delicious winter dish. It is inexpensive and can be left to simmer in a slow cooker.

Serve 4-6

2 oxtails, washed very well
½ cup (125 ml) oil
2 onions, chopped
2 sticks celery, diced
2 carrots, sliced
2 skinned and diced tomatoes
2 tsp (10 ml) salt
½ tsp (3 ml) pepper
1 tsp (5 ml) seasoning salt
1 tsp (5 ml) garlic salt
½ tsp (3 ml) ginger
2-3 cups (500-750 ml) water
15-oz can (425 g) baked beans in tomato sauce or northern butter beans

Heat oil in saucepan. Add chopped onions, celery, carrots and brown lightly. Add tomatoes and cook another 2-3 minutes. Add the oxtail, salt, pepper, seasoning salt, garlic salt, ginger, and water and allow to simmer on low for 5-6 hours or as long as it takes for the oxtail to become tender. Add more water during the cooking process, if necessary. Half an hour before serving, add baked beans.

Serve over rice or mashed potatoes.

KWV, Paarl or Springbok Shiraz or Groot Constantia Estate Shiraz

CRISPY ROAST OXTAIL

Serves 4-6

2 oxtails, washed well
2-3 Tbs (30-45 ml) oil
2 carrots, diced
2-3 sticks celery, diced
1-2 onions, diced
flour, salt and pepper
1 head garlic
few bay leaves and peppercorns
2-3 Tbs (30-45 ml) chopped parsley
1 cup (250 ml) red wine (KWV Paarl or Springbok Pinotage)
1 cup (250 ml) water
2-3 oz (50-75 g) margarine
bread crumbs

Trim excess fat from oxtail. Season with salt and pepper and dust with flour. Brown in oil. Remove and set aside. Add carrots, celery, and onions to saucepan, adding more oil if necessary and allow to sauté for 3-5 minutes. Return oxtail, head of garlic intact, bay leaves, peppercorns, parsley, wine, and water to cover to saucepan and bring to boil. Turn down heat and allow to simmer for a few hours or until meat is tender. Transfer meat and juice to casserole and refrigerate overnight.

The next day, skim off fat. Remove oxtail from juice. Drain on absorbent paper. Remove bay leaves and garlic from liquid. Strain liquid through sieve, pressing on vegetables to extract as much liquid as possible. Bring liquid to boil and thicken with a mixture of cornstarch and water until required consistency. This will be your gravy.

Meanwhile, brush drained oxtail with melted margarine or oil. Roll in bread crumbs and place in roasting pan. Roast in a 400°F (200°C) oven until crispy and brown. Serve with gravy

Selma Daniels
London, England

KWV, Paarl or Springbok Cabernet Sauvignon or Warwick Estate Cabernet Sauvignon

POTJIEKOS TOMATO BREDIE (A STEW)

Serves 6-8

2 lbs (1 kg) mutton (lamb ribs or cubed lamb—traditionally, ribs were used)
oil for browning
2 large onions, chopped
2 sticks celery, diced
1 carrot sliced
4 large tomatoes, skinned and diced
2-3 cloves garlic, crushed
salt and pepper
1 chicken or beef bouillon cube
2 cups (500 ml) water
4 potatoes, halved

Brown meat in oil and set aside. Sauté onions and celery. Add carrot, tomatoes, meat, seasonings, bouillon cube, and water. Cover and simmer slowly for ½ hour, adding a little more water only if necessary.

Add potatoes and continue to simmer over low heat for another 45 minutes to 1 hour. If desired, thicken with 1 tsp (5 ml) gravy mix or cornflour (cornstarch) mixed to a paste with a small amount of cold water. Adjust seasonings.

Serve over rice.

Cabbage Bredie (stew) can be made by adding ½ head coarsely diced cabbage when adding carrots, tomatoes etc.

Springbok Pinotage or Beyerskloof Pinotage

SOUTRIBBETJIES (CURED AND DRIED LAMB RIBS)

Delicious on the Braai (Barbeque)

Serves 6-8

2-3 lbs (1½ kg) breast of lamb
Ask your butcher to leave it in one piece but to slice through the bones so that you have no trouble in serving it.

Curing Mixture:
3 cups (750 ml) water
½ cup (125 ml) coarse salt
1½ tsp (7 ml) saltpeter or sodium nitrate (available at drug stores)
1½ Tbs (20 ml) sugar
1½ tsp (7 ml) baking soda (bicarb)
a few bay leaves, peppercorns and whole coriander

Combine curing ingredients in a saucepan and bring to a boil, cooking until sugar has dissolved. Strain and allow to cool thoroughly.

Place ribs in a Pyrex, earthenware, or plastic container. Pour over cooled curing solution. Cover with foil or plastic wrap and place in refrigerator for 2 days to marinate. Pat dry and hang in a cool place until dry. When dry, rinse meat well and then soak in cold water for ½-¾ hour to get rid of the excess salt. Pat dry again, season with ground coriander and black pepper and "Braai" (cook on barbecue) until crisp and brown.

KWV, Paarl or Springbok Shiraz or Saxenburg Shiraz

SOUTH AFRICAN MEAT LOAF

This is not traditional, but because people today are so health conscious, ground turkey can be substituted for the ground beef, in which case add 1 tsp (5 ml) garlic salt, 1 tsp (5 ml) seasoning salt, and 3 Tbs (45 ml) Worcestershire sauce.

Serves 4

2 lbs (1 kg) ground beef
1 bread roll 2-3 days old or 2 Tbs (30 ml) matzo meal
1 ripe tomato
1 medium onion
1 small Granny Smith apple, peeled
½ cup (125 ml) cold water
2 tsp (10 ml) salt
½ tsp (3 ml) ginger
dash garlic salt
½ tsp (3 ml) pepper
1 chicken bouillon cube-crushed
1 large tomato, sliced
1 large onion, sliced
roasting potatoes

Grate roll, tomato, onion, apple, and add to meat. Add water and spices and combine well with fork. Form into loaf with hands on foil-lined roasting pan. Arrange thick slices of tomato and onions on top of loaf and thick slices of potato around. Pour over 2-3 Tbs (30-45 ml) oil and bake for one hour in moderate oven.

KWV, Paarl or Springbok Merlot or Rust En Vrede Estate Merlot

SOSATIES (DUTCH KEBABS)

Yield: 12-14 kebabs

Dried apricots and drained, canned pineapple cubes
4-5 lbs (2-2½ kg) leg of lamb, deboned and cubed

Marinade:
2-3 onions chopped
1 cup (250 ml) water
1 cup (250 ml) red wine vinegar
1 Tbs (15 ml) sugar
2 Tbs (30 ml) brown sugar
2-3 Tbs (30-45 ml) curry powder (best if purchased from an Indian store)
2 tsp (10 ml) salt
1 tsp (5 ml) coarsely ground black pepper
pinch white pepper
2 tsp (10 ml) ground coriander
6-8 lemon leaves, coarsely chopped (available from the florist)
lemon leaves and sliced lemon for garnish

Prepare the lamb kebabs:

Thread lamb onto skewers alternating with apricots and pineapple cubes. Do not remove fat from lamb as this prevents the kebabs from drying out.

Marinade:

Combine marinade ingredients in a large saucepan. Bring to a boil, stirring constantly. Reduce heat and continue to simmer for another 5 minutes. Cool, pour over prepared lamb kebabs. Marinade for at least 48 hours before use—a few days is still better, turning every day. Remove kebabs from marinade, place marinade in saucepan, boil for 5 minutes, strain.

Cook and serve:

Grill kebabs over hot coals or under oven broiler for 15-20 minutes or until slightly pink in center, basting frequently with reserved marinade. Serve on a bed of rice or couscous and spoon remaining boiled marinade over. Surround serving platter with lemon leaves and twists of lemon.

KWV, Paarl or Springbok Pinotage or Groot Constantia Estate Pinotage

SWEET AND SOUR TONGUE

Serves 6-8

Boil pickled corned tongue until tender with 1 onion, 2 whole carrots, 2 sticks celery, and 2 cloves garlic. Remove tongue, strain and reserve stock.

2 onions
2 Tbs (30 ml) oil
6 gingersnaps
½ cup (125 ml) vinegar
1 Tbs (15 ml) Worcestershire sauce
½ cup (125 ml) brown sugar
1 chicken bouillon cube, crushed
handful of raisins
2 Tbs (30 ml) chutney
2 bay leaves
salt and pepper to taste
2½ cups (625 ml) stock

Prepare Sauce:
Brown onions in oil. Stir in crumbled gingersnaps. Add remaining ingredients and reserved stock and cook over gentle heat until thickened. Adjust seasoning.

Peel and slice tongue. Place in ovenware dish. Spoon over sauce and bake in a 350°F (180°C) oven for 25-30 minutes.

Cathedral Cellar Chardonnay or Boschendal Chardonnay

TONGUE IN MUSTARD SAUCE

Serves 6-8

1 pickled tongue, boiled until soft with bay leaves, 2 cloves garlic, peppercorns, carrots, and sliced onion. Peel and slice tongue and place in casserole dish.

2 Tbs (30 ml) oil
2 Tbs (30 ml) flour
¼ cup (60 ml) mustard powder
½ cup (125 ml) sugar
¾ tsp (4 ml) salt
¾ cup (180 ml) boiling water
¾ cup (180 ml) salad vinegar
¾ cup (180 ml) mayonnaise
juice of ½ lemon
¼ cup (60 ml) chopped gherkins

Place oil, flour, mustard, sugar, salt, and boiling water in double boiler, and stir until smooth. Add vinegar and continue to cook until well blended and thickened. Allow to cool slightly, then add mayonnaise, lemon juice, and gherkins.

Pour over tongue in casserole and bake in a 350°F (180°C) oven for 30-40 minutes.

This sauce is excellent to use over corned beef or brisket as well.

Sally Kallmeyer
Johannesburg, South Africa

KWV Springbok Paarl, Springbok Pinotage, or Backsberg Estate Pinotage

VEGETARIAN BOBOTIE

Serves 12

2-3 Tbs (30-45 ml) olive oil
2 medium onions, diced
2 leeks, sliced (white only)
2 sticks celery, sliced
½ lb (250 g) mushrooms, sliced
2 tomatoes, skinned and diced
2-3 zucchini, halved and sliced
2 yellow squash, halved and sliced
1 large eggplant, peeled and cubed
1 butternut squash, peeled, seeded and cubed
1 yellow bell pepper, sliced
1 red bell pepper, sliced
1 green bell pepper, sliced
1-2 tsp (5-10 ml) brown sugar
1 tsp (5 ml) tumeric
1-1½ tsp (5-7 ml) salt to taste
dash pepper
2 Tbs (30 ml) chutney
1 Tbs (15 ml) lemon juice
1 Tbs (15 ml) apricot or peach jam or preserves
1 Tbs (15 ml) Worcestershire sauce
1 Tbs (15 ml) curry powder
1 x 3" (7.5 ml) thick slice of brown bread, soaked in water and squeezed out
2 eggs
1½ cups (375 ml) milk
4 bay leaves
margarine or butter to dot on top (optional)

Heat oil in large saucepan. Add onions, leeks and celery and sauté until translucent. Add mushrooms, tomatoes, zucchini, yellow squash, eggplant, three bell peppers, and butternut squash and cook over medium low heat for approximately 30 minutes or until vegetables are tender. Add brown sugar, tumeric, salt, pepper, chutney, lemon juice, apricot preserves, and Worcestershire sauce and cook over low heat an additional 5-10 minutes. Lastly add bread and curry powder and continue to cook until well blended and thickened.

Spoon mixture into two ovenware dishes 8 x 12 inches (20 x 30 cms) which have been sprayed with non-stick spray.

Beat eggs and milk together and pour half the mixture on top of each dish.

Insert bay leaves, dot with margarine or butter, and bake in a 350°F oven (180°C) for 20-30 minutes or just until custard sets.

Cathedral Cellar Chardonnay or Boschendal Estate Chardonnay Light

VENISON MEAT PIE

This recipe could, of course, be used with beef or lamb as well.

Serves 6-8

Pastry:
3 cups (750 ml) flour
½ lb (250 g) butter
1 cup (250 ml) sour cream
½ tsp (3 ml) salt

Sift flour and salt. Rub in butter and make into a dough with cream. Refrigerate for a few hours. Roll out into rounds on a floured board and bake in a 400°F (200°C) oven for approximately 15 minutes or until nicely browned.

You may use commercial puff pastry, if you wish.

Meat:
3 lbs (1½ kg) cubed venison, marinated in buttermilk overnight (discard buttermilk)
3-4 Tbs (45-60 ml) olive oil
2 onions, diced
2 sticks celery, diced
2 leeks diced (white part only)
1 carrot, sliced
2-3 cloves garlic, crushed
½ cup (125 ml) wine vinegar
½ cup (125 ml) red wine (KWV Paarl or Springbok Pinotage)
½ cup (125 ml) water
few bay leaves and peppercorns
1 Tbs (15 ml) Dijon mustard
1 Tbs (15 ml) sugar
1-2 Tbs (15-30 ml) cornstarch mixed to a paste with cold water
Salt and pepper to taste
finely diced parsley for decoration

Brown meat in oil, remove and set aside. Add onions, celery, leeks, carrot, garlic, and cook until lightly browned. Return meat to pot with wine vinegar, red wine, water, bay leaves, and peppercorns and simmer slowly until tender. Add mustard, sugar, salt, and pepper to taste. Thicken as desired with cornstarch mixture.

Heat rounds of pastry in a 350°F (180°C) oven. Spoon over meat filling. Sprinkle with parsley and top with another pastry round.

Cathedral Cellar Triptych or Warwick Trilogy

BILTONG

The first known appearance of the word biltong is compiled from two words, Bil and Tong, which mean "buttock" and "tongue;" in other words, strips of lean meat (resembling tongue) dried in the sun. Because the word as well as the subject described is of Dutch origin, it is not surprising that so many Afrikaans words and idiomatic expressions are built around the word biltong.

Over the years, the biltong cult spread to all sections of the population and more and more English speaking South Africans acquired the custom of eating biltong.

The following are some interesting biltong recipes.

Use 1½ cups (375 ml) of the following mixture for 40 lbs (18 kg) meat:

Mixture:
2 lbs (1 kg) salt (coarse or fine)
½ cup (¼ lb; 225 g) brown or white sugar
1 Tbs (½ oz; 12 g) saltpeter—imparts bright red color to the biltong (also known as sodium nitrate)
1½ Tbs (25 ml) baking soda—counteracts the formation of mold
4 Tbs (60 ml) coarsely ground pepper
4 Tbs (60 ml) coarsely ground coriander
vinegar

Sprinkle meat with vinegar. Combine all mixture ingredients. Sprinkle meat with half the mixture, turn over and sprinkle with the balance of the mixture. Pack in layers in a plastic container and sprinkle between each layer with additional coriander. Let the meat remain in the salt mixture overnight. The next day, hang the meat in a cool place where there is a draught or a fan. It usually takes between 5 and 10 days to dry.

Thinner strips of biltong may be saltier than thicker strips.

Meat to use for the making of biltong:
Biltong is usually made from beef, venison or ostrich. The best cut of meat is the silverside (bottom round). Cut strips 1½" (3.5 cm) thick along the grain of the meat. Thick flank may also be used. Beef biltong can be stored successfully in the freezer once dried.

If you are a meat lover, you will love biltong! Biltong is a cured meat similar to jerky; but, the latter being a poor comparison. It is so popular with South Africans that there are a number of ex-South Africans living in various parts of the United States that make biltong and boerewors (a deliciously spiced sausage) as a business and ship it to ex-compatriots all over the country. They also carry a selection of South African groceries. The names and addresses of a few of these suppliers are listed under List of Suppliers on page ivx. So if you prefer not to attempt making it, it is still available!

BILTONG TART

Serves 8-10

1 cup (250 ml) flour
1 tsp (5 ml) salt
4 oz (125 g) butter
4 oz (125 g) cream cheese

Place flour and salt in food processor. Add butter and process until crumbly. Add cream cheese and blend to a dough. Refrigerate a few hours or overnight. Roll dough out fairly thinly and place in an ungreased 9" (22 cm) pie dish. Bake shell blind for 15 minutes in a 400°F (200°C) oven. (Cover dough with wax paper and weigh down with dried beans). Remove paper and beans and return to oven for an additional 5-10 minutes.

Filling:
2 Tbs (30 ml) flour
2 Tbs (25 g) butter
pinch salt
1 cup (250 ml) milk
2 oz (60 g) mushrooms
1 onion, finely chopped
1 Tbs (15 ml) butter
1 tsp (5 ml) lemon juice
1 tsp (5 ml) chopped parsley
2 eggs
¾ cup (200 ml) finely grated biltong (can substitute jerky)

Melt butter, then stir in flour and salt. Add the milk gradually and keep stirring until the sauce boils and thickens. Set aside. Sauté the mushrooms and onion in the tablespoon butter. Combine with the white sauce. Add lemon juice and parsley. Separate the eggs, beat the egg yolks, and add to the white sauce. Beat the whites until stiff and fold into the mixture. Add biltong. Spoon into partially baked shell and bake for a further 10 minutes at 400°F (200°C).

KWV, Paarl or Springbok Chardonnay or Groot Constartia Estate Chardonnay

BILTONG SCONES

Yield: 8-10

1⅔ cups (400 ml) flour
3 tsp (15 ml) baking powder
2 oz (60 g) butter
2 oz (60 g) finely grated biltong (can substitute jerky)
1 egg
½ tsp (3 ml) vegemite or marmite dissolved in 1 Tbs (15 ml) boiling water.
½ cup (125 ml) milk or cream

Sift together all dry ingredients, except the biltong. Rub in the butter until crumbly. Add the biltong. Beat egg, dissolved marmite, and milk together and blend to a dough. Roll out to ¼" (25 mm) thickness and cut into squares. Place squares on a slightly greased baking sheet and bake at 400°F (200°C) for 10-12 minutes. Spread scones with butter while still hot.

KWV, Paarl Springbok Chardonnay or De Wetshof Estate Lesca Chardonnay

SMOOR

A few years ago, we appointed Philip Zaacks to be our official taster. Phil was elected to this position because, not only does he know good food, but enjoys cooking, too. His duty was to taste, criticize, and suggest improvements for various foods, a task which he seemed to enjoy immensely and took very seriously. Phil was also forbidden by us prior to his visits to South Africa, to lose any weight, as we felt it would be a bad reflection on our cooking abilities, as the word was out that he was our official taster. However, his wife Lucille, assured us, and we quote, "You need have no fear—It will never happen!" Thanks Phil, most sincerely, for a job well done!

Serves 6

3-4 onions, diced
a few Tbs oil
2-3 cloves crushed garlic
5-6 large ripe tomatoes, skinned
Salt, pepper, Worcestershire Sauce and sugar to taste

Sauté onions in oil until nicely browned. Add garlic and cook a little longer. Add peeled tomatoes and simmer for 2-3 hours until totally disintegrated. Season with salt, pepper, and Worcestershire Sauce to taste. Combine 1 Tbs (15 ml) cornstarch with cold water to form a smooth paste and stir into sauce until desired consistency is attained. Adjust seasonings with salt, pepper, Worcestershire Sauce and sugar to taste. Serve over rice, pasta, or "pap."

Philip Zaacks
Cincinnati, Ohio

KWV Steen or Paarl Chenin Blanc

COOKED MEALIE MEAL (STYWE PAP)

This traditional food is usually served at a "braai" with a gravy made primarily of onions, tomatoes, and seasonings, or you may use Philip Zaack's "Smoor" on page 46. "Pap" is a thick cornmeal mixture like porridge which is cooked and eaten with the fingers. This is what distinguishes a South African braai from any other barbeque. It is delicious!

Serves 12

6 cups (1½ litres) water
2½ tsp (12.5 ml) salt
3 Tbs (45 ml) butter or margarine
3 cups (750 ml) mealie meal (cornmeal)

Bring the water, salt, and butter to boil. This can be done in a potjie (black cast iron pot) over hot coals or in a regular pot on the stove. Mix the cornmeal to a paste with additional cold water. Add paste to boiling water stirring gently with a fork; reduce heat and simmer approximately 1 hour stirring now and again.

CHRISTMAS PUDDING

While we were growing up in South Africa, hotels served Christmas pudding during the Christmas holidays—there were coins to be found in the pudding. In those days there were tickeys (3-cent silver coins), sixpence (6-cent silver coins), and shillings (a 12-cent silver coin) in it, and the thrill of finding one of them in your serving was such fun and considered to be extremely lucky! This custom was adopted from an English tradition. Probably, a few must have been swallowed in the process! For hygienic reasons, the coins were boiled for a few hours beforehand.

Serves 12

1 heaped (250 ml) cup flour
½ tsp (2 ml) salt
1 cup (250 ml) sugar
2 tsp (10 ml) baking powder
1 tsp (5 ml) cinnamon
½ tsp (2 ml) mixed spice (apple pie spice)
½ tsp (2 ml) ginger
2 heaped cups (500 ml) freshly made bread crumbs
½ lb (250 g) butter or margarine
4-5 cups (750 g) mixed fruit consisting of raisins, golden raisins, currants, mixed orange and lemon peel, dried cherries, glazed cherries, dates, pineapple, apricots et cetera plumped in boiling water
1 small carrot grated

2 eggs
¼ cup (60 ml) KWV or Paarl VSOP Brandy
1 Tbs (15 ml) syrup
½ cup (125 ml) marmalade
2 Tbs (30 ml) orange juice
grated rind of 1 orange

To prepare pudding:
Sift flour, salt, sugar, baking powder, cinnamon, mixed spice (or apple pie spice), and ginger. Combine with bread crumbs. Grate in butter or margarine; add eggs that have been lightly beaten with brandy, syrup, marmalade, orange juice and grated rind. Fold in mixed fruit and grated carrots and mix well.

Glaze:
1 cup (250 ml) sugar
1 cup (250 ml) boiling water
½ cup (125 ml) semi-sweet wine—Springbok Sauvignon Blanc

Combine sugar, boiling water and wine in saucepan and stir until sugar has dissolved.

Pour glaze into greased steaming molds and spoon pudding mixture into this. Seal containers with aluminum foil and a rubber band. Steam for 4 hours. This can also be done in a 350°F (180°C) oven in a bain marie (in a foil container or roasting pan filled with boiling water half way up sides).

This pudding can be prepared in advance and frozen or refrigerated for a couple of days and on the day you wish to serve, steam for a further 2 hours. Turn onto a serving platter. Serve with ice cream and custard. Garnish with toasted almonds and cherries.

KWV or Paarl VSOP Brandy

AUNTIE CELIE'S GRENADILLA (PASSION FRUIT) PUDDING

These succulent fruits grow on vines in many gardens in South Africa—they are delicious eaten freshly plucked from the vines. There is nothing quite like grenadillas (passion fruit) but fresh apricots (pureed) could be substituted. "Passion fruit" is occasionally found in U.S. supermarkets.

Serves 12

3⅜ pkg (96 g) lemon jelly (Jell-O)
3 cups (750 ml) boiling water
14-oz can (396 g) condensed milk, refrigerated overnight
juice of 1 large lemon
1 cup (250 ml) grenadilla pulp (passion fruit)

Dissolve jelly in boiling water. Beat condensed milk and lemon juice until light. Mix in cooled Jello and fold in grenadilla (passion fruit). Pour into a glass bowl and refrigerate overnight.

KWV Noble Late Harvest

CREME CARAMEL

Serves 8

¾ cup (200 ml) sugar
4 eggs
2 Tbs (30 ml) sugar
1 tsp (5 ml) vanilla
3 cups (750 ml) milk
   or 2 cups (500 ml) milk and 1 cup (250 ml) cream

Melt ¾ cup (200 ml) sugar over low heat in a heavy saucepan; then pour into 6 cup (1½ litre) Pyrex bowl.

Beat eggs with 2 Tbs (30 ml) sugar and vanilla just until blended, using a whisk. Scald milk (must be just under boiling point) and pour, very slowly into the egg mixture, beating all the time as you do so. Pour over cool caramelized sugar and place the Pyrex dish into a large baking tin, which has been half filled with boiling water. This is called a "bain marie."

Bake in a 350°F (180°C) oven for 50-60 minutes. Cool and refrigerate overnight.

To serve, loosen edges with knife and invert onto a serving platter. Pour over 2-3 Tbs (30-45 ml) KWV Van der Hum Liqueur just before serving and top with grated chocolate and/or swirls of whipped cream.

Serve with KWV Van Der Hum Liqueur

DESIREE'S SOUTH AFRICAN DESSERT

Serves 12

8 oz (227 g) cream cheese, at room temperature
1 cup (250 ml) whipping cream
Assorted exotic fruits:
bananas, sprinkle with lemon juice
litches
kiwi fruit, peeled and sliced
mangoes, peeled and cut in chunks
blueberries
strawberries
blackberries
16 oz (454 g) plain yogurt
7 Tbs (105 ml) honey

Beat cream cheese until soft. Add cream and whip until spreading consistency, adding more cream if necessary.

Layer in the following order in a glass trifle bowl:
Cream cheese and cream
Fruit
Yogurt
Honey drizzled over yogurt

Continue in this manner finishing with a layer of yogurt drizzled with honey. Sprinkle with flaked almonds.

Desiree Blumenthal
Cincinnati, Ohio

KWV 1975 Muscadel

GRAN'S PUDDING

Serves 4

1 egg
2 Tbs (30 ml) sugar
1 Tbs (15 ml) syrup
3 Tbs (45 ml) margarine
½ cup (125 ml) water or milk
1 cup (250 ml) flour
1 tsp (5 ml) baking powder
cinnamon and ground ginger
grated apple, sliced banana, jam, cinnamon and sugar

Beat together egg, sugar, syrup, and margarine. Add water or milk and sifted dry ingredients. Pour half the mixture into an 8" (20 cm) square greased ovenware dish. Place grated apple, sliced banana, cinnamon and sugar and dots of jam (preserves) over mixture. Cover with remaining batter and bake in a 350°F (180°C) oven for 25-30 minutes. Serve hot with custard.

KWV or Paarl VSOP Brandy

SOUTH AFRICAN BREAD PUDDING WITH CUSTARD OR BRANDY SAUCE

Serves 8-10

10-12 slices white bread or challah, crusts removed and halved diagonally
1½ cups (375 ml) cream   **½ cup (125 ml) golden raisins**
1½ cups (375 ml) milk   **1 tsp (5 ml) vanilla**
2 oz (50 g) butter   **½ tsp (3 ml) ground nutmeg**
3 eggs   **pinch salt**
½ cup (125 ml) sugar   **1 cup (250 ml) apricot jam**

Topping:
2 Tbs (30 ml) sugar
1 tsp (5 ml) cinnamon
2 oz (50 g) butter

Heat cream, milk, and butter until butter melts. Beat eggs and sugar together until light and creamy. Slowly beat in milk/butter mixture. Add raisins, vanilla, nutmeg, and salt. Spread jam thickly on bread and sandwich together. Grease 10" x 13" x 3" (25 cm x 32 cm x 8 cm) casserole dish very well with butter. Place bread in overlapping slices. Pour over egg/milk mixture. Sprinkle liberally with cinnamon sugar mixture. Dot with butter. Bake uncovered in a bain marie at 350°F (180°C) for 50-60 minutes or until set. Serve with the following custard or brandy cream sauce.

Custard:
5 egg yolks
2½ Tbs (37 ml) sugar
1 heaped Tbs (20 ml) cornstarch (cornflour)
pinch salt
1 tsp (5 ml) vanilla
2 cups (500 ml) milk scalded; i.e., brought to boiling point

Beat egg yolks and sugar. Beat in cornstarch and salt. Slowly add milk, whisking all the time while adding. Cook in double boiler whisking until thick (approximately 5 minutes). Add vanilla. Serve with pudding.

Brandy Sauce:
2 oz (50 g) butter
1 cup (250 ml) brown sugar
1 cup (250 ml) cream
½ cup (125 ml) KWV or Paarl VSOP Brandy
1-2 Tbs (15-30 ml) cornstarch (cornflour)

Melt butter. Stir in brown sugar, cream and brandy and then thicken slightly with cornstarch mixed to a paste with cold water.

KWV or Paarl Tawny Port

MALVA PUDDING

Although this pudding is baked in the oven, it has the taste and texture of a steamed pudding which is very popular in South African cuisine, especially served with custard!

Serves 6-8

1 egg
1 cup (250 ml) sugar
1 cup (250 ml) flour
1 tsp (5 ml) baking soda (bicarb)
pinch salt
1 Tbs (15 ml) apricot jam (preserves)
1 Tbs (15 ml) butter, melted
1 Tbs (15 ml) vinegar
½ cup (125 ml) milk

Sauce:
½ cup (125 ml) cream
3 oz (75 g) butter
½ cup (125 ml) sugar
¼ cup (60 ml) KWV Cream or Paarl Oloroso Sherry

Preheat oven to 350°F (180°C).

Beat egg and sugar together well. Sift flour, baking soda, and salt and set aside. Add jam. Melt butter, add vinegar and milk, and add alternately to egg mixture with sifted dry ingredients. Pour into a 8" (20 cm) square baking dish sprayed with nonstick spray and bake covered loosely with foil for 45-60 minutes.

Combine sauce ingredients in a saucepan and bring to a boil. Pour over pudding immediately after it comes out of the oven.

This pudding must be served warm with custard, cream or ice cream.

KWV or Paarl VSOP Brandy

TIPSY TART

Named this because you might feel a little tipsy from the brandy in it.

Serves 8-10

1 cup (250 ml) chopped, pitted dates
1 tsp (5 ml) baking soda (bicarb)
1 cup (250 ml) boiling water
1½ cups (375 ml) flour
½ tsp (3 ml) baking powder
½ tsp (3 ml) salt
1 tsp (5 ml) apple pie spice (mixed spice)
4 oz (125 g) butter
1 cup (250 ml) sugar
2 eggs beaten

Glaze:
1 cup (250 ml) sugar
¾ cup (200 ml) water
3 Tbs (50 g) butter
¾ cup (200 ml) KWV or Paarl VSOP Brandy
1 tsp (5 ml) vanilla extract

Garnish:
whipped cream
maraschino cherries
chocolate curls

Mix together dates, bicarbonate of soda (baking soda) and boiling water. Set aside. Sift together flour, baking powder, salt and apple pie spice (mixed spice). In another bowl cream the butter and sugar together. Add beaten eggs.

Add sifted dry ingredients to the egg mixture, then stir in date mixture. Pour into a well-greased baking dish 9" x 13" (22 cm x 32 cm) and bake in 350°F (180°C) oven for 35-45 minutes.

Glaze:
Boil together all ingredients. Pour while still boiling over tart, immediately after it has been taken out of the oven.

Serve warm with whipped cream.

KWV 10-Year-Old Brandy

TROPICAL FRUIT DESSERT

Serves 8-10

3-4 mangoes, peeled and sliced
2-3 kiwi fruit, peeled and sliced
pulp from 3-4 grenadillas (passion fruit)
½ cup (125 ml) liqueur, orange flavored (Van der Hum)
1 cup (250 ml) plain yogurt
1 cup (250 ml) cream, whipped
brown sugar

Combine mangoes, kiwi fruit and grenadilla in a glass bowl. Pour over liqueur. Combine yogurt and cream and carefully spoon over. Top with brown sugar. Refrigerate overnight to allow brown sugar to liquefy.

This is delicious using only mangoes.

KWV Noble Late Harvest

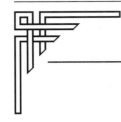
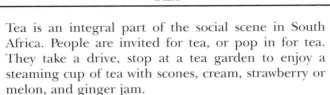

TEA

Tea is an integral part of the social scene in South Africa. People are invited for tea, or pop in for tea. They take a drive, stop at a tea garden to enjoy a steaming cup of tea with scones, cream, strawberry or melon, and ginger jam.

Tea in South Africa is not offered in a variety of flavors—just English Breakfast tea. The only questions is whether it is served with hot milk, cold milk, or black with lemon.

If you arrive unexpectedly at any South African home around tea time, you will always be offered a cup of tea accompanied by at least, a small plate of biscuits (cookies).

Tea is served from a teapot, whether it is porcelain, stainless steel, or silver. Presented on a tray lined with a freshly starched tray cloth is the way we were taught to serve tea. For more special occasions, the tea cups are placed on a doily-lined saucer. The tea cup itself is also very important. The finer the porcelain, the better the tea.

There is an art to making a cup of tea. First the teapot must be heated with boiling water. The boiling water is then thrown out and the tea and more boiling water are put in and allowed to brew until the right strength is reached. Meanwhile, the cup is heated with boiling water and the tea is poured into the cup. The milk is heated but not boiled and poured into the cup.

Such is the making of a perfect cup of tea!

TYPICAL SOUTH AFRICAN CHEESECAKE

1 cup (250 ml) crushed vanilla wafers or marie biscuits
2 oz (50 g) butter, melted
2 lbs (1 kg) cream cheese (soft farmer's cheese) or use 1 lb (½ kg) Philadelphia style
    cream cheese and 1 lb (½ kg) cottage cheese
1¼ cups (300 ml) sugar
4 eggs
½ cup (125 ml) cornstarch
1 cup (250 ml) cream
1 tsp (5 ml) vanilla

Blend crumbs and melted butter together and press onto base and up sides of 9" (23 cm) loose bottom pan.

Blend cheese only in food processor until smooth. Place cheese in a bowl and beat in sugar, eggs, cornstarch, cream, and vanilla, until well combined.

Pour into crust and bake in a 375°F (190°C) oven for 35 minutes. Turn oven off and without opening oven door leave cheesecake to set for 45-60 minutes. Remove from oven and cool.

Our friend, Cecilia Gleyher, makes her own cream cheese as follows and that would be good to use in this cheesecake:

4 cups (1 litre) buttermilk made from full cream milk
1 gallon (3.8 litres) full cream milk

Bring the above ingredients to boil over gentle heat, cover and allow to stand at room temperature for a day or two until the cheese sinks to the bottom of the pot. Strain through cheesecloth in a colander. Squeeze out excess liquid gently. Makes approximately 3 lbs (1½ kgs).

CHOCOLATE HOT MILK SPONGE

(Mercia Fine's famous Chocolate Cake)

A quick, easy and versatile cake. Hot milk sponges are very popular in South Africa. They are quick and easy to make and can be filled with a variety of fillings—usually whipped cream and/or fruit. This is the one that Myrna and her mom created as they found that the usual recipes in South Africa came out dry here in the States, probably because of the butter not being as rich. We think this one is really good!

Serves 10-12

1¼ cup (300 ml) flour
⅓ cup (80 ml) cocoa
pinch salt
2 tsp (20 ml) baking powder
5 eggs
1¼ cup (300 ml) sugar
2 Tbs (30 ml) oil
1 tsp (5 ml) vanilla
1 envelope Choc-O-Bake or 1 oz (30 g) dark chocolate, melted
½ cup (125 ml) milk
4 oz (125 g) butter

Sift flour, cocoa, salt, and baking powder and set aside. Beat eggs and sugar until thick and creamy. Add oil and vanilla and beat another 5 minutes. Add Choc-O-Bake or chocolate. Place milk and butter in saucepan and stir until butter has melted and mixture comes to a boil. Add alternatively to the egg mixture with sifted dry ingredients. Pour into two greased and floured 9" (23 cm) pans and bake in a 350°F (180°C) oven for 15-20 minutes.

Turn out onto cooling racks and fill and frost as desired. We would suggest a chocolate or plain cream filling topped with a chocolate glaze, such as Best Ever Chocolate Cake with Caramel Frosting on page 259.

Chocolate cream filling:
Beat 1 cup (250 ml) cream with 2 Tbs (30 ml) powdered (icing) sugar, 2 Tbs (30 ml) drinking chocolate, 1 Tbs (15 ml) cocoa, and tsp (5 ml) vanilla until of a spreading consistency.

Decorate with shavings of white chocolate.

FRUITCAKE

A wedding cake in South Africa is always a fruitcake. It is just taken for granted, and no other cake is even considered. It is covered with marzipan (almond paste) and then frosted with Royal Icing.

The bottom layer of the wedding cake is an artificial layer—-usually a round box that is iced (frosted) to look like a cake. The second and third layers are fruit cake that the bridal couple take home for souvenirs or to keep and eat on their first anniversary. It is a very practical cake to make because a fruit cake matures with age and actually tastes much better a few weeks after it has been made.

The cake for the guests is baked in advance, sliced into finger slices, with the marzipan icing layer on the top only and packaged in cellophane bags which are attractively tied with a ribbon. These are then placed in baskets on either side of the wedding cake and the bride and groom have a photograph taken as if they were cutting the bottom layer. They then proceed to throw the prepackaged slices to all the guests that have gathered around for the cutting of the cake. It is supposed to be lucky for a young, single lady to sleep with a slice of the wedding cake under her pillow! They say that whoever she dreams of, she will marry.

1 lb (250 g) butter
1 cup (250 ml) sugar
½ cup (125 ml) brown sugar
4 eggs
1 Tbs (15 ml) cream
2 Tbs (30 ml) oil
1 Tbs (15 ml) ground almonds (almond meal)
3 cups (750 ml) flour
1 tsp (5 ml) baking powder
½ cup (125 ml) orange juice combined with 1 tsp (5 ml) baking soda (bicarbonate of soda)
3½ lbs (1¾ kg) mixed fruit—raisins, sultanas (golden raisins), currants, glacé pineapple, ginger, cherries, mixed peel or whatever you wish
2-3 Tbs (30-45 ml) KWV 10-Year-Old brandy

Cream butter and sugars. Add eggs, one at a time. Add cream, oil, ground almonds, and then sifted flour and baking powder alternately with orange juice and baking soda combination. Fold in fruit. Bake in a sprayed and lined tin (double-layer parchment or wax paper) in 375°F (190°C) oven for ½ hour, then turn oven down to 250°F (125°C) and bake for 1½ hours. After removing from oven, pour over brandy.

Cool fruitcake in pan before turning out. If you are not coating with marzipan or Royal Icing, to store well it should be wrapped in aluminum foil or plastic wrap. Store fruitcake for at least a week before serving but preferably 3-4 weeks ahead of time. The cake can be kept in the refrigerator.

ALMOND PASTE AND FROSTING FOR FRUIT CAKE (WEDDING CAKE)

1 lb (500 g) almond paste
1½ cups (375 ml) powdered (icing) sugar
1 tsp (5 ml) vanilla
½ cup (125 ml) light corn syrup
(if light corn syrup is not available, boil together 1 cup (250 ml) sugar and ½ cup
(125 ml) water until it thickens and spins a thread when dropped from a spoon. Use
½ cup (125 ml) of this cooled mixture.

Crumble almond paste. Add powdered sugar and knead in well. Add vanilla to syrup.
Add to almond paste mixture and mix well to combine.

To assemble the cake with marzipan and frosting:
Heat 1 cup (250 ml) apricot jam and paint surface of the cake with this. Roll out
almond paste on surface sprinkled with powdered sugar. Mark outline of pan in which
cake was baked on rolled-out marzipan and cut out. Press cut circle onto cake.

Roll remaining paste into long rectangular strip. Trim one side evenly with knife, cut
away marzipan projecting from cake so that it is perfectly horizontal and forms sharp
edge around cake. Allow to dry before frosting with Royal Icing.

1. Royal Icing
    Use 1 egg white to each pound (500 g) of powdered sugar.
    Few drops acetic acid (2-3 drops) to each pound (500 g) of powdered sugar.

2. Royal Icing—This recipe provided by courtesy of Myrna's daughter, Desiree Rosen
    6 Tbs (90 ml) meringue powder
    6 cups (1½ lbs) powdered (icing) sugar
    12 Tbs (180 ml) lukewarm water
    4 Tbs (60 ml) light corn syrup
    ½ tsp (3 ml) vanilla (clear if available)

Combine ingredients. Beat in a food mixer for 10-12 minutes. Keep refrigerated in a
sealed plastic container.

CRUNCHIES

A traditional biscuit (cookie) savored by all.

4 oz (125 g) butter
1½ cups (375 ml) sugar
2 Tbs (30 ml) golden syrup or honey
2 cups (500 ml) rolled oats
2 cups (500 ml) desiccated coconut
1 cup (250 ml) unsifted cake flour
pinch salt
1 egg beaten
2 tsp (10 ml) baking soda (bicarb)

Preheat oven to 350°F (180°C).

Grease a 15½" x 11½" x 1" (40 cm x 30 cm x 2 cm) jelly roll pan or spray with nonstick. Melt butter, sugar, syrup or honey in a large saucepan over low heat.

Combine the oats, coconut, flour and salt in a mixing bowl. Allow the butter mixture to cool slightly. Quickly stir in the egg and bicarb and when the mixture becomes frothy, add the flour mixture and mix well.

Press the crumbly mixture into pan with a spatula and bake on the middle shelf of the oven for 20 minutes or until golden brown. Remove from oven and cut into squares while hot (allow to cool in the pan).

KICHEL

4 eggs
¾ cup (200 ml) vegetable oil
¾ cup (200 ml) sugar
approximately 3 cups (750 ml) flour
4 tsp (20 ml) baking powder
1½ tsp (7 ml) salt
little ground ginger

Make into a soft dough by beating together eggs, oil, and sugar. Add flour sifted with baking powder, salt, and ginger. Roll out thinly and cut out rounds with a glass. Sprinkle with sugar and press in with rolling pin. Place on lightly greased cookie tray.

Bake at 375°F (190°C) on middle rack. Watch carefully since they burn quickly. Turn over and bake a few more minutes.

Minnie Zaacks
Cape Town, South Africa

KOEKSUSTERS

This is similar to a doughnut that is plunged into cold syrup when hot and in so doing it becomes very crispy on the outside and oozes with syrup as you bite into it.

Yield: 36

1 oz (25 g) cake yeast
1 tsp (5 ml) sugar
¾ cup (200 ml) warm water
5 cups (625 g) flour
1 tsp (5 ml) salt
½ cup (125 ml) sugar
1 cup (250 ml) warm milk
½ cup (125 ml) butter or margarine, melted
½ tsp (3 ml) freshly grated nutmeg
2 eggs, lightly beaten
oil for frying

Syrup:
3 cups (750 ml) sugar
2 cups (500 ml) water
1 stick cinnamon
a touch of KWV 10-Year-Old Brandy

First prepare the syrup:
Combine ingredients in a saucepan and simmer without stirring for 10 minutes. Refrigerate overnight so that it is very cold when plunging koeksusters into it.

Method:
Liquefy yeast by mixing with 1 tsp (5 ml) sugar. Stir in a little of the measured warm water. Combine flour, salt, and sugar in a large bowl. Make a well in the center and add yeast and all other ingredients except oil. Mix into a dough and knead in a food mixer with a dough hook for approximately 10 minutes. Cover and leave to rise overnight. Roll out dough to approximately ½" (1.5 cm) and cut into strips 8" (20 cm) long. Fold in half lengthwise and twist. Allow to rise on a lightly floured board in a warm place for 15-20 minutes.

Deep fry in hot oil until golden brown. Plunge into cold syrup and drain on a wire cooling tray.

CRUSTLESS MELKTERT

Serves 8-10

2 Tbs (30 ml) butter
1 cup (250 ml) sugar
¾ tsp (3 ml) vanilla
3 eggs separated
4 cups (1 litre) milk
1 cup (250 ml) flour
1 tsp (5 ml) baking powder
pinch salt

Melt butter, beat in sugar and vanilla. Add egg yolks and beat well. Add milk and beat well. Beat in sifted flour, baking powder and pinch of salt. Beat egg whites stiffly and fold into mixture.

Pour into greased 9" (23 cm) square dish. Bake at 325°F (160°C) for 35-45 minutes.

MELKTERT WITH CRUST

Serves 8

Crust:
2 cups (500 ml) marie biscuit (or graham cracker) crumbs
4 oz (125 g) butter, melted

Combine crumbs and butter. Press onto bottom and sides of a 9" (23 cm) loose bottomed pan.

Filling:

2 cups (500 ml) milk
2 Tbs (30 ml) sugar
5 Tbs (75 g) butter
pinch of salt
1 tsp (5 ml) vanilla extract

dash of grated nutmeg
3 Tbs (45 ml) cornstarch
½ cup (125 ml) cream
3 egg yolks
cinnamon and sugar

Bring milk, sugar, butter, salt, vanilla and nutmeg to the boil. Blend corn flour (cornstarch) smoothly with cream. Pour boiling milk over cream mixture, stirring well.

Beat egg yolks and while beating, slowly pour some of the hot mixture into the egg yolks; return the whole mixture to the saucepan, blend well and cook, beating constantly with a whisk, until thickened. Remove and cool. (If too thick, add more milk.)

Pour cooled custard filling into shell. Sprinkle with cinnamon and sugar and bake in 350°F (180°C) oven for 15-20 minutes.

MICROWAVE FUDGE

¼ lb (113 g) butter
14 oz can (396 g) condensed milk
2 cups (500 ml) sugar
2 Tbs (30 ml) golden syrup (or lite syrup)

Place butter in large microwave-safe bowl and add remaining ingredients. Microwave for 11-12 minutes, stirring well every 3 minutes.

Remove from microwave and add one of the following:
1. 1 tsp (5 ml) vanilla, or
2. 2-3 Tbs (30-45 ml) instant coffee granules dissolved in 2 Tbs (30 ml) boiling water. Add 4½ oz (110 g) chopped pecans.

Pour into greased 13" x 9" (32 x 22 cms) jelly roll pan; cool and cut into squares.

Pam Cohen
Sydney, Australia

MILK BREADS (BABKE)

This is Minnie Zaacks' recipe as she gave it to us. We have also given our version of what to do. Minnie is 91 years young and a fabulous cook.

3 lbs (1½ kg) flour
1½ cups (375 ml) sugar
2½ tsp (12 ml) salt
a little ginger
½ lb (250 g) butter and some fish oil (we guess about ¼-½ cup [60-125 ml] of vegetable oil)
about 3½ cups (875 ml) warmed milk
3 eggs
2 cakes yeast or 3 tsp (15 ml) dried yeast
additional melted butter
cinnamon, sugar, and dried fruit

Sift dry ingredients. Make well in center and add melted butter, oil, milk, eggs, and yeast. Knead dough until smooth. Allow to rise, punch down, knead again adding additional melted butter. (Minnie says the dough must be soft.) Allow to rise again. Make into shapes by rolling out, spreading with additional melted butter, sprinkle with cinnamon, sugar and dried fruit and roll up. Allow to rise again until light and spongy and bake at 325°F (160°C) for 10-15 minutes.

OUMA'S RUSKS

Ouma is the Afrikaans word for grandmother and these rusks are great for "dunking" (dipping) into your tea or coffee to soften. We suppose a grandmother's teeth were not strong enough to bite into these as they are very dry and hard!

6 oz (175 g) margarine
6 cups (1½ lbs) whole wheat flour
5 tsp (25 ml) baking powder
1 tsp (5 ml) salt
¾ cup (200 ml) brown sugar

1 egg
1½ cups (375 ml) buttermilk
½ cup (125 ml) sunflower seeds
1 cup (250 ml) raisins
½ cup (125 ml) sesame seeds

Rub margarine into dry ingredients. Mix egg and buttermilk and add sunflower seeds and raisins.

Form into fingers and dip in sesame seeds. Bake at 350°F (180°C) for 45-50 minutes. Reduce heat to 200°F (100°C) to dry for approximately 1 hour.

PINEAPPLE TART

Serves 10-12

Dough:
1½ cups (375 ml) flour
2 Tbs (30 ml) sugar
pinch salt

1 tsp (5 ml) baking powder
½ lb (125 g) butter
2 egg yolks

Place flour, sugar, salt, and baking powder in food processor with butter and blend. Add egg yolks and if necessary, a little cold water to form a dough. Roll out and place in a 10" (25 cm) greased springform pan.

Filling:
2 apples, peeled, cored, and grated
2 pineapples, grated

4 Tbs (30 ml) sugar
2 Tbs (30 ml) custard powder or dessert mix

Combine pineapple, apple, sugar, and custard powder (or dessert mix). Simmer until thick, stirring constantly. Cool. Place in pastry shell. Bake at 350°F (180°C) for 25-30 minutes.

Meringue:
2 egg whites
pinch cream of tartar
½ cup (125 ml) sugar

Beat egg whites with cream of tartar until stiff; gradually add sugar and continue to beat until stiff and shiny. Arrange on top of tart and return to 350°F (180°C) oven for 5-10 minutes or until nicely browned.

PYRAMID CHEESE CAKE

Serves 8-10

30 tennis biscuits (cookies), chocolate graham crackers, or Kedem tea biscuits
1 x 3⅜ oz (96 g) package vanilla instant pudding
1 cup (250 ml) cream
1 cup (250 ml) milk
1 lb (500 g) soft smooth cream cheese
1 egg
4 ozs (125 g) butter
3/4 cup (180 ml) castor (superfine) sugar or granulated sugar
1 tsp (5 ml) vanilla
1 Tbs (15 ml) KWV VSOP Brandy
maraschino cherries

Glaze:
4 Tbs (60 ml) sugar
¼ cup (60 ml) water
2 Tbs (30 ml) cocoa powder
1 x 12 oz (375 g) large slab dark chocolate
3 Tbs (45 ml) butter

Beat together vanilla instant pudding, cream, and milk until thickened. Add cheese and egg. Set aside.

Cream together the butter and sugar. Add vanilla and brandy and fold into pudding mixture.

Lay a large piece of heavy duty foil on counter and place 3 rows of 5 biscuits per strip on foil. Spread with half the cheese mixture. Top with another 3 rows of biscuits and spread the remaining filling down the center row. Press a row of cherries along the center. Fold up long sides of the foil so that the cake forms a triangle. Place in freezer to set.

Prepare glaze by boiling together sugar, water, cocoa, and chocolate for a few minutes. Add butter and blend. Pour and spread over cake and place in refrigerator to set.

Decorate by placing the dark, milk, and white chocolate in separate plastic bags. Melt chocolate in bag in microwave oven on defrost for 2-3 minutes. Snip off corner of bag and drizzle lines of chocolate over top of cake. May omit glaze.

Esme Isaacs
Johannesburg, South Africa

PUMPKIN FRITTERS

Yield: 12-16

2 cups (500 ml) cooked pumpkin (may use canned)
½ cup (125 ml) flour
2 tsp (10 ml) baking powder
½ tsp (3 ml) freshly grated nutmeg
½ cup (125 ml) sugar
½ tsp (3 ml) salt
2 eggs lightly beaten
oil for frying
cinnamon and sugar for sprinkling

Combine all ingredients to form a batter. Drop by tablespoons into hot oil and fry on both sides until crisp and golden. Drain on absorbent paper.

Serve sprinkled with a mixture of cinnamon and sugar.

SCONES

Scones bring back wonderful memories of Constantia Nek Restaurant in Cape Town with its old Cape Dutch design and its thick, dark wooden rafters, with the smell of burning pine logs emanating from its enormous fireplace and munching on their incredible scones served with freshly whipped cream and a variety of jams, with hot tea. On many a cold Sunday afternoon in Cincinnati, we have said "Let's go to Constantia Nek for tea and scones...."

Makes 12

2 cups (500 ml) flour
4 tsp (20 ml) baking powder
pinch salt
1 Tbs (15 ml) sugar

4 oz (125 g) butter
1 egg, beaten
1 cup (250 ml) cream

Sift dry ingredients. Cut in the butter with a knife or grate in. (This may also be done in the food processor.) Add beaten egg and cream.

Drop spoonsful into muffin pans and bake at 400°F (200°C) for 10-15 minutes.

Serve warm or freshly baked with cream and preserves.

Variations:

1. Add 1 Tbs (15 ml) grated orange rind.

2. Add 1 cup (250 ml) chopped dates or mixed dried fruit

3. Add ½ cup (125 ml) chocolate chips and ½ cup (125 ml) dried tart cherries

SOUR MILK PANCAKES

Of course if you already have milk that has soured, this is a great way to use it!

Serves 4

1 cup (250 ml) milk, left out of the refrigerator to curdle
pinch salt
1 egg
pinch cinnamon
2-3 Tbs (30-45 ml) sugar
1 Tbs (15 ml) cream
enough flour to mix to a batter consistency
cinnamon and sugar

Mix sour milk, salt, egg, cinnamon, sugar, and cream together. Add flour gradually to make a soft dough. Drop spoonful in hot, buttered pan. When bubbles appear around edges, turn over and allow to brown on other side.

Serve with mixed cinnamon and sugar.

TEIGLACH—FOOL PROOF RECIPE

This is a South African Jewish recipe which originated from Myrna's Grandmother, who came to South Africa from Latvia.

It is absolutely essential that the right pot is used to ensure the success of these teiglach. It must be a copper-bottomed 12-quart stockpot.

Yield: 36-40

12 eggs (must be jumbo) less 3 whites
2 tsp (10 ml) sugar
1 Tbs (15 ml) ground ginger
4 Tbs (60 ml) oil

2 Tbs (30 ml) KWV or Paarl VSOP Brandy
finely grated rind of 1 or 2 oranges
1 box cake meal

Syrup:
6 x 11 oz (275 g) bottles syrup or 4 x 1 lb (500 g) tins of golden syrup
8 cups (4 lbs/2 kg) sugar
10 cups (2½ litres) water
2 Tbs (30 ml) ground ginger to be added at end

Prepare syrup by placing sugar, syrup and water in saucepan, stirring until thoroughly combined. Bring to a boil. Turn off heat until ready to add teiglach.

Beat eggs and sugar in a food mixer until light and fluffy. Add ginger and oil and beat in well. Add brandy and orange rind and blend well. Sift the cake meal and add about 2 cups (500 ml) to the mixture. Turn out onto a board and knead in all except about ½ cup (125 ml) of the cake meal. Roll into balls, the size of a golf ball, and make a hole in the middle using the handle of the wooden spoon.

Tie a clean dish cloth around the lid of the pot (this prevents the moisture from dripping back on the teiglach.) Bring the syrup to a fast boil on high heat, add the teiglach quickly, being careful not to splash yourself with the boiling syrup. Cover with the lid and allow to boil on high for 30 minutes without opening the pot.

After 30 minutes, open pot, give a quick stir, and cook again, still on high, for another 15 minutes. At this point, if they are browning too quickly, turn heat down to medium. You have to use your own judgment on this. Continue to open pot and stir every 10 minutes after this. These teiglach can take from one hour to an hour and a half to cook. To test whether they are done, remove one from pot when nicely browned and if it does not fall back, they are ready. Finally, stir in the 2 Tbs (30 ml) ground ginger, remove one at a time, turning the heat down to very low, and place on a cooling rack, sprinkle with flaked almonds, shredded coconut or crushed cornflakes.

To use the syrup again to make another batch of teiglach, add 8 cups (2 litres) water and 6 cups (1½ kg) sugar. Heat and strain and it is ready to use.

SPRINGBOK TOFFEE

This toffee is named for the Springbok, a beautiful gazelle found only in Southern Africa on the Central Plains. In 1906, it became the official emblem of the South African Rugby team and since then appears as the emblem of many sports teams and Societies and until recently was emblazoned on the tail section of South African Airways aeroplanes. It has now been replaced by the new South African flag.

To see a herd of these animals "pronking" on the Central Plains is an unforgettable and awesome sight.

1½ cups (375 ml) sugar
¼ lb (125 g) butter
3 Tbs (45 ml) syrup
1 can condensed milk
vanilla essence

Boil sugar, butter, and syrup together for 4 minutes. Add condensed milk and essence. Boil for 30 minutes or until mixture is a nice brown. Stir constantly while boiling. Place on a baking sheet, cut and cool.

STUFFED MONKEYS

This is basically a fruit biscuit. Where the name "Stuffed Monkeys" came from we have no idea!

1¼ cups (300 ml) flour
pinch salt
½ cup (125 ml) sugar
¼ lb (125 g) butter

2 eggs, slightly beaten
1 tsp (5 ml) vanilla
1 Tbs (15 ml) cream
melted butter, cinnamon, and sugar

Filling:
1 lb (500 g) currants
1 lb (500 g) raisins
½ lb (250 g) sultanas (golden raisins)

¼ lb (125 g) candied peel (optional)
1 Tbs (15 ml) apricot jam
1 Tbs (15 ml) KWV or Paarl VSOP Brandy

Glaze:
Beaten egg, sugar, and chopped nuts

Place flour, salt, and sugar in food processor. Add butter and blend until crumbly. Add eggs, vanilla and cream. Roll dough on slightly floured board thinly into strips about 3" (7.5 cm) wide. Brush with melted butter, sprinkle with cinnamon and sugar, and spread with combined filling ingredients. Roll up like swiss roll (jelly roll) and slice about 1" (2.5 cm) long on the diagonal. Brush with additional beaten egg and sprinkle lightly with sugar or chopped nuts. Bake in a 400°F (200°C) oven for 8-10 minutes.

CAPE SEED BREAD

2 cups (500 ml) wholewheat flour
1 cup (250 ml) cracked wheat*
1 cup (250 ml) roasted sunflower seeds (salted or unsalted)
1 tsp (5 ml) salt
1 tsp (5 ml) bicarbonate of soda (baking soda)
2-3 Tbs (30-45 ml) honey
2 cups (500 ml) plain yogurt or buttermilk
sesame and poppy seeds for sprinkling

Combine flour, cracked wheat, sunflower seeds and salt. Add bicarbonate of soda (baking soda) and honey to yogurt and allow to stand a few minutes. Add to dry ingredients and mix well. Spoon into a greased loaf pan. Sprinkle with sesame and poppy seeds. Bake at 400°F (200°C) for 45 minutes. Turn oven off and leave another 15 minutes.

*If cracked wheat is not available, bran may be used in its place.

Nola Miller
Atlanta, Georgia

GERT'S KITKE (CHALLAH)

1 cake yeast or 1 pkg yeast
2 Tbs (30 ml) sugar
½ cup (125 ml) warm water
6 cups (750 g) flour
¼ cup (60 ml) sugar
2 tsp (10 ml) salt

1 tsp (5 ml) baking powder
2 eggs
½ cup (125 ml) oil
2 cups (500 ml) warm water
sesame or poppy seeds for sprinkling

Mash yeast with sugar until it liquefies. Stir in warm water. Cover and set aside for 10 minutes. Sift dry ingredients. Make well in center and add eggs, oil, yeast mixture, and 2 cups (500 ml) warm water—enough to make a sticky consistency. Knead until smooth. Leave to rise about 1 hour.

Push down and leave to rise again until double, and then shape into 3 medium or 2 large kitkes. Leave to rise again in a warm place for about 1 hour or until spongy.

Brush with egg wash (egg beaten with 2 Tbs [30 ml] water). Sprinkle with sesame or poppy seeds. Bake at 375°F (190°C) for 30 minutes.

For Jewish holidays, double the amount of sugar and add raisins.

Gertrude Michel
Johannesburg, South Africa

APPLE OR APRICOT CHUTNEY

2½ lbs (1¼ kg) sliced apples or dried apricots or a combination of both
¾ lb (750 g) brown sugar
1 Tbs (15 ml) salt
pinch of cayenne pepper
1 Tbs (15 ml) ground ginger
1 Tbs (15 ml)) mustard seeds
¾ lb (750 g) sultanas
2 cloves garlic, bruised
2 cups (500 ml) vinegar

Place all the ingredients in a large saucepan and stir constantly until the mixture boils. Allow to simmer gently until the required thickness is attained—approximately 1½-2 hours, stirring occasionally to prevent burning. Pour into sterilized containers and cover while hot.

WATERMELON KONFYT (WATERMELON JAM)

The type of watermelon best suited to konfyt is one which is not completely ripe; and therefore, when the ripe pieces of melon have been cut away, use the thick, uncolored pieces of the melon adhering to the skin.

Peel off the green skin very thinly. Cut the melon into whatever size preferred, remembering that the thicker the pieces, the better. Now take a fork and puncture the melon thoroughly, so that when soaking in lime* water, the lime will penetrate right through. You will require 2½ Tbs (40 ml) of lime (which can be purchased from any pharmacy) to 1 bucket or bowl of water.

Dissolve the lime in the water and allow to stand for about an hour, so that the lime water when ready to use is quite clear. Place the prepared peels into the lime water and soak overnight. It is advisable, before placing the melon into the syrup, prior to boiling, to bring the melon to a boil in clean, cold water in order that surplus lime is disposed of. If this is done, it will also be noticed that a scum forms on top of the water. It is preferable to avoid having this in the actual preserves (jam). Bruise four pieces of ginger and place in the syrup, which is made thus:

6 lbs (2¾ kg) white sugar to every 4 lbs (2 kg) of watermelon. Add water so that when boiling, the syrup is not too thick. Boil the melon until the pieces are transparent, crisp and juicy.

When cooked, it is ready for use or preserving. The syrup will also by this time have thickened.

*Must use pickling lime.

Appetizers

AVOCADO TURNOVERS

Serves 10-12

6 avocados, peeled and halved and sprinkled with lemon juice
1 green pepper, chopped
1 red pepper, chopped
1 small can sliced black olives
2 Tbs (30 ml) chopped parsley
shrimp or imitation crab meat, cut into bite size pieces

Combine all ingredients except avocados. Toss with a little of the following dressing. Refrigerate. Refrigerate remaining dressing for another use. Place avocado face down on a bed of lettuce on serving platter. Spoon over chilled dressing and serve.

Dressing:
1 cup (250 ml) balsamic vinegar
2 Tbs (30 ml) brown sugar
½ cup (125 ml) olive oil
2-3 cloves garlic, crushed
salt and pepper to taste

Combine all ingredients in blender.

Myrna Diamond
Baltimore, Maryland

Springbok Sauvignon Blanc or Groot Constantia Sauvignon Blanc

BEAN TORTE

Serves 12-14

1 cup (250 ml) black beans
4 chicken or vegetable bouillon cubes
7 cups (1¾ L) water
1 cup (250 ml) kidney beans
½ cup (125 ml) store bought or homemade pesto
½-1 cup (125-250 ml) bottled or homemade salsa
4 oz (125 g) crumbled feta cheese

Rinse and pick over black beans. Place in a large pot and add 2 chicken or vegetable bouillon cubes and 3 cups (750 ml) water. Bring to a boil. Cover and simmer approximately 2 hours until beans are tender. Stir occasionally. Drain liquid.

Rinse and pick over kidney beans. Soak overnight. The following day, cover beans with 4 cups (1 L) water and 2 chicken or vegetable bouillon cubes and simmer approximately 1-1½ hours until tender, stirring occasionally. Drain liquid.

Line a 9" (23 cm) springform pan with plastic wrap with edges overlapping rim. Combine black beans and kidney beans and mix together gently. Gently press ⅓ bean mixture into pan. Smooth over. Spread pesto over bean mixture. Press another ⅓ layer of bean mixture over pesto making the bean layer smooth. On top of beans, make an even layer of salsa. Sprinkle with crumbled feta cheese. Top with remaining beans, pressing down gently to make it smooth. Cover tightly with plastic wrap and refrigerate until firm or overnight.

Invert onto a platter and remove plastic wrap. Decorate with a dollop of sour cream and basil leaves. Serve with tortilla chips.

Pesto:
4 large cloves garlic, peeled
2 cups (500 ml) lightly packed basil leaves
1 tsp (5 ml) coarsely ground black pepper
½ cup (125 ml) Parmesan cheese
½ cup (125 ml) pine nuts
¾ cup (200 ml) olive oil

Process all ingredients in food processor until mixture is well blended and smooth.

KWV Cream Sherry or Paarl Oloroso Sherry

BEEF FRY STUFFED MUSHROOMS

Serves 6

6 large portabella (black) mushrooms
1 x 6 oz (170 g) pkg kosher beef fry
1 onion, chopped
2 cloves garlic, crushed
2-3 Tbs (30-45 ml) fresh bread crumbs
1 Tbs (15 ml) chopped parsley
salt and fresh ground black pepper

Wash mushrooms and dry. Cut out stems and discard. Fry beef until crisp. Remove and set aside. Add onion and garlic to pan and cook until soft. Add crumbs, crumbled meat, chopped parsley, and season to taste with salt and freshly ground pepper.

Stuff mushrooms and bake in a 350°F (180°C) oven for 15-20 minutes until hot.

KWV Renasans Sherry or Paarl Pale Dry Sherry

CHINESE LOBSTER PANCAKES

Serves 8-10

Crepes:
1½ cups (375 ml) flour
pinch salt
½ tsp (3 ml) baking powder
3 eggs
2½ cups (625 ml) cold water

Sift flour, salt, and baking powder. Beat eggs and water well. Add flour mixture. Beat until smooth. Grease pan with oil and fry lightly on one side.

Filling:
¼ lb (125 g) freshly sliced mushrooms
vegetable oil
2-3 lobster tails, cut into chunks
1 tsp (5 ml) freshly grated ginger
4 chopped green onions
salt and pepper to taste

Sauté mushrooms in oil. Add lobster and sauté approximately 2-3 minutes. Add ginger and onions and sauté lightly. Add salt and pepper to taste. Spoon filling onto cooked side of crepe, fold crepes in half and serve with the following sauce spooned over.

Sauce:
1 onion, finely chopped and sautéed in 1 oz (25 g) butter
½ tsp (3 ml) paprika
⅓ cup (80 ml) KWV Renasans Sherry
¾ cup (200 ml) fish stock or chicken stock
1 bay leaf
½ cup (125 ml) heavy cream
1 oz (25 g) butter
salt and freshly ground pepper
extra chopped lobster

In saucepan, combine onion, paprika, sherry, fish stock, bay leaf. Simmer until reduced by two-thirds. Add cream and reduce by half. Strain; whisk in remaining butter. Season with salt and pepper. Fold in extra chopped lobster. Keep warm. (Do not boil as it will curdle.)

KWV Paarl or Springbok Sauvignon Blanc

CHUTNEY CHEESE SPREAD

1 lb (500 g) cream cheese
4 oz (125 g) butter
juice of ½ orange and 1 tsp (5 ml) orange rind
1 heaped Tbs (20 ml) curry powder
¼ cup (60 ml) orange marmalade
¼ cup (60 ml) apricot preserves
½ cup (125 ml) chutney
1 cup (250 ml) toasted cashew nuts

Dampen two 9" (22 cm) squares of cheesecloth with water, wring dry, and smoothly line a small loaf pan with a double thickness of cheesecloth.

Combine cream cheese, butter, rind, and juice in a food processor or electric mixer and beat until fluffy. Remove half of the mixture and reserve. Add curry powder to remaining mixture and blend until thoroughly mixed. Spoon ⅓ of the reserved mixture into lined mold, pressing with a spatula to compress the mixture. Add ⅓ of curry mixture, pressing in the same manner. Spread half marmalade and apricot preserves mixture over cheese in mold. Repeat ending with layer of orange flavored and then curry mixture. Bring excess cheesecloth up over the top to cover the cheese completely and chill until the cheese is firm. (May be wrapped, at this point, in plastic wrap for up to two days.)

Before serving, invert the mold onto a serving plate and gently pull off the cheesecloth.

Place the chutney in a small saucepan and melt over low heat. Gently press the nuts into the surface of the cheese. Remove the chutney from the heat and cool to room temperature, then spoon over the cheese to cover completely. Spread evenly over the sides. Refrigerate for about 30 minutes to allow glaze to set. Garnish with orange zest.

Serve with bagel crisps or wheatmeal crackers.

(Chef's tip: A light colored chutney is preferable.)

KWV Renasans Sherry or Paarl Pale Dry

EGGPLANT SPREAD

Serves 12-14

1 lb (½ kg) eggplant (aubergines)
1 tsp (5 ml) hot chile oil
1 Tbs (15 ml) sesame oil
2 medium shallots
2 tsp (10 ml) minced garlic

4 green onions, chopped
2 Tbs (30 ml) soy sauce
1 Tbs (15 ml) balsamic vinegar
1 Tbs (15 ml) sugar

Prick eggplants with a sharp fork and place on a baking dish in the center of a 400°F (200°C) oven. Bake the eggplants for 40-50 minutes, turning after 20 minutes, or until they are uniformly soft. Remove from the oven. When they are cool enough to handle easily, cut off both ends and peel off skin. Drain any liquid that seeps out and put flesh into food processor and pulse it on and off.

Mix chile oil and sesame oil in pan. Sauté finely chopped shallots until soft and lightly browned. Add garlic and set aside to cool. Mix green onions with remaining ingredients. Combine shallot/garlic mixture with green onion mixture. Stir into chopped eggplant. Serve with pita bread sliced into quarters. This spread is even better if made a day in advance to allow the flavors to blend.

KWV Cream Sherry or Paarl Oloroso Sherry

EGGPLANT TIMBALES

Serves 8-10

2-3 eggplant (aubergines) thinly sliced
olive oil
salt and pepper
1 bunch spinach leaves, cleaned and blanched in boiling water
8 oz (250 g) smoked mozzarella or gouda cheese
1 14½ oz (411 g) can pasta-ready tomatoes with basil, garlic, and oregano
Parmesan cheese
toasted pine nuts for garnish

Brush eggplant slices with olive oil, and place on foil-lined baking sheet under oven broiler until nicely browned on both sides. Cool and place in dish. Season with salt and pepper. Pour over another 1-2 Tbs (15-30 ml) oil and allow to marinate for a few hours or keep refrigerated until required.

Sandwich two slices of eggplant together with a few spinach leaves and 2-3 thin slices of cheese in-between. Place in a casserole dish which has been sprayed with nonstick spray. Spoon over tomatoes, sprinkle liberally with Parmesan cheese and bake in a 400°F (200°C) oven for 20-25 minutes, or until cheese has melted. Sprinkle with pine nuts. These can be made in individual timbale dishes or in one large 8" x 12" (20 x 30 cm) casserole dish.

Cathedral Cellar Chardonnay or De Wetshof d'Honneur Chardonnay

FIERY LAYERED MEXICAN DIP

A fiery twist to an old favorite

Serves 10-12

Layer in the following order on the bottom of a 9" (22 cm) springform pan, or spread in a ring on a large platter.

Can bean dip
Can frozen guacamole-defrosted
7-oz bottle (210 g) hot peppers, drained
1 cup (250 ml) hot salsa
6-oz can (175 g) pitted olives, drained and chopped
¾ cup (200 ml) sour cream
8 oz (250 g) grated Monterey Jack cheese

Serve surrounded by corn chips.

May be made a day in advance and kept refrigerated.

KWV Cream Sherry or Paarl Oloroso

FIGS WITH GORGONZOLA SAUCE

With thanks to Frattini Restaurant, Sydney, Australia

Lesley tasted this unusual and delicious dish in Sydney, Australia. The chef, Frank Totaro (Chichov), was kind enough to share the recipe.

Serves 8

10-12 fresh figs
½ cup (125 ml) cream
1 Tbs (15 ml) butter
3 oz (75 g) gorgonzola or mild blue cheese
1½ Tbs (125 ml) Parmesan cheese

Combine cream, butter, gorgonzola and Parmesan cheeses and bring to a boil and then turn to low and allow to simmer until reduced and thickened, about 20 minutes.

Serve hot sauce spooned over figs.

Boschendal Estate Le Grand Pavillon Sparkling Wine

FILO BAKED BRIE

Serves 12

1 x 4½ oz pkg (135 g) cheese with garlic and herbs (Rondele or Boursin)
2 Tbs (30 ml) whipping cream
1x8 oz (250 g) brie
3 sheets filo
melted butter

In mixing bowl, beat spiced cheese and cream until smooth. Spread on top of brie, covering the top evenly and completely.

Butter one sheet of filo and place it carefully on baking sheet. Continue with the rest of pastry sheets, making sure points do not overlap but fan out like a star. Place cheese in centre of pastry and lifting sides of pastry all around, tie into a loose bundle at the top with a cotton string. Fluff out the tops. Brush outside with more melted butter and refrigerate until firm.

Bake at 400°F (200°C) for about 20 minutes until pastry is golden. Cool 10 minutes before serving.

May be frozen. Bring to room temperature before baking.

KWV Paarl or Springbok Sauvignon Blanc, or Saxenburg Sauvignon Blanc

FRENCH ONION ROUNDS

Serves 12

1 loaf party rye bread
¼ cup (60 ml) mayonnaise
1 can French fried onion rings
Worcestershire Sauce
Parmesan cheese
few drops tabasco
dash of onion powder

Mix mayonnaise, onion rings, Worcestershire sauce, tabasco, and onion powder. Spread on rye rounds. Sprinkle with Parmesan cheese.

Place under broiler for a few minutes. Watch carefully as it burns easily. Serve immediately.

Ethel Grayce
Cincinnati, Ohio

KWV, Paarl, or Springbok Sauvignon Blanc

GRILLED POLENTA WITH ROASTED PEPPER ANCHOVY TOPPING

Serves 10-12

**4 cups (1 L) chicken stock or 4 cups (1 L) water and 2 crushed chicken bouillion
cubes or just plain water, if you prefer**
1 cup (250 ml) fine yellow cornmeal
1 Tbs (15 ml) butter or margarine

Bring chicken stock or water with or without cubes and butter or margarine to a boil.
Slowly add cornmeal and whisk constantly over medium low heat. Cook until thickened.
Turn to low and allow to cook another 20 minutes. Pour into 9" x 13" pan (23 x 33 cm)
which has been sprayed with nonstick (garlic flavored, if available). Cool thoroughly,
then cut into squares, triangles or rounds (using a cookie cutter). Place polenta on a
foil-lined baking sheet. Brush lightly or spray with olive oil and grill on both sides,
directly under broiler, until crisp and golden.

Sauce:
2 red bell peppers
2 yellow bell peppers
1 can anchovy fillets, drained, reserving oil
4 cloves garlic, chopped
4 large tomatoes, peeled, seeded and cut into small chunks
½ tsp crushed red pepper
¼ cup (60 ml) coarsely chopped parsley
fresh basil leaves for garnish

Roast the peppers directly under the broiler, turning until charred all over. Transfer
the peppers to a plastic bag, close tightly and allow to cool. Peel off the blackened skin
and discard seeds and membrane. Chop coarsely. Brush the bottom of a 9" (22 cm)
Pyrex dish with olive oil and arrange a layer of the peppers on bottom. Chop the
anchovies. Sprinkle a little anchovies, garlic and tomato over the peppers. Sprinkle
with crushed red pepper. Continue layering the ingredients until all are used up, and
pour over the reserved anchovy oil. Top with chopped parsley and bake in a 350°F
(180°C) oven for 20 minutes. Can use hot or cold.

Top grilled polenta with a mound of pepper anchovy mixture. Garnish with fresh basil
leaves.

Cathedral Cellar Chardonnay or Weltevrede Estate Chardonnay

HERRING IN MUSTARD SAUCE

Serves 12-14

32-oz (1 kg) jar Party Herring in Wine Sauce, drained and liquid reserved.

Mustard Mayonnaise:
¼ cup (60 ml) mayonnaise
¼ cup (60 ml) sour cream
2 Tbs (30 ml) sweet mustard
2 Tbs (30 ml) dijon mustard
¼ cup (60 ml) vinegar drained from herring
4 Tbs (60 ml) fresh dill
1 Tbs (15 ml) granulated sugar
¼ cup (60 ml) oil
salt and freshly ground pepper

Combine mayonnaise and sour cream. With a wire whisk, whisk together mustards, vinegar, dill, and sugar. Slowly add oil and blend until thick and creamy. Stir in mayonnaise and sour cream, salt and pepper to taste.

Pour over herrings and marinate 4-5 hours or overnight.

Boiled new potatoes are the perfect accompaniment.

Paarl Chenin Blanc or Groot Constantia Estate Weisser Riesling

HUMMUS, TEHINI, AND SALSA APPETIZER

Serves 12

Hummus:

15-oz can (432 g) chick peas, drained reserve 1 Tbs (15 ml) peas
3 Tbs (45 ml) fresh lemon juice
2 cloves garlic
1 tsp (5 ml) salt
½ tsp (2 ml) black pepper
½ cup (125 ml) sesame seed paste (tehini)
pinch cumin

Combine ingredients in a food processor or blender.

Tehini:

½ cup (125 ml) sesame seed paste (tehini)
juice of 1 lemon
2-3 cloves garlic
salt to taste
2 Tbs (30 ml) parsley
water

Place in a blender to make thin dressing, adding water if mixture is too thick.

Salsa:

Refer to page 169.
Place hummus onto plate around rim. Fill center of plate with tehini. Spoon over dollops of salsa. Decorate with reserved chick peas and sprigs of cilantro.

Serve with pita bread.

KWV Renasans Sherry or Paarl Pale Dry Sherry

ISRAELI EGGPLANT SPREAD

Serves 12

3 whole eggplants, grilled until skin is blistered and charred
3-4 cloves garlic, peeled
juice of 1 lemon
1 small onion
½ cup (125 ml) mayonnaise
salt
parsley for garnish

Peel cooked eggplant and squeeze out as much of bitter juice as possible. Place in blender or food processor. Add garlic, lemon juice, onion and mayonnaise. Blend to a puree and season to taste with salt. Garnish with parsley. Serve with pita bread.

KWV, Paarl or Springbok Chardonnay, or Backsberg Estate Chardonnay

KOREAN CHICKEN WINGS

Season 1 lb (½ kg) chicken wings with the following:

1 tsp (5 ml) salt
1 tsp (5 ml) coarsely ground black pepper
4 cloves garlic, crushed
2 Tbs (30 ml) rice wine vinegar
1½ Tbs (22 ml) fresh ginger juice extracted from grated ginger root

Allow to marinate in the refrigerator overnight.

1 cup (250 ml) cornstarch
1 cup (250 ml) water

Combine cornstarch and water and allow to separate then drain water off top. Dip chicken in this remaining cornstarch and deep fry until cooked. Before serving, dip in cornstarch mixture again and fry again. Combine twice fried chicken wings with the following sauce.

Sauce:
2-3 Tbs (30-45 ml) oil
2 banana peppers, seeded and sliced
1 red pepper, seeded and sliced
1 green pepper, seeded and sliced

½ cup (125 ml) soy sauce
½ cup (125 ml) water
½ cup (125 ml) sugar

Heat oil. Fry banana pepper, red and green peppers for 2 minutes. Set aside. Boil soy sauce, water and sugar together until thickened. Combine with peppers and pour over chicken wings.

KWV Paarl, Springbok Sauvignon Blanc or Boschendal Sauvignon Blanc

MARINATED GINGER SQUID

Serves 8-10

3 lbs (1½ kg) baby squid, cleaned and cut into rings
2 sticks celery, diced
½ each red, green and yellow pepper, seeded and diced
lettuce, finely shredded
2 green onions, diced

Dressing:
1 jalapeño chili, seeded
2 Tbs (30 ml) rice wine vinegar
1 Tbs (15 ml) sesame oil
¼ cup (60 ml) lime juice
2 tsp (10 ml) sugar
2 Tbs (30 ml) Thai fish sauce
1 tsp (5 ml) grated ginger
2 cloves garlic, peeled
garlic powder

Place squid in a bowl and pour over enough boiling water to cover. Allow to stand for 5 minutes, then drain and dry thoroughly.

Place the dressing ingredients into a food processor and blend well. Combine squid, celery and peppers, spoon over dressing and mix well. Refrigerate until needed. Place a little shredded lettuce on individual plates or dishes. Spoon over squid in marinade and garnish with diced green onion.

Cathedral Cellar Sauvignon Blanc or Neil Ellis Sauvignon Blanc

ONION QUICHE

Serves 8-10

Crust:
¼ lb (125 g) butter
1 Tbs (15 ml) sugar
1½ cups (375 ml) flour

Filling:
3 cups (750 ml) grated onions
(drain off the juice by allowing to stand in a colander after grating)
2 eggs
1 cup (250 ml) cream
¼ lb (125 g) butter

Topping:
Grated cheddar cheese

Combine butter, sugar, and flour to form a dough. Line 9" (23 cm) ovenware dish with the pastry. Bake crust at 350°F (180°C) for about 20 minutes.

Simmer onions in butter over low heat for about 45 minutes. Allow to cool. Beat eggs well and add the cream. Season with salt and pepper. Combine onions with egg and cream mixture and pour into shell. Sprinkle heavily with cheddar cheese and bake in a 325°F (160°C) oven for approximately 20 minutes or until custard has set.

Shirley Levy
Cincinnati, Ohio

KWV, Paarl or Springbok Chardonnay

OVEN FRIED ROESTI

Serves 10-12

2 lbs (1 kg) baking potatoes (approx. 2 large) or 2 x 1¼lb (567 g) pkgs shredded potatoes
2 cups (500 ml) cold water
1 egg, lightly beaten
1 small onion, grated
1 rounded Tbs (20 ml) cornstarch
1 tsp (5 ml) salt
freshly grated nutmeg
½ cup (125 ml) oil

Grate potatoes coarsely and cover with cold water. (This is not necessary in using commercial shredded potatoes but you will need to use an additional 1 Tbs [15 ml] cornstarch.) Allow to stand 5-10 minutes. Strain water off potatoes and reserve. Dry grated potatoes very well, squeezing in dish cloth. Place dry potatoes in bowl and add egg, onion, cornstarch, salt, and nutmeg and mix well. Pour water off the potato water and add sediment to mixture. Mix well.

In large oven skillet or roasting pan, heat 2 Tbs (30 ml) oil until hot. Drop the mixture by half cup (125 ml) measures into hot oil, flattening slightly. Bake in a 475°F (230°C) oven for 20 minutes or until golden. Turn and bake another 10 minutes. Transfer onto a sheet of absorbent paper and then place on a platter and keep warm while cooking the remaining roesti as before.

Top with smoked salmon, sour cream and caviar, or chopped onions.

KWV, Paarl or Springbok Chardonnay, or De Wetshof Estate Bon Vallon Chardonnay

PIROSHKI

Yield: 24 approx.

Dough:
2 cups (500 ml) flour
pinch salt
8 oz (125 g) butter
8 oz (125 g) cream cheese

Filling:
2 oz (50 g) butter
2 shallots, finely chopped
2 green onions, sliced
8 oz (125 g) mushrooms
2 Tbs (30 ml) flour
4 oz (125 g) cream cheese
¼ cup (60 ml) cream
1 beaten egg
salt and pepper to taste
1 egg white for wash
sesame seeds

Dough:

Sift flour and salt, grate in butter or process in a food processor. Add cream cheese and blend to a dough. Place in a plastic bag and refrigerate overnight.

Filling:

Melt butter in a pan, add shallots and green onions, and sauté lightly. Add mushrooms and cook until liquid has evaporated. Stir in flour, add cheese and cream, and stir constantly over low heat until smooth. Add a few tablespoons of the hot mixture to the beaten egg, stir in and blend, and return the egg mixture to the pan. Stir until blended and thickened. Remove from heat and season with salt and pepper to taste. Allow filling to cool thoroughly.

Roll out dough. Cut into rounds. Place a spoonful of filling in the center of each round. Moisten edges with water and press together well forming semi-circles. Brush with egg white, sprinkle with sesame seeds and bake in 400°F (200°C) oven for 20-25 minutes or until golden.

These piroshki may be baked earlier in the day and reheated in a 400°F (200°C) oven (not microwave) before serving, approximately 5-10 minutes.

KWV Renasans Sherry or Paarl Golden Medium Sherry

SALMON CUCUMBER STRATA

Serves 12

Line an 8" (20 cm) loose bottom pan or 9" x 5" x 3" (20 x 12.5 x 7.5 cm) loaf pan with plastic wrap.

Cucumber Mixture:
8 oz (250 g) cream cheese
½ cup (125 ml) sour cream
salt and few drops tabasco to taste
medium cucumber—pared, seeded, and shredded
1 small onion, finely chopped
1 Tbs (15 ml) snipped fresh dill or 1 tsp (5 ml) dried dill

Salmon Mixture:
15-oz can (437 g) good quality salmon, drained, skinned, and bones removed
¾ cup (375 ml) mayonnaise
1 small onion, finely grated
juice of 1 lemon
2 Tbs (30 ml) prepared horseradish
2 Tbs (30 ml) chopped parsley
1 tsp (5 ml) salt
½ tsp (3 ml) paprika
2 Tbs (30 ml) gelatin
½ cup (125 ml) boiling water
1 cup (250 ml) whipped cream
few drops of red coloring

Cucumber layer:
Beat cream cheese in medium bowl until soft and smooth. Beat in sour cream, salt, and tabasco. Stir in cucumbers, onions, and dill. Set aside.

Salmon layer:
Flake salmon into large bowl. Combine with mayonnaise, onion, lemon juice, horseradish, parsley, salt and paprika. Dissolve gelatin in a little cold water [about 1 Tbs (15 ml)] and then stir in ½ cup (125 ml) boiling water and stir until thoroughly dissolved. Stir 3 Tbs (45 ml) gelatin liquid into cucumber mixture. Pour into prepared pan. Chill while finishing salmon (approximately ¾ hour).

Stir remaining gelatin and coloring into salmon. Fold in whipped cream. Carefully spoon over cucumber layer in pan. Cover. Chill 6 hours or overnight.

Lucille Zaacks
Cincinnati, Ohio

KWV, Springbok, or Paarl Sauvignon Blanc

SALMON MOUSSE

Serves 12

15 oz (180 g) salmon, drained and flaked
salt, pepper and paprika
1 envelope [1Tbs (15 ml)] gelatin
⅓ cup (80 ml) boiling water
½ cup (125 ml) mayonnaise
½ cup (125 ml) cream, thickly beaten

1 tomato, chopped
½ English cucumber, chopped
1 hard-boiled egg, chopped
1 Tbs (15 ml) grated onion
1 pickled cucumber, chopped
ketchup (tomato sauce)

Mash salmon with salt, pepper and paprika. Dissolve gelatin with boiling water. Mix gelatin with mayonnaise. Fold in cream and add all ingredients. Add ketchup until mixture is right color. Season to taste. Pour into greased mold. Allow to set in refrigerator. Serve with avocado pear or plain yogurt combined with chopped cucumber.

Pam Cohen
Sydney, Australia

Groot Constantia Estate or Backsberg Estate Sauvignon Blanc

SAVORY BLUE/ROQUEFORT CHEESECAKE

Serves 12

½ cup (125 ml) fine dry bread crumbs
1 lb (500 g) cream cheese
8 oz (250 g) blue or roquefort cheese, crumbled
2 cups (500 ml) sour cream—divided
½ tsp (3 ml) salt
½ tsp (3 ml) pepper
3 eggs
2 Tbs (30 ml) cornstarch (cornflour)
1 onion, grated and sautéed in 1 oz (30 g) butter until golden brown

Preheat oven to 300°F (150°C). Butter or spray with non stick a 9" (22 cm) loose bottomed spring form pan. Sprinkle bread crumbs evenly over the bottom and set aside.

Mix together by hand, cream cheese, blue cheese, 1 cup (250 ml) sour cream, salt, pepper, eggs, and cornstarch until blended. Fold in onion. Pour mixture into prepared pan and bake for 1 hour or until set. Remove from oven. Allow to stand for 5 minutes. Spread with remaining sour cream and return to oven for another 10 minutes.

Cool in pan on wire rack. This cake may be served warm or at room temperature or even chilled, if you wish.

Optional: Spoon a little salsa (see salsa recipe on page 169) on each serving, if desired.

KWV Cream Sherry or Paarl Golden Medium Sherry

SEAFOOD EXOTICA

Serves 6-8

2 shallots, finely chopped
2 Tbs (30 ml) butter
4 cloves garlic, crushed
½ lb (250 g) mushrooms, thinly sliced
2 Tbs (30 ml) flour
1 cup (250 ml) cream stirred with juice of half lemon
1 tsp (5 ml) dijon mustard
seasoning, salt and pepper to taste
½ cup (125 ml) grated Swiss cheese
¼ cup (60 ml) grated Parmesan cheese
1 Tbs (15 ml) finely chopped green onion tops
1 Tbs (15 ml) chopped parsley
¼ lb (125 g) cooked crab meat, flaked
¼ lb (125 g) cooked shrimp, diced
½ pkg (500 g) ready-made puff pastry

Sauté shallots in butter until lightly browned. Add garlic and mushrooms. Add flour and cook until thickened. Add the cream and lemon juice, mustard and seasonings and cook and stir constantly over low heat until sauce is thick. Stir in the Swiss cheese, Parmesan cheese, green onions and parsley. Allow to cool. When cooled, stir in crab meat and shrimp.

Roll out pastry to measure a 12" x 14" (27 x 34 cm) rectangle and cut in half, lengthwise. Place first half on a 10" x 15" (25 x 34 cm) jelly roll pan. Spread filling on top, leaving a 1" (2 cm) border. Cover with second half of pastry. Seal edges with the tines of a fork and scallop the edges. Prick top with fork.

Brush top with beaten egg. Bake in 350°F (180°C) oven for about 30 minutes or until top is golden brown and pastry is puffed. Cut into slices.

Note: Drained, flaked salmon or tuna may be substituted for seafood, especially in kosher households.

May be frozen before baking. Bake frozen.

KWV, Paarl or Springbok Sauvignon Blanc or Neil Ellis Sauvignon Blanc

SUNDRIED TOMATO AND ROASTED GARLIC SPREAD

Serves 12

2 red peppers
1 small onion
4-5 cloves garlic, roasted
½-1 jalapeño pepper, to taste, seeded and chopped
16 oz (500 g) cream cheese or ricotta cheese
2 Tbs (30 ml) parsley
2 Tbs (30 ml) basil
2 Tbs (30 ml) coarsely chopped sundried tomatoes

Broil peppers under broiler until skin blackens and blisters. Remove from oven and place in plastic bag for 10 minutes, then skin, discard seeds and membrane and dice flesh. Combine all ingredients in food processor or blender.

Serve with crackers or vegetables.

Note:
To roast garlic, preheat oven to 400°F (200°C). Cut small slice off top and place in small baking dish. Drizzle lightly with olive oil. Bake uncovered for 15-20 minutes or until soft when squeezed.

This could be made into a dip substituting 2 cups (500 ml) plain yogurt for the cream cheese.

KWV Renasans Sherry or Paarl Pale Dry Sherry

SUNDRIED TOMATO AND CHEESE BREAD TWIST

Serves 10-12

2 pkgs dry yeast
1½ Tbs (20 ml) sugar
¼ cup (60 ml) water (115°F/50°C)
3-4 cups (375-500 g) all-purpose flour
2 tsp (10 ml) salt
4 oz (125 g) butter
¾ cup (200 ml) luke warm milk

Sprinkle yeast and ½ Tbs (7 ml) sugar over ¼ cup (60 ml) very warm water. Set aside for a minute or two, then stir until yeast is dissolved. Let rest about 5 minutes until mixture doubles in volume.

Place the following in food processor and blend using steel blade: flour, remaining tablespoon of sugar and salt, then butter and yeast mixture. With machine running, add milk through the feed tube, until mixture reaches a ball form. Remove steel blade and use plastic blade to continue kneading. When dough is smooth and elastic, place it in a well-greased bowl and cover. Let rise until doubles in bulk (approximately 1 hour). When dough has risen, punch down and shape as follows. Punch center and pull in sides. Roll into a circle 22" (49 cm) in diameter. If not a perfect circle, work out with hands. Allow to stand for 5 minutes. Place circle in a 9" or 10" (22 cm) glass Pyrex dish which has been greased, stretching dough as you are putting it in. Push dough down into dish and press air out. Put filling on top of dough. Pleat the dough into loose folds (try to make the pleats even) and then gather together the ends of the dough that meet in the center and twist. Squeeze into a small knob and tuck under. Brush with egg yolk and a tsp (5 ml) of water. Cover the loaf and set aside for 10-15 minutes.

Bake for 1 hour at 375°F (190°C) on lowest shelf. Turn bread onto wire rack and cool an hour or two before serving.

Filling:
2 Tbs (30 ml) softened butter
1 egg
1 lb (500 g) Muenster cheese, finely grated
1 lb (500 g) Mozzarella cheese, finely grated
1 Tbs (15 ml) fresh oregano (or dried)
1 Tbs (15 ml) fresh basil (or dried)
6-8 finely chopped sundried tomatoes

Combine butter and egg. Mix remaining ingredients (except sundried tomatoes) until smooth. Place sundried tomatoes on bottom of dough and place cheese mixture on top. Proceed as directed above. Allow dough with filling to stand for 10 minutes before baking.

KWV, Paarl or Springbok Chardonnay or Neil Ellis Chardonnay

SUNDRIED TOMATO, CHEESE AND BASIL STRUDEL

Serves 16

3 oz (75 g) sundried tomatoes
4 shallots, finely chopped
1 clove garlic, crushed
1-2 Tbs (15-30 ml) olive oil
1 lb (500 g) cream cheese
2 eggs
¼ cup (60 ml) fresh basil, finely chopped, or 1 tsp (5 ml) dried basil
4 oz (125 g) feta cheese
½-1 tsp (3-5 ml) coarsely ground black pepper
1/3 cup (80 ml) pine nuts, toasted
1 lb (500 g) phyllo pastry
melted butter or margarine

In a small bowl, pour boiling water over tomatoes and allow to stand until softened. Drain well and chop into pieces. Set aside. Sauté shallots and garlic in olive oil. Beat cream cheese until softened. Add eggs and then shallots garlic mixture, chopped basil, feta cheese, and pepper. Fold in tomatoes and pine nuts.

Place the sheets of phyllo on waxed paper on work surface. Cover with a second sheet of wax paper and then a damp (not wet) cloth. Keep stack covered while you work to prevent the phyllo from drying out. Remove one of the sheets from the stack and place in front of you. Brush with melted butter (not too much), rather sparingly. Place a second sheet of phyllo on top of the first and again brush with melted butter. Repeat in this way until you have stacked 5 sheets. Spread ¼ of the cheese mixture lengthwise on sheet, tuck in ends, and roll up. Place seam side down on ungreased baking sheet. Brush top with butter and make diagonal slits across top of pastry about 2" (5 cm) apart. Repeat the whole procedure to make 4 strudels in all.

Bake at 375°F (190°C) for 30 minutes. Allow to rest for 5-10 minutes before serving.

KWV, Paarl or Springbok Chardonnay or Neil Ellis Chardonnay

SPINACH AND CHEESE CUPS

Yield: 24

1 medium onion, chopped
1 Tbs (25 g) butter
2 eggs
4 oz (125 g) ricotta
4 oz (125 g) feta, crumbled
8 oz (250 g) cream cheese, softened
1 x 10 oz (310 g) pkg spinach, defrosted
1 Tbs (15 ml) fresh chopped parsley
pinch dill weed
salt and freshly ground pepper
1 lb (½ kg) phyllo dough, thawed or 4 boxes mini phyllo dough shells, if available
melted butter

Chop onion and sauté in butter until softened.

Combine eggs, onion, and cheeses and blend in food processor until smooth. Squeeze all the water out of spinach and add to mixture. Mix in parsley, dill, salt and pepper. Refrigerate 1 hour.

Brush 4 sheets of phyllo with melted butter and place on top of one another. Cut into 3" (7 cm) squares. Push into 2" (5 cm) diameter muffin (patty) pans which have been sprayed with nonstick cooking spray. Fill with filling and bake at 400°F (200°C) for about 20-25 minutes or until brown. If using store-bought shells, fill with filling and bake as instructed on box.

If desired, these can also be made into spanokapita by cutting phyllo into lengthwise strips, 2" (5 cm) wide, keeping unused phyllo sheets covered with a damp towel. Brush with melted butter. Place a rounded teaspoon of filling on one end and fold like a flag to the other end. Bake at 400°F (200°C) for about 20 minutes.

KWV, Paarl or Springbok Sauvignon Blanc or Saxenburg Sauvignon Blanc

TOMATO SALSA WITH BRUSCHETTA

To be used as a delicious nonfat dip or with barbecued fish, meat or poultry as a sauce or with humus and tehina.

Serves 8

1 onion, preferably red, quartered
2 green chilies, halved and seeds removed
1-2 cloves garlic
¾ cup (200 ml) cilantro (dunia)
2-3 tomatoes
1 Tbs (15 ml) olive oil
½-1 tsp salt (3-5 ml)
1 tsp (5 ml) coarsely ground black pepper

Place onion, chilies, garlic, cilantro, salt and pepper in food processor. Process until finely chopped. Coarsely dice tomatoes and mix with their juice and the processed ingredients. Stir in olive oil and add additional salt to taste.

As a Dip:
Serve with tortilla chips, plain chips, brushetta (Italian garlic toast) and toasted pita chips.

Toasted Pita Chips:
Halve and quarter pita bread. Open out. Brush with olive oil, sprinkle with garlic salt and place under broiler until golden brown and crisp.

Bruschetta:
Slice French loaf on the diagonal in 1" (2.5 cm) slices, brush with olive oil and toast under broiler on both sides. Peel a clove of garlic, cut in half and rub onto the cut side of the toast.

KWV Cream Sherry or Paarl Oloroso

TURKEYTISERS IN PHYLLO

Yield: approx. 40

1 oz (25 g) butter or margarine
1 medium onion, chopped
2 shallots, chopped
2-3 cloves garlic minced
1 lb (½ kg) freshly ground turkey
⅓ cup (80 ml) red cooking wine (Springbok Pinotage)
1 Tbs (15 ml) dried parsley
28-oz can (825 g) Italian tomatoes with basil, drained
½-1 tsp (3-5 ml) salt
1 tsp (5 ml) freshly ground pepper
2 bay leaves
½ chicken bouillon cube
1 tsp (5 ml) chopped jalapeño chile or chile powder
1 egg, lightly beaten
1 lb pkg (450 g) phyllo
1 stick (125 g) butter or margarine, melted
sesame seeds for sprinkling

Melt butter or margarine in a large pan over medium heat. Add onion, chopped shallots, and half of minced garlic and sauté 3-4 minutes. Stir in ground turkey and cook until no longer pink. Pour in all but 2 Tbs (30 ml) wine and simmer 2-3 minutes. Reduce heat to medium low and add parsley, tomatoes, salt, pepper, bay leaves, bouillon cube, and jalapeño chili or chili powder and simmer for 15 minutes. Drain fat from meat. Add remaining garlic and wine. Allow to cool. Add beaten egg.

Place phyllo on work surface. Remove 3 sheets from stack and keep remaining sheets covered with a damp cloth to prevent drying out. Remove one sheet of phyllo and brush with melted butter. Repeat with remaining two sheets. Cut into 4 strips with scissors. Place 1 tsp (5 ml) of filling at bottom end and fold like a flag to the other end. Repeat procedure with remaining phyllo and filling.

Brush triangles with melted butter and sprinkle with sesame seeds. Bake in a 400°F (200°C) oven for approximately 20-25 minutes until golden brown. Serve hot.

KWV, Paarl, or Springbok Sauvignon Blanc

Soups

ASPARAGUS POTATO SOUP

Serves 10-12

2 Tbs (30 ml) olive oil
2 onions, diced
3 leeks, sliced
3 shallots, chopped
2 sticks celery, sliced
2-3 cloves garlic, crushed
2 lb (1 kg) green asparagus—snap off bottoms of stalks
2 large potatoes, cubed
2 vegetable bouillon cubes
2 tsp (10 ml) salt and pepper to taste

Heat oil in large pot. Add onions, leeks, shallots and celery and sauté until limp. Add garlic, asparagus, potatoes, vegetable bouillon cubes, salt, pepper and water to cover. Simmer over low heat until tender. Blend in food processor until smooth. Adjust seasonings. Garnish with fresh diced herbs or black pepper.

KWV or Paarl Sauvignon Blanc or Boschendal Estate Sauvignon Blanc

BOMBAY CURRIED BANANA CHICKEN SOUP

Serves 10-12

2 oz (50 g) butter or margarine
1 medium onion, chopped
2 sticks celery, chopped
1 Tbs (15 ml) flour
1-1½ tsp (5-7 ml) curry powder
3 cups (750 ml) chicken broth
¾ cup (200 ml) light cream or nondairy creamer
1 tsp (5 ml) salt
1½ cups (375 ml) cooked chicken, diced
2 bananas, peeled and diced
toasted coconut and chopped raisins for garnish

Melt butter in large saucepan and stir in onion and celery. Cook until vegetables are limp. Stir in flour and curry powder. Mix well and cook slightly. Stir in chicken broth, cream and salt; simmer a few minutes. Add chicken and bananas. Heat but be careful not to boil.

May be served hot or cold. Serve with toasted coconut and chopped raisins.

KWV Late Harvest or KWV Golden Vintage or Groot Constantia Estate Gewürztraminer

BUTTERNUT SOUP

Serves 6-8

1 Tbs (15 ml) butter
2 onions, chopped
2 leeks, sliced
2 large butternut squash, peeled and diced
1 Tbs (15 ml) flour
1-2 tsp (5-10 ml) curry powder
4-6 cups (1-1½ liters) chicken stock
1 cup (250 ml) apple juice
grated rind and juice of 1 orange
salt and pepper
crème Fraîche
chopped parsley or chives

Saute onions and leeks in butter until translucent. Add butternut and saute for approximately 3 minutes, stirring occasionally. Add flour and curry and cook for a few minutes. Add chicken stock, apple and orange juice, and grated rind and simmer slowly for 15-20 minutes or until vegetables are soft. Liquidize in food processor. Season with salt and pepper. If desired 1 cup (250 ml) cream or skim milk may be added.

Serve with a dollop of cream Fraîche and sprinkle with parsley or chives.

CARROT GINGER SOUP

Serves 10-12

2 Tbs (30 ml) olive oil
2 large onions, diced
1 leek, sliced
1 Tbs (15 ml) grated peeled gingerroot
2½ lbs (1 kg) baby carrots
8 cups (2 liters) water
2 chicken or vegetable bouillon cubes
2 tsp (10 ml) salt
1 tsp (5 ml) pepper
1-2 Tbs (15-30 ml) brown sugar or 2 envelopes sweetener
grated rind of 1 orange
1 cup (250 ml) orange juice
1 cup (250 ml) cream or nondairy creamer (optional)

In a large saucepan, heat oil. Add onion and leek and cook until tender and golden, about 20 minutes. Add remaining ingredients except cream and allow to simmer on medium-low heat for 1 hour or until carrots are tender. Adjust seasoning. Blend soup in small batches in blender until pureed.

Return to saucepan and heat to serve. Adjust seasoning and if desired, add cream or non-dairy creamer.

KWV, Paarl Chenin Blanc

CREAMY CRAB AND CORN SOUP

Serves 8-10

2-3 Tbs (30-45 ml) olive oil
2 sticks celery, diced
1 large onion, diced
1 carrot, diced
1 leek, sliced
1 cup (250 ml) clam juice
2 cups (500 ml) vegetable stock
**   (made by dissolving 2 vegetable bouillon cubes in boiling water)**
1 can corn kernels, drain and reserve liquid
½ cup (125 ml) KWV, Paarl, or Springbok Sauvignon Blanc
1 can creamed corn
1 cup (250 ml) whipping or heavy cream
8 oz (250 g) jumbo lump crab meat or imitation crab meat
1 Tbs (15 ml) cornstarch (cornflour), mixed to a paste with a little cold water
salt and pepper
2 green onions, chopped
2-3 Tbs (30-45 ml) chopped parsley

In a large saucepan, heat olive oil, add celery, onion, carrot, and leek and sauté until lightly browned. Add clam juice, vegetable stock, reserved liquid from corn, and wine. Bring to a boil and simmer for 30-40 minutes or until vegetables are tender. Add corn and creamed corn, reduce heat, and stir in cream and crab meat. Add cornstarch mixture, if necessary to thicken only, and return to a gentle simmer. Season to taste with salt and pepper.

To serve, sprinkle with green onion and parsley and serve with crusty bread.

KWV, Paarl, or Springbok Sauvignon Blanc or Weltevrede Estate Prive Du Bois

CURRIED CREAM OF TOMATO SOUP

Serves 8-10

2 carrots, diced
1 leek, diced
1 onion, diced
3 oz (75 g) butter
1 Tbs (15 ml) flour
1-2 tsp (5-10 ml) curry powder, or to taste
2 lbs (1 kg) fresh tomatoes, skinned and diced
2 Tbs (30 ml) tomato puree
1 cup (250 ml) vegetable or chicken stock, using a bouillon cube
1 tsp (5 ml) salt
dash black pepper
1 Tbs (15 ml) sugar
1-2 bay leaves
1 cup (250 ml) coconut cream or coconut milk*
½ cup (125 ml) cream
basil or mint leaves for garnish

Sauté carrots, leek and onion in butter until limp. Remove from heat and stir in flour and curry. Add tomatoes and tomato puree and stir in. Return to low heat and stir in stock, salt, freshly ground pepper, sugar, bay leaves and coconut cream or milk. Simmer for 15-20 minutes and when vegetables are soft, remove from heat and allow to cool slightly, remove bay leaves and then blend in food processor or blender. Return to saucepan and add cream. Adjust seasonings and serve hot, garnished with basil or mint leaves.

Coconut Milk:
Pour 1 cup (250 ml) boiling water over 2 cups (500 ml) coconut and allow to infuse for a few hours. Strain, pressing down hard to release all the liquid.

KWV Renasans Sherry or Paarl Pale Dry

GARLIC ZUCCHINI SOUP

Serves 10-12

2 shallots
4 cloves garlic, crushed
2 leeks, washed well and sliced
2 medium onions, chopped
2 Tbs (30 ml) butter or margarine
2¼ lbs (1 kg) zucchini (baby marrows), thinly sliced
8 cups (2 L) boiling water
4 chicken or vegetable bouillon cubes
1 tsp (5 ml) freshly ground pepper
4 medium size red potatoes, peeled and thinly sliced
8 oz (250 ml) sour cream (optional)
3 Tbs (45 ml) chopped green onion
salt to taste

Sauté shallots, garlic, leeks and onions in butter or margarine in large pot over medium heat until tender. Add zucchini, water, bouillon cube, pepper and potatoes and bring to a boil. Cover, reduce heat and simmer 30 minutes or until potato is tender. Season to taste with salt.

Add half of mixture to food processor or blender and process until smooth. Repeat with remaining mixture. Serve soup warm or cold. If desired, top each serving with a dollop of sour cream and sprinkle with chopped green onions.

*To enhance the color of the soup, the zucchini may be peeled and then at the very end you may tint the soup a pale delicate green, using food color very sparingly, a drop at a time.

KWV Steen or Paarl Cape Riesling

HUNGARIAN FISH SOUP

Serves 8-10

2 onions, chopped
2 leeks, sliced
4 large whole carrots, sliced
1 tomato, sliced
2 sticks celery, diced
2 large potatoes, sliced
1 finely diced chili (optional)
4 lbs (2 kg) mixed fish, cleaned and cut into 1" (2½ cm) cubes (the weight of the fish includes the heads)
1 Tbs (15 ml) paprika
salt and pepper to taste

Simmer onions, leeks, carrots, tomato, celery, potatoes, chili and fish heads in enough water to generously cover for 1½ hours. Strain and place in large saucepan. Puree remaining vegetables and add to fish stock with fish cubes, paprika, salt and pepper. Cook gently until cubed fish is cooked—about 3-4 minutes.

Serve with hot crusty bread.

KWV Late Harvest or Golden Vintage or Groot Constantia Estate Weisser Riesling

LETTUCE SOUP

Serves 4-6

2 onions, chopped
2 leeks, washed very well and sliced
1 Tbs (15 ml) butter or olive oil
3½ cups (900 ml) finely chopped iceberg lettuce
1-2 vegetable bouillon cubes
4 cups (1 liter) water
½ cup (125 ml) cream
freshly ground nutmeg
salt and freshly ground pepper

Sauté onions and leeks in butter. When slightly soft, add lettuce. Add vegetable cubes and water and simmer covered, until tender, for about 10-15 minutes. Add cream. Simmer slowly for a further 10-15 minutes. Add nutmeg and season to taste with salt and pepper.

KWV, Paarl, Springbok Sauvignon Blanc, or Backsberg Sauvignon Blanc

MYRNA'S MOM'S VEGETABLE SOUP

Serves 10-12

1 can cream of vegetable soup
1 can cream of tomato soup
1 can beans in tomato sauce
1 can northern beans (butter beans)
2 chicken bouillon cubes
approximately 6 cups (1½ L) boiling water
1 cup (250 ml) cooked fine noodles
½ cup (125 ml) grated cabbage (optional)
salt and pepper

Simmer all together until well blended. Taste for seasoning.

Cathedral Cellar Chardonnay or Boschendal Estate Chardonnay

NATURE'S SOUP

Serves 10-12

2 Tbs (30 ml) olive oil
2 onions, chopped
3 shallots, chopped
2-3 leeks, sliced
1 parsnip, peeled and diced
1 turnip, peeled and diced
2-3 cloves garlic, chopped
4-6 carrots, diced
4 zucchini, sliced
4 yellow squash, sliced
1 cup (250 ml) diced butternut
1 cup (250 ml) peas
2 large potatoes, peeled and diced
1 cup (250 ml) diced broccoli (optional)
2-3 vegetable bouillon cubes
salt and pepper to taste

In a large pot sauté onions, shallots and leeks in olive oil for 5-10 minutes or until limp. Add remaining vegetables and garlic with water to cover. Bring to the boil. Turn down heat. Add bouillon cubes and simmer soup for 1½-2 hours until veggies are tender. Season to taste and sprinkle with diced fresh herbs of your choice. You may puree if you wish.

Paarl Riesling or Springbok Chardonnay

PASTA FAGIOLI

Serves 12

2 Tbs (30 ml) oil
1 large onion, chopped
¼ cabbage, shredded
1 large leek, sliced
1 clove garlic, crushed
2 sticks celery, chopped
1 large carrot, diced
1 can whole tomatoes, chopped
2 chicken, beef or vegetable bouillon cubes
1 large potato, diced
1 can butter beans (northern) with juice
1 can peas, with juice
8 oz (250 g) fusilli, orzo, small shells, or penne pasta
shavings of Parmesan cheese

Heat oil. Sauté onions, cabbage, leeks, garlic, celery and carrots until soft. Add can tomatoes, chicken, beef or vegetable bouillon cubes, potato, and water to cover. Simmer gently until potato is tender—about 30-45 minutes. Add can of beans with juice, can of peas with juice and pasta. Cook stirring occasionally for approximately 10 mins. until pasta is al denté. Garnish with shavings of Parmesan cheese.

KWV Renasans or Paarl Pale Dry Sherry

PORTABELLA MUSHROOM SOUP

Serves 6

1 lb 10 oz (750 g) portabella mushrooms
4 oz (125 g) butter
2 cloves garlic, crushed
4 Tbs (60 ml) fresh parsley, finely chopped
5 slices white bread, crusts removed

4 cups (1 L) chicken stock
nutmeg, freshly grated
salt and pepper
½-1 cup (125-250 ml) cream

Wipe mushrooms and chop roughly.

Melt butter in saucepan. Add mushrooms, garlic and parsley. Cover and cook slowly for 10 minutes. Crumble bread into saucepan. Add stock and seasonings. Bring to boil, stirring and simmer 10 minutes.

Blend half in food processor. Return to saucepan with remaining soup and add cream. Reheat gently but do not boil. Serve hot, garnished with additional sautéed mushroom slices.

Desiree Blumenthal
Cincinnati, Ohio

KWV, Paarl, Springbok Sauvignon Blanc, Groot Constantia Estate Sauvignon Blanc

ROASTED PEPPER AND GARLIC SOUP

Serves 10-12

3 lbs (1½ kg) red bell peppers, roasted
1 large onion, diced
2 leeks, diced
2 Tbs (30 ml) oil
4 large cloves garlic, crushed
¼ tsp (1 ml) onion powder
½ tsp (2 ml) salt
few drops tabasco
6 cups (1½ l) strong chicken stock
½ cup (125 ml) cream
4 oz (125 g) spiced Gournay Cheese or Herbed Boursin or any cream cheese with
  herbs and spices, at room temperature

Preheat broiler and place peppers on foil-lined pan. Broil peppers, turning until charred on all sides. Transfer peppers to plastic bag and seal. When peppers are cool enough to handle, peel, discard seeds and membrane and dice. Sauté onion and leeks in a large saucepan in oil until limp. Add crushed garlic and sauté 2 minutes longer.

Add seasonings, peppers, chicken stock and allow to simmer gently 30 minutes. Add cream and cheese and stir until thoroughly combined. Cool. Process in food processor.

Serve hot or cold. Season to taste with salt and pepper. If necessary, you may add more chicken stock.

KWV, Paarl Springbok Chardonnay or De Wetshof Estate Bon Vallon Chardonnay

SEAFOOD GEZPACHO

Serves 12

1 large yellow pepper, coarsely chopped
6 lbs (3 kg) large ripe tomatoes, peeled, seeded, and chopped
1 large red pepper, coarsely chopped
1 English cucumber, coarsely chopped
1 large red onion, coarsely chopped
4 cloves garlic, chopped
1 cup (250 ml) buttermilk
1 tsp (5 ml) rice wine vinegar
½ tsp (2 ml) cayenne pepper
Salt and freshly ground pepper
1 lb (450 g) fresh salmon, cooked and cubed
1 cup (250 ml) frozen corn kernels, cooked and drained
dash tabasco, to taste
8-oz can (225 g) tomato juice, poured into ice cube tray and frozen

Combine the tomatoes, peppers, cucumber, red onion, chopped garlic, buttermilk, rice vinegar and cayenne pepper. Working in batches, process in food processor until blended but still chunky. Transfer to a large bowl and season with salt, freshly ground pepper and tabasco to taste. Cover and refrigerate overnight.

Before serving, stir in salmon and corn. Ladle soup into serving dishes and add tomato juice ice cubes.

KWV, Paarl, or Springbok Sauvignon Blanc or Boschendal Estate Sauvignon Blanc

ZUPPA DE PESCA

Serves 6-8

2 Tbs (30 ml) olive oil
1 large onion, chopped
1 stick celery, chopped
½ cup (125 ml) KWV Renasans or Paarl Pale Dry Sherry
2 tsp (10 ml) finely chopped garlic
1 x 16-oz (425 g) can whole tomatoes, with juice
1 bay leaf
½ chicken bouillon cube, crushed
1 Tbs (15 ml) freshly chopped oregano
1 tsp (5 ml) dried or 1 Tbs (15 ml) fresh chopped parsley
freshly ground black pepper
1 lb (500 g) fish such as cod, hake, or snapper cut into cubes
12-oz pkg (375 g) cooked shrimp

Heat oil in large saucepan. Add onion and celery and sauté until limp. Add sherry, garlic, tomatoes with juice, bay leaf, bouillon cube, herbs and pepper and heat to boiling. Reduce heat and simmer for 10-15 minutes. Add fish and shrimp and cook another 5 minutes to poach fish.

Spoon fish and broth into bowls. Sprinkle with additional chopped parsley. Serve with brushetta or crusty garlic bread.

KWV Steen or Paarl Cape Riesling or Boschendal Estate Chardonnay Light

White Chocolate Cheesecake

photo by Joseph Braun, Bronze Photography, Cincinnati, Ohio

Clockwise: Tortellini Salad; Chinese Chicken Salad and Exotic Lettuce, Sundried Tomato and G
Cheese Salad

photo by Alain Proust, Cape Town, South Africa
food stylist: Macushla Falkiner, Cape Town, South Africa

Sosaties (Dutch Kebabs), Bobotie, Samoosas, Souped up Chicken

photo by Alain Proust, Cape Town, South Africa
food stylist: Macushla Falkiner, Cape Town, South Africa

Mussels Marniere, Cape Pickled Fish, Thai Crispy Snapper

photo by Alain Proust, Cape Town, South Africa
food stylist: Macushla Falkiner, Cape Town, South Africa

Grilled Prawns (Portuguese Style), Mixed Vegetable Grill, Onion Quiche, Very Berry Salad

photo by Alain Proust, Cape Town, South Africa
food stylist: Macushla Falkiner, Cape Town, South Africa
photo location: KWV Farm, Laborie Estate, Paarl, South Africa

Koeksusters; Cape Seed Bread; Melktert with Crust; Pumpkin Fritters; Ouma's Rusks

photo by Alain Proust, Cape Town, South Africa
food stylist: Macushla Falkiner, Cape Town, South Africa

Almond Chocolate Layer Cake; Chocolate Raspberry Slice; 2 Tone Creme Brulee; Sacher Te
Chocolate Glazed Banana Cake

photo by Joseph Braun, Bronze Photography, Cincinnati, Ohio

Millionaire's Nut Tart; Cream Pound Cake; Kadiyif with Custard; Ginger Almond Tart; Austr
Caramel Logs; Chinese Chews; Cream Tartlets; Desiree Rosen's Chocolate Cream Truffles; E
Almond Coffee Tartlets; Shortbread Jam Cookies; Caramel Apple Kuchen

photo by Joseph Braun, Bronze Photography, Cincinnati, Ohio

Tropical Fruit Dessert; Frozen Lemon Meringue; Lemon Glazed Cheesecake; Hawaiian Grilled Fruit with Coconut Vanilla Sauce; Mango Roulade with Passion Fruit Glaze

photo by Joseph Braun, Bronze Photography, Cincinnati, Ohio

Seafood

ANCHOVY FLAVORED GRILLED HALIBUT STEAKS

Serves 4

4 halibut steaks (kingklip may also be used) about 1" (2.5 cm) thick
½ tsp (3 ml) garlic powder
juice of 1 lemon
½ tsp (3 ml) dried oregano
½ tsp (3 ml) dried parsley
1 tsp (5 ml) Old Bay Seasoning or fish spice
2 cloves crushed garlic
1 tsp (5 ml) cracked pepper
½ tsp (3 ml) concentrated hot pepper paste—or half a jalapeño pepper, seeded
1 tsp (5 ml) creme d'anchois or ½ can anchovies
½ cup (125 ml) olive oil

Place halibut or kingklip steaks in a tupperware or plastic container. Place remaining ingredients in blender and pour over steaks. Allow to marinate for at least a few hours or overnight. Place on foil-lined baking sheet directly under oven broiler and broil for 5-7 minutes on each side or until nicely browned. This can also be grilled on the barbecue.

Serve garnished with anchovies and capers.

Cathedral Cellars Chardonnay or De Wetshof Estate d'Honneur Chardonnay

BAKED SEA BASS

Serves 4

2 x 2 lbs (1 kg) whole sea bass, scaled and gutted*
juice of 1 lemon
salt, pepper, garlic powder and fish spice
2-3 Tbs (30-45 ml) olive oil
1 large onion, diced
1 tsp (5 ml) crushed garlic
1 leek, sliced
2 sticks celery, sliced
1 green pepper, coarsely diced
1 red pepper, coarsely diced
1 yellow pepper, coarsely diced
2 skinned tomatoes, diced
1 can mushrooms, drained
1 Tbs (15 ml) chopped parsley or herbs of choice

Wash and dry fish thoroughly, place in a foil-lined baking tray or roasting pan. Sprinkle with lemon juice and season generously with salt, pepper, garlic powder and fish spice.

In a large saucepan, heat olive oil, add onion, garlic, celery, leek and peppers and sauté 5-10 minutes. Add tomatoes and mushrooms and sauté another 5 minutes. Add parsley, allow vegetable mixture to cool. Place half of the mixture underneath the fish and the rest on top.

Cover with foil and bake in a 400°F (200°C) oven for 45-60 minutes or until fish is easily pierced with fork. Serve over pasta or with baked potatoes.

*If you don't want to be bothered with bones in the fish, you may have the fish filleted (do not remove skin) and sandwich the two halves together with the half vegetable mixture in the middle and the rest spooned on top. Bake as above.

KWV, Paarl or Springbok Sauvignon Blanc or Neil Ellis Sauvignon

DELICIOUS AND TASTY GRILLED HALIBUT, KINGKLIP, OR SWORDFISH

Serves 4

2 lbs (1kg) halibut steaks, 1" (2.5 cm) thick (with the bone)
3 cloves garlic, crushed
½ tsp (3 ml) chopped jalapeño peppers
2 tsp (10 ml) coarsely ground black pepper
3 Tbs (45 ml) olive oil
juice of ½ lemon
1 tsp (5 ml) garlic powder
1 tsp (5 ml) dried or fresh oregano
1 tsp (5 ml) dried or fresh basil
1 tsp (5 ml) salt

Combine garlic and remaining eight ingredients and rub over both sides of the fish. Allow to marinate for at least 2 hours. Place on foil-lined baking sheet and broil directly under broiler until very well browned and crispy on both sides. Spoon the juices over the fish. This can also be cooked on the barbecue.

Serve with pasta or new potatoes and roasted* or steamed asparagus.

*To roast asparagus: Break off wooded ends. Brush with olive oil (preferably garlic-flavored oil), and place on a foil-lined pan and place in a 500°F (260°) oven for 5-10 minutes until cooked.

KWV, Springbok or Paarl Chardonnay or Backsberg Estate Chardonnay

FETTUCINI WITH SCALLOPS, SHRIMPS, MUSSELS AND MAHI-MAHI

Serves 8-10

1 lb (500 g) mahi-mahi or kabeljou (a South African fish)
1 lb (500 g) shrimp (prawns)
½ lb (250 g) scallop
2 lbs (¾ kg) mussels
1 large onion, finely chopped
6 cloves garlic, finely chopped
3 Tbs (45 ml) olive oil
1 cup (250 ml) white wine
1½ cups (250 ml) chicken stock
125 g (4 oz) butter
2 Tbs (30 ml) Pernod liquor
juice of lemon
1 tsp (5 ml) dried or 1 Tbs (15 ml) freshly chopped parsley
½ tsp (3 ml) dried thyme
½ tsp (3 ml) garlic salt
black pepper to taste

Sauté onion and garlic in olive oil 3-5 minutes. Add wine, chicken stock, and bring to the boil. Add mahi-mahi and cook 2-3 minutes. Add shrimp and cook another 2-3 minutes. Remove shrimp and mahi-mahi and set aside.

Add mussels and allow mixture to steam until the shells open—about 5 minutes. Discard unopened shells. Remove cooked mussels and set aside. Reduce the broth by half by simmering gently. Add butter, Pernod, lemon juice, herbs, garlic salt and black pepper to taste. Place scallops in the liquid and poach for 1-2 minutes. Add the mahi-mahi, shrimp and mussels and heat through thoroughly.

Serve on a bed of cooked fettucini and sprinkle with additional fresh chopped parsley and garnish with twists of lemon.

Cathedral Cellar Chardonnay or Backsberg Estate Chardonnay

FISH STEAKS AU POIVRE

Serves 4

4 cod steaks (or other firm fleshed fish such as halibut or kingklip)
salt and fish spice—Old Bay Seasoning
4 Tbs (60 ml) mixed peppercorns (pink, green, and black)
1 Tbs (15 ml) flour
2 Tbs (30 ml) oil
2 oz (50 g) butter
1 cup (250 ml) fish stock or chicken stock
¼ cup (60 ml) KWV Renasans Sherry
1 Tbs (15 ml) soy sauce
1 Tbs (15 ml) KWV VSOP or 10-Year-Old Brandy
1 cup (250 ml) heavy cream

Season the fish with salt and fish spice. Crush peppercorns, mix with flour, and press this mixture onto the fish steaks. Heat the oil and butter in a large saucepan and cook the steaks on each side until crisp and golden. Remove from pan and set aside.

Pour the stock, sherry, soy sauce and brandy into the pan and reduce until about 1 cup (250 ml) of mixture remains. Add cream and continue to cook until further reduced. Adjust seasonings if necessary and pour over steaks.

Serve on a bed of angel hair pasta or with boiled new potatoes.

KWV, Paarl or Springbok Sauvignon Blanc or Saxenburg Sauvignon Blanc

FRIED FISH WITH MORE THAN TARTARE SAUCE

Serves 6-8

2 lbs (1 kg) fresh fish (cod loin, orange roughy, kingklip, hake, or sole
½ cup (125 ml) plus 1 Tbs (15 ml) flour
½ cup (125 ml) flat beer
1 Tbs (15 ml) cider vinegar
½ tsp (2 ml) baking soda
¾ tsp (4 ml) salt
¼ tsp (1 ml) pepper
¼ tsp (1 ml) fish spice
oil for frying

Rinse fish in cold water and dry thoroughly on absorbent paper.

Whisk flour, beer, vinegar, and baking soda in medium bowl until well blended. Season with salt, pepper, and fish spice.

Pour oil into pan to a depth of ½" (1.25 cm). Heat oil on high until hot. Dip fish into batter, letting excess run off into bowl. Place fish in oil and immediately turn heat to medium. Cook on both sides until golden brown. Drain on absorbent towels. Serve with the following sauce:

More than Tartare Sauce:
½ cup (125 ml) low fat plain yogurt
½ cup (125 ml) mayonnaise
¼ cup (60 ml) sweet bread and butter chip dill, chopped
**   (May use a combination of sweet and dill pickles)**
1½ jalapeño peppers, seeded and chopped
2 cloves garlic, minced
½ cup (125 ml) chopped red onion
salt to taste

Combine all ingredients gently with spoon. Make several hours or a day in advance to allow flavors to blend. Do not chop vegetables too finely.

KWV, Paarl, or Springbok Chardonnay or Weltevrede Estate Chardonnay

GRILLED BLACKENED SALMON AU BEURRÉ BLANC

Serves 6

6 salmon steaks, rubbed with olive oil and sprinkled generously with blackened seasoning (recipe following or use store-bought variety)

Place steaks on foil-lined baking sheet and broil on both sides until crisp and nicely browned.

Beurré Blanc Sauce:
1 cup (250 ml) white wine (Springbok Chardonnay)
1 cup (250 ml) cream
2 shallots, finely chopped
1 Tbs (15 ml) lemon juice
1 Tbs (15 ml) chopped parsley
a sprig of thyme
6-8 peppercorns
3 oz (90 g) butter

Place wine, cream, shallots, lemon juice, parsley, thyme and peppercorns in a heavy saucepan and bring to a boil. Reduce heat and cook until reduced by half. Strain into another small saucepan, pressing down firmly on solids to extract as much liquid as possible. Set over very low heat and whisk in 1 piece of butter at a time until all butter is melted and sauce is smooth.

Spoon half of sauce onto serving platter. Place salmon steaks on top and drizzle remaining sauce over top. Garnish with slices of lemon and fresh sprigs of herbs.

Blackened seasoning:
2 Tbs (30 ml) sugar
2 Tbs (30 ml) dry mustard powder
½ tsp (3 ml) cinnamon
3 Tbs (45 ml) paprika
1 Tbs (15 ml) cocoa
1 cup (250 ml) chili powder
1 Tbs (15 ml) ground cumin
2 Tbs (30 ml) ground black pepper
½ cup (125 ml) kosher salt

Combine all ingredients.

Cathedral Cellar Chardonnay or Boschendal Estate Chardonnay Reserve

GRILLED CRAB CAKES WITH LOW-FAT MUSTARD SAUCE

Serves 4-6

8 oz (250 g) can Premium Jumbo Lump Crab Meat (can use imitation crab meat)
1½ lb (¾ kg) Alaskan or snow crab, removed from shells and picked over for cartilage
and shell, well drained on absorbent towels
½ cup (125 ml) fresh breadcrumbs, lightly packed
2 Tbs (30 ml) Worcestershire Sauce
2 Tbs (30 ml) lemon juice
1 tsp (5 ml) fish spice or to taste
pinch cayenne pepper
½ tsp (3 ml) freshly ground pepper to taste
2 Tbs (30 ml) freeze-dried or fresh chives
2 tsp (10 ml) dry mustard

Place all ingredients in mixing bowl and stir to combine. Shape into 8 x 2½" (6 cm) diameter patties. If mixture is still wet, add more bread crumbs or blot between paper towels. Spray crab cakes with nonstick olive oil spray and place on foil-lined pan and place immediately under broiler. Cook for approximately 5 minutes on each side until golden brown. When turning over, spray second side with nonstick olive oil spray. Remove and place on paper towel to drain. Makes 12 crab cakes. Serve with low fat mustard sauce.

Sauce:
¼ cup (60 ml) dijon mustard
2 Tbs (30 ml) red wine vinegar
1 Tbs (15 ml) sugar
pinch salt
¼ cup (60 ml) plain yogurt
1 Tbs (15 ml) minced chopped dill or 1 tsp (5 ml) dried

Blend all ingredients together thoroughly. Chill several hours for flavors to blend.

KWV, Paarl, or Springbok Sauvignon Blanc, or Groot Constantia Estate Sauvignon Blanc

GRILLED FISH STEAKS WITH PINEAPPLE BANANA SALSA

Serves 4-6

2 lbs (1 kg) salmon, swordfish or tuna steaks
salt
black pepper
garlic powder
Italian herbs
juice of 1 lemon
½ cup (125 ml) olive oil

Season fish with salt, black pepper, garlic powder, herbs, lemon juice and olive oil. Line a pan with foil and spray well with cooking spray. Cook fish under broiler skin side up first and then turn over, approximately 5-7 minutes on each side. Can also be done on the barbecue.

Transfer fish to platter and top each steak with 2 Tbs (30 ml) salsa and serve extra salsa on side. Sprinkle lightly with additional chopped cilantro (dunia).

Pineapple Banana Salsa:
½ cup (15 ml) cilantro (dunia)
1 clove garlic
1 small onion
1 small green chili, seeds removed
½ red pepper
½ tsp (3 ml) salt
1 tsp (5 ml) black pepper, coarsely ground
20-oz (567 g) can pineapple tidbits with juice
1 banana

Combine first seven ingredients in food processor. Stir in pineapple and sliced banana.

Cathedral Cellar Sauvignon or Neil Ellis Sauvignon Blanc

GRILLED GRAVILAX

Serves 4

1 salmon side [approx. 1½ lb (¾ kg)]
1 Tbs (15 ml) sugar
1 Tbs (15 ml) coarse kosher salt
2 tsp (10 ml) freshly ground black pepper
1 Tbs (15 ml) vodka
1 large bunch fresh dill
olive oil for brushing

Combine sugar, salt and pepper, and set aside. Sprinkle vodka over salmon and then rub with mixed dry ingredients. Place dill on top, cover with foil, weigh down, and chill overnight, turning once.

Drain liquid off fish. Pat dry. Remove excess salt and dill, brush with olive oil and grill until cooked (approximately 3-5 minutes per side).

KWV, Paarl, or Springbok Sauvignon Blanc, or Boschendal Estate Sauvignon Blanc

GRILLED MAHI-MAHI WITH LOBSTER CREAM SAUCE

Serves 4-6

2 lbs (1 kg) mahi-mahi (salmon may also be used)
juice of 1 lemon
salt, pepper and garlic powder
melted butter or olive oil

Sprinkle lemon juice over both sides of fish, season with salt, pepper, and garlic powder. Brush with melted butter or olive oil. Place on a cookie sheet lined with foil and broil skin side up first, then turn over and continue to broil until brown and crusty. Can also be done on the barbecue.

Lobster cream sauce:
1 onion, diced
3 cloves garlic, crushed
1 Tbs (15 ml) fresh grated ginger
1-2 jalapeño chilies, seeded and diced
2-3 Tbs (30-45 ml) olive oil
1 tomato, skinned and diced
1 cup (250 ml) coconut milk
½ chicken bouillon cube, crushed
1 Tbs (15 ml) curry powder
¼-1 cup (125-250 ml) heavy cream
diced lobster, crab, shrimp or scallops (one or all, as you wish)

Sauté onion, garlic, ginger, and jalapeño pepper in olive oil until onion is lightly browned. Add tomato, coconut milk, bouillon cube and curry powder (the latter must be mixed to a paste with a little cold water) and simmer for 15-20 minutes. Cool. Place in blender or food processor until smooth. Add cream (as much as you think necessary). Return to heat and simmer until slightly thickened. Add diced seafood.

Spoon over grilled fish.

Any leftover sauce may be frozen and kept for later use.

Cathedral Cellar Chardonnay or Backsberg Estate Chardonnay

GRILLED SALMON WITH SAFFRON CREAM SAUCE AND PUREED ROASTED PEPPER

Serves 6

6 salmon fillets
juice of ½ lemon
salt
pepper
garlic powder
2-3 Tbs (30-45 ml) olive oil

Sprinkle lemon juice over fish. Season with salt, pepper and garlic powder. Pour over olive oil and allow to marinate a couple of hours or overnight.

Sauce:
½ cup (125 ml) white wine (Springbok Chardonnay)
1 cup (250 ml) fish stock or chicken stock
2 bay leaves
6 peppercorns
sprinkling of dried parsley
½ tsp (3 ml) saffron threads
2 egg yolks
1 cup (250 ml) heavy cream
salt and pepper to taste

Pour wine, fish or chicken stock, bay leaves, peppercorns, parsley, and saffron into saucepan. Bring to a boil and then simmer gently until reduced to half. Strain.

Beat egg yolks with cream just until combined. Add reduced stock whisking all the time and cook over low heat until slightly thickened. If necessary, thicken with a paste of 1 tsp (5 ml) cornstarch mixed to a paste with cold water.

Place a pool of sauce on plates, place salmon on top and decorate with a puree of roasted red peppers which have been placed in a plastic bag with one corner snipped off and pipe lines over salmon. Place a sprig of any fresh herb on top.

To roast peppers:
Place under broiler on foil-lined pan and turn until skin is charred on all sides. Cool in a paper or plastic bag. Peel off skin and remove seeds and place flesh in blender to puree. Season with salt and pepper to taste, if desired.

KWV, Paarl or Springbok Chardonnay or De Wetshof Estate d'Honneur Chardonnay

144

GRILLED SALMON OR TUNA WITH ROASTED RED PEPPER SAUCE

Serves 6

6 salmon or tuna steaks

Season both sides with salt, pepper, garlic powder, juice of 1 lemon and drizzle with 2 Tbs (30 ml) oil.

Sauce:
3 or 4 bell peppers
1 jalapeño pepper
2 Tbs (30 ml) olive oil
1 onion, chopped
3 cloves garlic, crushed
1 Tbs (15 ml) freshly chopped parsley
¼ tsp (1 ml) ground cumin
½ tsp (3 ml) celery salt
½ chicken bouillon cube, crushed
½ cup (125 ml) water
1 Tbs (15 ml) lemon juice

Preheat broiler. Cover pan with foil and place bell peppers on foil under broiler rack approximately 4" (10 cm) from heat, turning until peppers are charred all over. Place in brown paper bag, seal and allow to cool. When cool enough to peel, discard seeds and membranes and chop coarsely. Set aside.

Sauté onion and garlic in olive oil until softened (approx. 5 minutes). Add roasted peppers and all remaining ingredients. Cook approximately 5-7 minutes. Remove mixture from heat. Cool and place in blender to combine. Do not puree completely. Sauce must be slightly chunky.

Fish:
Place fish steaks on foil-lined pan immediately under broiler and broil until slightly crispy and brown on both sides, approximately 4-6 minutes on each side depending on thickness of steak [total cooking time—10 minutes per inch (2 cm)].

Garnish with twists of lemons and sprigs of dill or basil on each steak and serve with sauce on side. Sauce may be served at room temperature.

KWV Steen or Paarl Cape Riesling or Groot Constantia Estate Constantia Blanc

MARINATED FISH

Serves 8

4-5 lbs (2kg) red snapper or stump nose (ask fishmonger to scrape scales and remove eyes). Season fish inside and out with fish seasoning and salt and pepper.
Lightly slash fish diagonally—not too deep.

Mix and place inside fish:
3 green onions, diced
1 red chili
1 Tbs (15 ml) sliced gingerroot
½ cup (125 ml) fresh cilantro

*A note about cilantro: A green, lemony herb (also known as Coriander and Chinese parsley and in South Africa, it is referred to as Dunia).

Marinade:
1 Tbs (15 ml) KWV Renasans Sherry
½ cup (125 ml) olive oil
2 Tbs (30 ml) lite soy sauce
juice of 1 lemon
1 tsp (5 ml) garlic powder
½ tsp (2 ml) salt
½ tsp (2 ml) pepper

Combine ingredients and pour over fish.

Allow to marinate at least 3 hours. Grill as follows:

When grilling fish, use a barbecue fish basket, spray with nonstick cooking spray, and grill as follows:

1. Preheat the grill for 15 minutes on high and turn down to medium when ready to cook.
2. Place a few lemon or lime slices between the fish and the basket.
3. To test fish for doneness, insert a bamboo skewer in meat. If it penetrates the fish easily, it is done. Pierce the fish when raw for comparison.
4. General rule of thumb for fish is 10 minutes total cooking time per inch; measure at the thickest portion.
5. When cooking whole fish, use indirect method as follows:
    Heat grill on high for about 20 minutes. When ready to cook, turn off one side only of grill, put a drip pan of water under grid, and place fish on grill over turned off side.

KWV, Paarl or Springbok Chardonnay or De Wetshof Estate Lesca Chardonnay

MERCIA'S SIMPLE BUT DELICIOUS FISH

Serves 4

2 lbs (1 kg) fish fillets (sole, hake, snapper, grouper, or orange roughy)
1 lemon
salt, pepper, fish spice (Old Bay Seasoning)
flour for dusting
2 Tbs (30 ml) oil
2 Tbs (50 g) butter
2 bananas, halved and sliced lengthwise
1 orange, cut in slices with skin
1 tsp (5 ml) ginger, freshly grated
½ cup (125 ml) cream
½ cup (125 ml) orange juice

Sprinkle fish with lemon juice. Season with salt, pepper and fish spice. Dust lightly with flour. Heat oil and butter in large frying pan. Fry fish until golden brown and crisp on each side. Remove and drain on absorbent paper.

Add sliced bananas to pan and fry until softened. Place fish on platter; top with bananas and keep warm. Add orange slices to pan as well as ginger, cream and orange juice. Cook until reduced and slightly thickened and pour over fish.

KWV, Paarl or Springbok Sauvignon Blanc, or Saxenburg Sauvignon Blanc

MEXICAN GRILLED FISH

Serves 4

1 red snapper, stump nose or line fish 3-4 lbs (1½-2 kg) leave fish whole, just have
    it gutted and eyes and scales removed.
2-3 cloves garlic
1 jalapeño pepper, seeded
2 large tomatoes
1 tsp (5 ml) salt
1-2 tsp (5-10 ml) chili powder
2 Tbs (30 ml) olive oil
½ cup (125 ml) cilantro (dunia)

Place garlic, jalapeño pepper, tomatoes, salt, pepper, olive oil, and cilantro in food processor. Place fish on large sheet of foil. Rub fish all over, inside and out, with this mixture and allow to marinate for a couple of hours or overnight. (This is not necessary if you are in a hurry.) Place fish, wrapped in foil, on baking tray in a 400°F (200°C) for 30 minutes; open foil, brush with additional olive oil (or dot with butter) and place under broiler until crispy and well browned and flakes easily when pierced with a fork.

Serve on a bed of angel hair pasta with the accumulated juices spooned over.

KWV Chenin Blanc or Boschendal Petit Pavillon

MUSSELS MARNIERE

Serves 4-6

6-7 lbs (3 kg) mussels
6 finely chopped shallots
4 cloves finely chopped garlic
3 Tbs (45 ml) olive oil
1 cup (250 ml) red wine—Springbok Cabernet Sauvignon
1 cup (250 ml) chicken stock
dill and thyme
¼ lb (125 g) butter
2 Tbs (30 ml) Pernod liquor
juice of 1 lemon
salt and pepper, if needed
½ cup (125 ml) chopped parsley

Wash mussels well, scrape off beard and then rinse thoroughly. In a large saucepan, sauté shallots and garlic in olive oil.

Add mussels, wine, chicken stock, dill and thyme. Cover tightly and steam using medium heat until the shells open—5 minutes or so. Discard unopened shells. Take cooked mussels and set aside to keep warm.

Cook the broth until it is reduced by half. Add the butter, Pernod and lemon juice. Taste for seasoning and correct accordingly.

Transfer mussels to deep plates or bowls and pour broth over them. Sprinkle with chopped parsley and serve with warm, crusty garlic bread.

Cathedral Cellar Chardonnay or Neil Ellis Chardonnay

PASTA WITH SMOKED SALMON AND LOBSTER

Serves 8-10

½ lb (250 g) penne pasta (or other shaped pasta)
2 Tbs (30 ml) olive oil
2-3 cloves garlic, crushed
4 chopped spring onions (white only)
1 large tomato, peeled, seeded and diced
(can use 4 finely diced sundried tomatoes, if desired)
1 Tbs (15 ml) freshly chopped basil
1 Tbs (15 ml) freshly snipped dill
½ tsp (3 ml) dried red pepper or peri-peri chilies
1 cup (250 ml) cream
2 Tbs (30 ml) vermouth or cooking wine—KWV Renasans Sherry
salt and pepper to taste
1½ cups (375 ml) cooked chopped lobster
4 oz (125 g) finely chopped smoked salmon (lox)
½ lb (250 g) fresh asparagus—steamed but still crisp—sliced diagonally.
2-3 Tbs (30-45 ml) freshly grated parmesan cheese and a few sprigs of dill for garnish
caviar for garnish

Cook pasta according to package directions. Drain and rinse with cold water and set aside.

Heat oil in heavy saucepan. Add garlic and onion and sauté 2-3 minutes. Add tomato, basil, dill, dried red pepper, cream and cooking wine. Cook until liquid has reduced and thickened (about 5 minutes over med-low heat). Adjust seasoning with salt and pepper. Stir in pasta, lobster, smoked salmon and asparagus. Cook over low heat, stirring constantly until heated through.

Arrange on a serving platter and sprinkle with parmesan cheese, sprigs of dill and dollops of caviar.

Cathedral Cellar Chardonnay or Boschendal Chardonnay

PASTRY WRAPPED MOUSSE FILLED SALMON WITH PAPAYA BASIL SAUCE

Serves 10-12

1 whole salmon, filleted into two sides
1 lemon
1 tsp (5 ml) salt
1 pkg commercially prepared puff pastry 1 lb (500 g)

½ tsp (3 ml) pepper
1 tsp (5 ml) garlic powder
½ tsp (3 ml) fish spice

Sprinkle fillets with juice of 1 lemon. Season with salt, pepper, garlic powder, and fish spice

Fish Mousse:
1 lb (500 g) orange roughy or stock fish
2 egg whites
1 cup (250 ml) cream
½ tsp (3 ml) salt
½ tsp (3 ml) pepper, freshly ground
dash cayenne or a few drops tabasco
1 Tbs (15 ml) freeze-dried chives or fresh chives
½ lb (250 g) mushrooms, chopped and sautéed in 2 oz (30 g) butter until liquid evaporates

Prepare mousse by placing fish in food processor with metal blade and process. Add egg whites, cream, seasonings, and chives. Fold in mushrooms. Spread mousse between the two salmon fillets like a sandwich.

Roll out pastry into a rectangular shape large enough to encase the whole salmon, reserving extra pastry scraps for decoration. Place salmon on pastry and seal. Turn seam side down onto baking sheet. Shape the tail end of pastry into a fan to resemble a fish tale and place black olive where eye would be. Roll out remaining scraps of pastry and cut into little rounds. Brush pastry rounds with beaten egg and place in overlapping pattern in rows lengthwise on pastry to resemble scales. Bake at 400°F (200°C) for 45-60 minutes until brown and a tester easily pierces right through the thickest part of fish.

Papaya basil sauce:
¾ cup (200 ml) fish stock or vegetable stock
¾ cup (200 ml) dry white wine (Springbok Sauvignon Blanc)
4 oz (113 g) stick butter
salt and pepper
1 Tbs (15 ml) Vermouth
¾ cup (200 ml) papaya, diced
1 Tbs (15 ml) chopped basil

In saucepan, cook stock and wine until reduced by half. Over low heat, whisk in chilled, cut up butter. Add salt, pepper, and 1 Tbs (15 ml) vermouth or to taste. Fold in papaya and basil. Serve sauce with fish.

KWV, Paarl or Springbok Chardonnay or Backsberg Estate Chardonnay

POACHED SALMON OR SOLE WITH CITRUS BEURRÉ BLANC

Serves 8-10

12 medium rolled soles or 3" (7 cm) salmon fillets or plait (braid) strips of sole and salmon for each serving
½ cup (125 ml) water
½ cup (125 ml) orange juice—must be freshly squeezed
½ cup (125 ml) vermouth or dry white wine (KWV Renasans Sherry)
2 bay leaves
½ tsp (3 ml) freshly grated ginger
few peppercorns
1 small shallot, chopped
⅛ tsp (3 ml) salt
⅓ cup (80 ml) cream
4 oz (125 g) butter, cut into 6 pieces
pepper to taste
dash orange-flavored liquor such as KWV Van der Hum Liquor
6 prebaked puff pastry rounds 3" (8 cm) in diameter

Bring water, orange juice, wine, bay leaves, ginger, peppercorns, shallots and salt to a boil in wide frying pan. Add fish or braid to liquid. Reduce heat to medium and cook covered approximately 3-4 minutes. Remove fish from liquid to a greased ovenware platter and set aside.

Strain liquid into small saucepan and continue to cook on high until reduced to ½ cup (125 ml). Reduce heat to low; stir in cream; whisk in butter in four batches adding each one when previous one is incorporated; season to taste with pepper; add liquor. Continue to cook on medium/low heat, whisking constantly until sauce further reduces and thickens slightly.

To serve, place fish in microwave on high for about 20-30 seconds to heat. Heat pastry rounds in 400°F (200°C) oven. Cut in half horizontally; place 2 fillets of fish onto each round; spoon a little sauce over fish and around base of each pastry case and place pastry lid on top and garnish.

Delicious!

Cathedral Cellar Sauvignon Blanc or Boschendal Sauvignon Blanc

QUICK AND EASY BAKED FISH

Serves 6

6 fish fillets of your choice, with skin
garlic, french dressing, vinaigrette or any Italian dressing

Marinate for 20 minutes

Drain fish, place in greased dish and dot with butter. Bake at 400°F (200°C) until crisp—approximately 15-20 minutes.

Eve Berger
Johannesburg, South Africa

KWV, Paarl or Springbok Sauvignon Blanc or Backsberg Estate Sauvignon Blanc

SALMON OR SOLE A LA CAVIAR

Serves 4-6

2 lbs (1 kg) salmon or sole fillets, cut into strips about 2" (5 cm) wide and 6"-8" (15 cm-20 cm) long and rolled up
3-oz (75 g) jar caviar
1 can anchovy fillets, drained and finely chopped
2 Tbs (30 ml) chopped fresh dill
3 Tbs (45 ml) chopped chives
1 cup (250 ml) cream
freshly ground black pepper
butter

Place rolled fish close together in greased ovenproof dish.

Sauce:
Stir together caviar, anchovies, dill, chives, cream and freshly ground pepper to taste.

Pour over fish. Dot with butter and bake at 475°F (225°C) oven for 15-20 minutes.

KWV, Paarl, or Springbok Chardonnay or De Wetshof Estate Lesca Chardonnay

SEA BASS EN PAPILOTE WITH MUSHROOMS, GINGER, AND SCALLIONS

Serves 6

6 fillets of sea bass or 1 whole fish filleted—do not remove skin*
salt and pepper
garlic powder
1 tsp (5 ml) lemon grass
2 tsp (10 ml) nam pla (Thai fish sauce)
3 tsp (15 ml) sesame oil
8 ozs (250 g) sliced mushrooms
1 leek, thinly sliced
1 tsp (5 ml) crushed garlic
24 slices of fresh peeled ginger
12 scallions (green onions) sliced
sesame seeds (optional)
6" x 9" (23 cms) pieces of aluminum foil

Spray foil with nonstick spray. Season fish generously with salt, pepper, garlic powder and lemon grass. Sprinkle lightly with nam pla and then sprinkle with sesame oil.

Combine mushrooms, leeks, garlic, ginger and scallions and place a little on each foil square. Top with fish. Sprinkle with remaining mushroom mixture.* Enclose and seal packages and bake in a 400°F (200°C) oven for approximately 30-45 minutes or until fish pierces easily with a wooden skewer.

*Can sprinkle each portion with sesame seeds, if desired.

*To make larger portions you may sandwich two fillets together with vegetable mixture in the middle and on top.

KWV, Paarl, or Springbok Sauvignon Blanc or Neil Ellis Sauvignon Blanc

SOUTHWESTERN GRILLED FISH

Rub fish steaks of your choice with olive oil and then coat generously with the following combined mixture:

3 Tbs (45 ml) chili powder
2 Tbs (30 ml) paprika
2 Tbs (30 ml) sugar
2 Tbs (30 ml) kosher salt
1 Tbs (15 ml) cocoa powder
2 tsp (10 ml) ground cumin
1 tsp (5 ml) dried oregano
2 Tbs (30 ml) mustard powder
1 tsp (5 ml) coarsely ground black pepper
½ tsp (3 ml) ground cinnamon

Place fish on a foil-lined baking sheet and grill directly under oven broiler on both sides until crusty and cooked on both sides. Drizzle with prepared hot mustard.

This is particularly good on fresh salmon. There should be enough dry spice rub for 6-8 large fish portions.

Cathedral Cellar Chardonnay or Weltevrede Estate Chardonnay

THAI CRISPY SNAPPER

Serves 4

1 x 2-3 lbs snapper or line fish (1-1½ kg) scaled, eyes and fins removed
salt, pepper and fish spice (Old Bay Seasoning)
flour
oil for frying

Season fish with salt, pepper, and fish spice and pat generously with flour. Fry in hot oil until crisp and golden on both sides. Drain well on absorbent paper. Place fish on serving platter, sprinkle with the combined diced topping ingredients and pour hot sauce over.

Sauce:
2 tsp (10 ml) dried lemon grass
2-3 Tbs (30-45 ml) nam pla (fish sauce). May use anchovy paste diluted to a liquid
     with cold water
1 Tbs (15 ml) sugar
3 cloves garlic, crushed
½-1 cup (125-250 ml) coconut milk made by pouring 2 cups (500 ml) boiling water
     over 1 cup (250 ml) coconut—allow to stand 20 minutes—strain and reserve liquid
1-2 tsp (5-10 ml) cornstarch mixed to a paste with water or coconut milk

To prepare sauce, combine all the ingredients except cornstarch and bring to a boil. Thicken slightly with cornstarch. Keep warm or reheat when ready to use.

Topping:
1 stick celery, finely diced
½ red pepper, seeded and diced
1 jalapeño pepper, seeded and diced
½ green pepper, seeded and diced
a handful of cilantro (dunia), finely chopped

Serve on a bed of linguini which has been tossed with a mixture of diced green onion (spring onions), diced tofu, scrambled egg which has been torn into small pieces and crushed salted peanuts.

Neil Ellis Sauvignon Blanc or Boschendal Estate Sauvignon Blanc

Poultry

AUNTIE CELIE'S DELICIOUS ROAST TURKEY

Make a paste in food processor of 2 oz (50 g) fresh, peeled gingerroot and 6 cloves of peeled garlic. Add 2 Tbs (30 ml) oil. Store in a jar and keep refrigerated. This is good to use on all roasts.

1-5 lb turkey (*see below for larger turkey)
juice of 1 lemon
1 tsp (5 ml) each salt and pepper
1 tsp (5 ml) chicken spice
1 tsp (5 ml) dry mustard (approx.)
flour
1 onion
juice of 1 or 2 oranges, depending on size of turkey
½ cup (125 ml) oil

Wash turkey well inside and out in cold water and dry thoroughly. Rub inside and out with lemon juice and 2 tsp (10 ml) of the ginger-garlic mixture. Season thoroughly inside and out with salt, pepper, chicken spice and dry mustard. Sprinkle the outside with a little flour. Place onion inside, cover and leave to marinate in refrigerator overnight.**

Preheat oven to 400°F (200°C). Spray the roasting pan with nonstick spray. Place turkey in pan and pour over oil and roast uncovered for 1 hour, basting every 20 minutes and turning over after half an hour.

Pour over orange juice and place the lid over the turkey but DO NOT CLOSE COMPLETELY—just cover a little so that the turkey cooks through. Continue to cook for about ½ hour and then remove from oven. Remove turkey, skim fat off gravy and make a paste of 2 tsp (10 ml) cornstarch, 1 tsp (5 ml) gravy powder and ½ cup (125 ml) cold water. Cook until thickened on top of stove. Strain.

*For a turkey of 7-10 lbs (3-4 kg), cook for 2½ hours, basting with orange juice the last ½ hour only.

**Auntie Celie says that you must use a deep oven roasting pan with a lid for roasting.

Myrna roasted a 17 lbs (7-8 kg) turkey for 3 hours at 350°F (180°C) and did not cover at all.

Lesley roasted a turkey breast on the barbecue seasoned as above and marinated overnight. When ready to grill, brush turkey with oil and place turkey breast side up using indirect method as described on page 180. Cook turkey 11-14 minutes per pound. You need not baste or turn. Turkey is done when temperature registers 170°F (77°C) to 180°F (82°C) with meat thermometer inserted in thickest part of breast, not touching the bone.

Cathedral Cellar Chardonnay or Weltevrede Estate Chardonnay

CASHEW CHICKEN

Serves 4

4 chicken breasts, skinned and deboned
½ tsp (3 ml) salt
1 Tbs (15 ml) cooking wine or sherry (KWV Renasans Sherry)
1 Tbs (15 ml) cornstarch
1 tsp (5 ml) sesame oil
3-4 Tbs (45-60 ml) oil
½ cup (125 ml) water
1 Tbs (15 ml) ground dried chilies (optional)
2 cloves garlic, thinly sliced
1 tsp (5 ml) freshly grated ginger
1 large can bamboo shoots (cubed)
3 sticks celery, cubed
1 can water chestnuts, drained and sliced
1 cup (250 ml) salted cashew nuts, toasted
3-4 Tbs (45-60 ml) caramel sauce

Cut chicken breasts into cubes. Sprinkle with salt and cooking wine and then stir in cornstarch. Allow to stand for about ½ hour. Mix in sesame oil.

Heat oil in wok or large frying pan. Add chicken and first cook over high heat and then turn down to medium heat until lightly browned and cooked through. Remove from wok and set aside. Add water to wok scraping bottom and bring to boil. Pour over chicken. Add more oil to wok and sauté chilies, garlic and ginger for about 1 minute. Add bamboo shoots, celery, water chestnuts and cashew nuts. Stir fry for 1-2 minutes. Add chicken and juices. Lastly, stir in caramel sauce. Adjust seasoning with salt, if desired.

Serve with steamed rice.

Caramel Sauce:
Combine ½ cup (125 g) sugar with 4 Tbs (60 ml) water. Bring to boil over medium heat and let boil until it changes color. Turn to low and cook until brown. Add ½ cup (125 ml) water to mixture and stir until sugar has dissolved. Remove from heat and store in glass jar in refrigerator.

KWV, Paarl, or Springbok Chardonnay or Backsberg Chardonnay

CHICKEN IN BALSAMIC BARBECUE SAUCE

This sauce is delicious heated and spooned over roast poultry, beef, or lamb.

Serves 6-8

2 chickens cut into portions or 8-10 chicken breasts, skinned and deboned
1 small onion, finely grated
¼ cup (60 ml) vegetable oil
¾ cup (200 ml) balsamic vinegar
3 Tbs (45 ml) sugar
6 Tbs (90 ml) ketchup
2 Tbs (30 ml) Worcestershire sauce
4 green onions, chopped
½ chicken bouillon cube, crushed
1 tsp (5 ml) salt
1 tsp (5 ml) freshly ground pepper
1 tsp (5 ml) dry mustard
2-3 cloves garlic, grated or crushed
few drops tabasco

Combine all ingredients, except chicken. Marinate chicken in half the sauce for a few hours or overnight. Put remaining half of marinade aside. Remove from marinade (discard this remaining marinade) and place chicken on a foil-lined pan and broil on middle rack of oven on both sides until nicely browned—approx. 25 minutes per side. Heat marinade that has been reserved and pour over chicken.

KWV, Paarl or Springbok Sauvignon Blanc or Groot Constantia Estate Sauvignon Blanc

CHICKEN OR BEEF FAJITAS

Serves 6

2 lbs (1 kg) chicken or steak strips
2 cloves garlic, crushed
1 tsp (5 ml) ground cumin
1 tsp (5 ml) coarsely ground black pepper
1 tsp (5 ml) salt
juice of ½ lemon

1 tsp (5 ml) chili powder
1 tsp (5 ml) dried oregano
2 Tbs (30 ml) vegetable oil
1 large onion, halved and sliced
1 large green pepper, sliced
flour tortillas

Mix garlic, cumin, black pepper, salt, lemon juice, chili powder and oregano and marinate chicken or steak for a few hours or overnight.

Heat skillet with oil until hot. Add onions and peppers and sauté until tender. Remove and keep warm. If necessary, add additional tablespoon (15 ml) or two of oil to pan. Stir fry chicken or beef until cooked, approximately 5-7 minutes. Serve chicken or beef in tortillas. Spoon over onion and pepper mixture. If desired, serve with tomato salsa.

KWV, Paarl, or Springbok Pinotage or Backsberg Pinotage

CHICKEN THAILAND WITH RICE

Serves 4

4-6 chicken breasts, split
1 large onion
1 or 2 jalapeño chilies, seeded
3 Tbs (45 ml) grated gingerroot
just under ¼ cup (60 ml) lemon juice
1 tsp (5 ml) fish sauce (nam pla)
½ tsp (3 ml) salt
4 Tbs (60 ml) soy sauce
2 Tbs (30 ml) sesame oil
2 Tbs (30 ml) sugar
½ cup (125 ml) coconut milk*
1 chicken bouillon cube, crushed

In food processor, combine onions, chilies, gingerroot, lemon juice, fish sauce, salt, and soy sauce. Process until smooth. Add sesame oil and sugar and blend well. Marinate chicken in mixture overnight. Grill, basting often with marinade.

Combine remaining marinade with coconut milk and chicken bouillon cube. Bring to a boil and simmer until smooth and thick, stirring constantly. Serve chicken with sauce and rice.

Rice:
1½ cups (375 ml) long-grain rice
½ tsp (3 ml) salt
2 cups (500 ml) water
1 cup (250 ml) coconut milk*

Combine rice, salt, water and coconut milk in a microwave-safe dish. Cook on 100% power for 20 minutes. Reduce heat to 50% power and cook for a further 15 minutes. Remove from oven and fluff up with fork.

* Coconut milk may be purchased or may be made by pouring 2½ cups (625 ml) boiling water over 2 cups (500 ml) coconut. Cover and stand until mixture is just warm. Mix through and then strain squeezing out as much liquid as you can.

KWV, Paarl, or Springbok Sauvivnon Blanc or Boschendal Sauvignon Blanc

CHICKEN TIKKA

Serves 6-8

8 skinless, boneless chicken breasts

Marinade:
1 Tbs (15 ml) vermouth or white wine vinegar
2 Tbs (30 ml) balsamic vinegar
1 tsp (5 ml) salt
½ tsp (2 ml) oregano
½ tsp (2 ml) cumin
1½ tsp (7 ml) ground coriander
½ tsp (2 ml) turmeric
3 Tbs (45 ml) tomato paste mixed with a little hot water to make a smooth paste
¼ tsp (1 ml) curry powder
1 cup (250 ml) plain yogurt
1 tsp (5 ml) freshly grated ginger
2 Tbs (30 ml) olive oil
1 tsp (5 ml) crushed dried red chili
juice of ½ lemon
2 tsp (10 ml) dried cilantro
2 onions, cut into chunks
2 green peppers, cut into chunks

Combine marinade ingredients and marinate chicken pieces for a few hours—for a more intense flavor marinade overnight.

Grill or barbecue chicken basting with marinade.

Heat up remainder of marinade and add chunks of onions and green peppers.

Bring to simmer. Combine chicken with sauce. Serve with rice.

KWV Late Harvest or Paarl Golden Vintage

DUCK WITH PINEAPPLE AND GINGER

2 ducks
salt, pepper, garlic salt and ground ginger
2 whole onions
1 cup (250 ml) water
2 x 16 ozs (453 g) cans of pineapple chunks in their own juice, drained, reserving juice
1 cup (250 ml) orange juice
finely grated rind of 1 orange
2 Tbs (30 ml) ginger liquor
2 Tbs (30 ml) KWV VSOP brandy
2 Tbs (30 ml) Van Der Hum
1 chicken bouillon cube, crushed
3 Tbs (45 ml) tomato ketchup
2 Tbs (30 ml) soy sauce
1x10.5 ozs (300 g) bottle ginger in syrup
1-2 Tbs (15-30 ml) sugar
2 Tbs (30 ml) cornstarch dissolved in a little pineapple juice
salt and pepper to taste

Season ducks with salt, pepper, garlic salt, and ginger and place one whole onion in each duck. Prick ducks well all over, to allow the fat to drain. Place on roasting rack over roasting pan and roast in a 350°F (180°C) oven for 1½ to 1¾ hours, turning halfway through the cooking period.

Cool and cut into serving portions.

Arrange duck in a SINGLE LAYER (this is very important), skin side up in a casserole dish.

Pour fat off roasting pan, place roasting pan on top of stove over medium heat and add water, 2 cups (500 ml) reserved pineapple juice, orange juice, orange rind, ginger liquor, brandy, VAN DER HUM, chicken bouillon cube, ketchup, soy sauce, ½ cup (125 ml) syrup from ginger, sugar and cornstarch, to the pan. Stir until thickened. Adjust seasoning with salt, pepper and sugar. Strain and pour over ducks. Chop up several pieces of ginger and add to duck with pineapple chunks. Bake uncovered in a 350°F (180°C) oven for about one hour, basting occasionally. This dish may be prepared in the morning and left to marinate until ready to bake.

Note: Any canned fruits may be substituted, such as cherries or figs, and the appropriate liquor used.

KWV, Paarl, or Springbok Pinotage or Groot Constantia Pinotage

EXTRA CRISPY DUCK CHERIE

Serves 4

1 duck seasoned with salt, pepper, garlic powder and ground ginger [about a tsp (5 ml) of each]. Prick all over.

Place on a roasting rack and roast at 350°F (180°C) until light brown and then increase oven temperature to 400°F (200°C) and baste with the following mixture:

½ cup (125 ml) marmalade
1 Tbs (15 ml) soy sauce
juice of 1 orange

Continue cooking until crispy and well browned. Cut into portions and serve with cherry sauce.

Cherry Sauce:
1 Tbs (15 ml) cornstarch
1 tsp (5 ml) gravy powder or browner
1 tsp (5 ml) salt
½ chicken bouillon cube, crushed
½ cup (125 ml) red wine (KWV Springbok Pinotage)
1 cup (250 ml) orange juice
1 can dark sweet pitted cherries, undrained
2 Tbs (60 ml) brown sugar
1-2 Tbs (15-30 ml) KWV Ruby Port or KWV Muscadel

Combine cornstarch and gravy powder with salt, bouillon cube, and mix to a paste with wine and orange juice. Place mixture in a saucepan with cherries and brown sugar and cook over medium heat, stirring constantly until thick. Stir in ruby port or muscadel.

KWV, Paarl, or Springbok Pinotage or Groot Constantia Pinotage

GRILLED CHICKEN BREAST WITH BLACK BEAN SALSA

Serves 6-8

6-8 chicken breasts—marinated overnight in Italian dressing

Salsa:
1 15-oz can (475 g) black beans, drained
1 15-oz can (432 g) corn kernels, drained
1 red pepper, diced
3 tomatoes, diced (preferably plum)
⅔ cup (160 ml) red onion, diced
1 jalapeño or serrano chili, seeds removed and diced
1 Tbs (15 ml) freshly squeezed lemon juice
1 tsp (5 ml) salt
1 Tbs (15 ml) olive oil
1 tsp (5 ml) coarsely ground black pepper
½ cup (125 ml) cilantro, finely chopped

Place chicken on a foil-lined pan and broil as close to the heat as possible until nicely browned on both sides. Combine salsa ingredients and spoon on top of chicken breasts.

Delicious and low calorie!

KWV, Paarl, or Springbok Chardonnay, or Weltevrede Estate Chardonnay

GRILLED JERK CHICKEN

Serves 6

6 chicken breasts
6 medium jalapeño peppers, seeded
½ cup (125 ml) olive oil
3 green onions, chopped
1 tsp (5 ml) mustard powder
2 Tbs (30 ml) dried rosemary

1 tsp (5 ml) dried thyme
1 tsp (5 ml) pepper
2 tsp (10 ml) jerk seasoning
¼ cup (60 ml) fresh lemon juice or lime juice
¼ cup (60 ml) soy sauce
6 Tbs (60 ml) olive oil

Place all ingredients, except chicken, in bowl of food processor with metal blade. Process 2 to 3 minutes or until smooth. Marinate breasts for at least 2-3hours.

Grill chicken on both sides until nicely browned, basting with marinade.

This marinade could also be used on a boneless butterflied turkey breast.

KWV, Paarl or Springbok Chardonnay or Neil Ellis Chardonnay

GRILLED CHICKEN BREAST WITH SALSA

Serves 6-8

6-8 chicken breasts, skinned and deboned
garlic powder
2 Tbs (30 ml) sesame oil
½ cup (125 ml) soy sauce
1 tsp (5 ml) black pepper—freshly ground

Season chicken liberally with garlic powder. Combine remaining ingredients and marinate for at least one hour. Broil under oven broiler on foil-lined baking sheets on both sides until nicely browned. Sprinkle with sesame seeds a minute before removing from oven. Serve with the following salsa.

Salsa:
1 onion (preferably purple onion)
1 Tbs (15 ml) olive oil
¼ cup cilantro
1 chili pepper (seeds removed)
½ tsp (3 ml) salt
½ tsp (3 ml) freshly ground pepper

Place all of the above ingredients in food processor and blend, not too fine. Add 2 diced tomatoes.

The above salsa may be served as an appetizer with tortilla chips.

KWV, Paarl or Springbok Sauvignon Blanc or Saxenburg Sauvignon Blanc

INDONESIAN STIR FRY

Serves 6

6 skinless, boneless chicken breasts cut in strips and seasoned with salt, pepper, garlic salt and seasoning salt
2 green peppers, halved and sliced
1 red pepper, halved and sliced
1 onion, cut in wedges
3 cloves garlic, chopped
2-3 dried chilies or 2-3 jalapeño chilies, chopped
1 Tbs (15 ml) grated ginger
1 chicken cube, dissolved in 1 cup (250 ml) boiling water
1 Tbs (15 ml) peanut butter
1 cup (250 ml) coconut milk or coconut cream
1 Tbs (15 ml) sugar
1 Tbs (15 ml) curry powder
1 Tbs (15 ml) cornstarch, dissolved in a little water
2 green onions (spring onions)

Stir fry chicken in a little oil in wok until nicely browned. Remove and set aside. Sauté green pepper, red pepper, onion, garlic, chilies and ginger in a little more oil for 2-3 minutes. Add all other ingredients, except chicken. Simmer together for 3-4 minutes. Add chicken.

Serve over angel hair pasta. Sprinkle with diced onion.

To make coconut milk, page 164.

KWV, Paarl or Springbok Chardonnay or Welterede Estate Prive Du Bois

JAMAICAN CHICKEN

Serves 8

8 chicken breasts
½ red hot chili [may use 1 tsp (5 ml) dried]
1 tsp (5 ml) garam marsala
1 Tbs (15 ml) grated gingerroot
4 cloves garlic, crushed
1 tsp (5 ml) freshly ground pepper, to taste
1 tsp (5 ml) ground coriander
½ tsp (3 ml) ground cumin
½ tsp (3 ml) cumin seeds
juice of 1 lemon
½ cup (125 ml) olive oil

Combine all ingredients except chicken. Marinate chicken overnight. Grill under broiler on foil-lined pan or on outdoor grill.

Serve with baked crispy sweet potato prepared by baking potato until done: cut in half, brush with olive oil and place on hot grill until brown and crispy.

KWV Chenin or Groot Constantia Weisser Riesling

JAVANESE CHICKEN

Serves 4-6

3 whole chicken breasts, boned and cubed
1 red bell pepper, cut into squares
1 green bell pepper, cut into squares
pineapple chunks
1 red onion, cut into chunks
¼ cup (60 ml) oil
⅓ cup (80 ml) molasses
⅓ cup (80 ml) soy sauce
salt and pepper to taste
1-2 cloves minced garlic
½ tsp (3 ml) cumin
1 crushed bay leaf
juice of ½ lemon

Combine oil, molasses, soy sauce, salt, pepper, garlic, cumin, bay leaf and lemon juice. Marinate chicken overnight.

Put on skewers with vegetables and pineapple chunks and broil by placing on a foil-lined pan under broiler or on the barbecue.

KWV, Paarl or Springbok Sauvignon Blanc or Boschendal Sauvignon Blanc

MARINATED TURKEY BREAST

Have your butcher debone a turkey breast. Wash and dry with paper cloth.

Serves 10-12

6 oz (175 ml) frozen orange juice, defrosted
6 oz (175 ml) soy sauce
6 oz (175 ml) honey
4 Tbs (60 ml) oil
1 Tbs (15 ml) freshly grated ginger
dash of red pepper

Combine marinade until well blended. Pour over turkey breast and marinate overnight.

Cook on the grill over indirect heat as described on page 180.

This marinade can be used on a boneless leg of lamb omitting oil. Barbeque as above.

Cathedral Cellar Chardonnay or Weltevrede Estate Chardonnay

QUICK AND EASY CAJUN CHICKEN WITH PASTA

Serves 6

Marinate 4-6 chicken breasts in commercially prepared cajun marinade for at least 24 hours.

1 large onion, peeled, cut into eight wedges and then separated
1 red pepper, seeded and sliced
1 yellow pepper, seeded and sliced
1 green pepper, seeded and sliced
4 cloves garlic, crushed
2-3 Tbs (30-45 ml) olive oil
8 oz (250 g) penne pasta or fettuccini, cooked al denté

Line a baking sheet with foil, spray with nonstick vegetable spray and place chicken breasts onto foil with quite a few spoons of the marinade over the chicken.

Place directly under oven broiler (grill) and grill on both sides until nicely browned, adding more marinade if necessary (only while cooking—do not use the marinade the chicken was in without bringing it to a boil).

Slice chicken breasts into strips, mix well with the marinade left on the foil and set aside.

Sauté onion, peppers, and garlic in oil for a few minutes. Combine with chicken and pasta.

KWV, Paarl or Springbok Pinotage or Beyerskloof Pinotage

SIMPLE CHICKEN CURRY

Serves 6

3 onions, chopped
2 cloves garlic, chopped
2 Tbs (30 ml) oil
1 Tbs (15 ml) flour
2 Tbs (30 ml) curry powder (or to taste)
2 cups (500 ml) chicken stock
½ apple, cored, peeled and sliced
2 tomatoes, peeled, and diced
1 tsp (5 ml) salt
1 tsp (5 ml) sugar
dash of ground cinnamon
dash of ground nutmeg
1 Tbs (15 ml) coconut
1 Tbs (15 ml) chutney
squeeze lemon juice
handful raisins
2½-3 lbs (1-1½ kg) cooked chicken

Cook onions and garlic slowly in oil. When soft but not brown, stir in flour. Add curry powder and cook slowly, stirring so that onions do not stick. If too dry, add a little chicken stock. Add apples and simmer gently for a few minutes. Add tomatoes with all their juices. Add stock and boil gently. Add salt, sugar, cinnamon, nutmeg, coconut, chutney, raisins, lemon juice and a little more stock. Simmer slowly for appox. 20-30 mins. Add chicken and warm gently.

You may use left over chicken, turkey or any firm fish. You may also toss in some cooked pasta.

To poach chicken:
Place chicken in a large casserole dish and sprinkle with salt and pepper. Place a stick of celery, a carrot, sprig of parsley and a small onion, cut in pieces, into dish with chicken. Pour white wine to a depth of ½" (2½ cms). Spray a piece of wax paper long enough to cover the casserole with a nonstick spray. Place sprayed side directly on chicken. Tuck edges into dish and bake at 350°F (180°C) for 20-25 minutes or until no longer pink inside. Cut chicken into strips.

Chicken cooked in this manner makes a delicious chicken salad.

KWV Steen or Paarl Chenin Blanc or Groot Constantia Estate Weisser Riesling

SLOW ROASTED OR GRILLED CHICKEN

This recipe requires fresh herbs for the ultimate taste.

Serves 6-8

2 chickens
2 tsp (10 ml) salt
2 Tbs (30 ml) fresh thyme
2 Tbs (30 ml) fresh rosemary
2 Tbs (30 ml) fresh oregano
2 Tbs (30 ml) fresh basil
2 Tbs (30 ml) fresh parsley
2 Tbs (30 ml) fresh marjoram
juice of 1 lemon
6 cloves garlic
2 tsp (10 ml) dry mustard
2 bay leaves
2 tsp (10 ml) coarsely ground black pepper
3-4 Tbs (45-60 ml) olive oil

Place all ingredients, except chicken and bay leaves, in food processor and blend well. Crush bay leaves and fold in. Rub chickens inside and out and also under the breast skin with mixture. Place in plastic bags and allow to marinate overnight.

To slow roast:
Preheat oven to 450°F (220°C). Split chickens down the back and place skin side up on a rack which has been sprayed with non stick over a roasting pan which has been lined with foil for easy cleaning. Place in a 450°F (230°C) oven for 10-15 minutes. Turn oven temperature down to 300°F (150°C) and allow chicken to roast for another 2-3 hours or until crisp and deep golden brown.

Absolutely Delicious!

To barbecue:
Do indirect cooking as described on page 180.

KWV Paarl or Springbok Cabernet Sauvignon

SOUPED-UP CHICKEN

Serves 6-8

2 frying chickens, can be cut into portions
1 large or 2 small onions, chopped
1 green pepper, chopped
1 can mushrooms, drained
1 can cream of tomato soup

1 can cream of mushroom soup
¾ cup (200 ml) chutney
1 chicken bouillon cube, crushed
1 Tbs (15 ml) curry
2 Tbs (30 ml) brown sugar

Combine all ingredients except chicken.

Season chicken with salt, pepper and garlic salt. Pour mixture over chicken and bake uncovered at 400°F (200°C) for one hour; then cover and leave another ½ to ¾ hour.

Chunks of unpeeled butternut squash can be placed on top before baking.

KWV, Paarl or Springbok Chardonnay or De Wetshof Estate Bon Vallon Chardonnay

TOMATO COCONUT CHICKEN CASSEROLE

Serves 10-12

12-14 chicken portions
salt, pepper, garlic powder, seasoning salt, and flour
2 Tbs (30 ml) oil
1 large onion, diced
2-3 cloves garlic, minced
1 Tbs (15 ml) freshly grated ginger
1 tsp (5 ml) chili powder
1 can 14½ oz (411 g) stewed tomatoes or 4 fresh tomatoes, skinned and diced
½ chicken bouillon cube dissolved in 1 cup (250 ml) water
½ cup (125 ml) flaked coconut
1 cup (250 ml) coconut cream, nondairy creamer or coconut milk

Season chicken portions with salt, pepper, garlic powder, seasoning salt and dust liberally with flour. Rub all over with oil and brown under broiler on both sides.

Place chicken in casserole and prepare sauce.

Sauté onions and garlic in oil until soft. Add ginger, chili powder, tomatoes, and chicken bouillon mixture. Pour over chicken and bake covered in 350°F (180°C) oven for ¾ hour.

Add coconut, cover and continue cooking until chicken is tender. Add coconut cream or nondairy creamer or coconut milk and stir into the sauce and return to oven for another 10-15 minutes until sauce thickens.

KWV Steen or Paarl Chenin Blanc

MUSTARD SAUCE FOR CHICKEN

1 cup (250 ml) Dijon mustard
½ cup (125 ml) teriyaki sauce
½ cup (125 ml) peanut oil
5 cloves garlic
black pepper, crushed

Put in blender for 20 seconds.

Baste on fish or chicken while cooking.

Hilary Isakow
Bloomfield Hills, Michigan

Beef, Lamb and Veal

BEEF SATAY

Serves 4

1½ lbs (750 g) top sirloin or tenderloin, cubed

Marinade:
1 small onion, finely grated
1 tsp (5 ml) fresh grated ginger
1½ Tbs (20 ml) soy sauce
2 Tbs (30 ml) brown sugar
2 Tbs (30 ml) lemon juice or 1 tsp (5 ml) finely chopped lemon grass
¼ tsp (2 ml) cayenne pepper
1 tsp (5 ml) ground coriander
½ tsp (3 ml) cumin
2 Tbs (30 ml) peanut oil
½ tsp (3 ml) salt
½ tsp (3 ml) garlic powder

Combine all marinade ingredients. Pour over beef, cover with plastic wrap and allow to marinate at least 3-4 hours or preferably overnight. Rub bamboo skewers with oil to prevent meat from sticking. Thread meat onto skewers and barbecue until well browned all over.

Sauce:
¾ cup (175 ml) roasted unsalted peanuts
2 Tbs (30 ml) peanut oil
2 Tbs (30 ml) soy sauce
1 Tbs (15 ml) ground coriander
½ tsp (3 ml) turmeric
2 cloves crushed garlic
1 red chili, finely chopped
½ tsp (3 ml) salt
¼ cup (60 ml) water
½-¾ cup (125-175 ml) coconut milk
1 Tbs (15 ml) lemon juice

Blend peanuts in food processor until finely chopped. Combine peanuts and all remaining ingredients in a small saucepan. Bring to boil and then simmer for 2-5 minutes or until thick.

Spoon some of the sauce onto platter and top with skewered beef.

KWV, Paarl, Roodeberg or Groot Constantia Rood

BUTTERFLIED LEG OF LAMB

Serves 8

Have your butcher butterfly a 4 lbs (± 2 kg) leg of lamb. Rub with dry mustard.

4 large cloves garlic, peeled and halved
juice of 1 lemon
1 cup (250 ml) olive oil
2 Tbs (30 ml) fresh thyme
2 Tbs (30 ml) fresh rosemary
1 Tbs (15 ml) fresh oregano
1 Tbs (15 ml) fresh mint
1 tsp (5 ml) freshly ground black pepper
3 bay leaves, coarsely crushed
peppercorns

With a sharp pointed knife, make slits in lamb and insert garlic cloves. Put all remaining ingredients in food processor except peppercorns and bay leaves. Pour marinade over lamb and add peppercorns and bay leaves. Marinade in refrigerator for at least 24 hours. Turn occasionally.

Remove from marinade. Grill lamb and occasionally baste with marinade. Cook 25 to 35 minutes. Thermometer should register 140°F (70°C) for rare and 160°F (80°C) for medium. Remove meat. Stand covered for about 15 minutes before slicing.

Indirect grilling (Gas Grill):
Heat grill on high for about 20 minutes. When ready to cook, turn off one side only of grill. Put a drip pan filled with water under meat and place meat on grid over turned off side.

Oven cooking:
Place meat on greased rack over a pan in 450°F (200°C) oven for approx. 25 mins. per side. Place under broiler until nicely browned.

KWV Paarl or Springbok Shiraz or Rust En Vrede Estate Shiraz

FRUITED LAMB IN CURRY SAUCE

Serves 10-12

1 leg of lamb, 4-5 lbs (2-2½ kg)
2 tsp (10 ml) salt
1 tsp (5 ml) black pepper
1½ tsp (7 ml) garlic powder
2 tsp (10 ml) mustard powder
1 tsp (5 ml) ginger
1 tsp (5 ml) cayenne pepper
½ tsp (3 ml) seasoning salt
2 Tbs (30 ml) curry powder
3 cloves garlic, crushed
2 medium onions, finely chopped
juice of 1 lemon
6½ oz (200 g) apricot juice
2 x 15 oz (439 g), apricots, drained, reserving juice
2 x 15 oz (439 g), pineapple chunks, drained, reserving juice
1 Tbs (15 ml) cornstarch (cornflour), mixed to a paste with a little cold water
maraschino cherries
mint leaves

Season lamb with salt, pepper, garlic powder, mustard powder, ginger, cayenne pepper, seasoning salt, and then rub with curry powder. Combine crushed garlic, chopped onion, lemon juice, apricot juice, and drained juices from apricots and pineapple. Pour over lamb and allow to marinate for 48 hours, turning occasionally.

Remove from marinade, reserving marinade, and place in roasting pan. Pour over ½ cup (125 ml) oil and roast in 350°F (180°C) oven for 45 minutes. Drain fat from pan. Pour marinade over lamb, cover and return to oven for a further 2 hours. When done, remove meat from pan and add cornstarch (cornflour) to the pan to thicken juices.

Use remaining fruit on skewers and alternate with maraschino cherries for color. Place in oven to heat thoroughly. Place meat on serving platter; pour over fruit sauce then insert fruited skewers into the lamb. Garnish with mint.

When serving, each guest should be presented with a fruit skewer with the meal.

KWV, Paarl or Springbok Pinotage or Saxenburg Pinotage

GRILLED CRUSTED TENDERLOIN

Serves 8-10

1 whole tenderloin
4-5 cloves garlic
2 tsp (10 ml) salt
2 heaped tsp (15 ml) mustard powder
1 tsp (5 ml) pepper medley
½ tsp (3 ml) garlic powder
1 tsp (5 ml) oregano or 1 stem fresh oregano (leaves only)
1 tsp (5 ml) parsley flakes
3 Tbs (45 ml) green peppercorns
1 tsp (5 ml) coriander
1 Tbs (15 ml) lemon juice
⅓-½ cup (80-125 ml) olive oil

Rinse meat—wipe dry well with paper towel. Score very lightly with sharp knife. Blend seasonings, lemon juice and olive oil well in food processor ensuring the peppercorns are finely crushed. Rub mixture well into meat. Wrap meat in foil or plastic and marinate overnight.

Bake at 450°F (230°C) for 35-45 minutes.

KWV, Paarl or Springbok Cabernet Sauvignon or Warwick Estate Cabernet Sauvignon

HERB CRUSTED RACK OF LAMB

Serves 6

2 racks of lamb, approximately 7 chops each
salt and freshly ground black pepper
2 Tbs (30 ml) olive oil
2 finely chopped shallots
4 cloves garlic, crushed
4 Tbs (60 ml) fresh herbs—combination of rosemary, parsley, basil, thyme, and marjoram
1 Tbs (15 ml) mustard
1 cup (250 ml) bread crumbs
4 Tbs (60 ml) olive oil

Preheat oven to 450°F (220°C) Season lamb with salt and black pepper. Combine oil, shallots, garlic, herbs and mustard in food processor and rub mixture evenly over lamb. Sprinkle with bread crumbs on meaty side and press down firmly. Place meat, fat side down in roasting pan and sprinkle with additional 4 Tbs (60 ml) oil and roast approximately 25 minutes until done or a meat thermometer inserted in the thickest part of the meat registers 130°F (70°C) for rare or 150°F (80°C) for medium. Baste occasionally.

When done, cover tips of bone with frills and allow meat to rest for 5 minutes before serving.

KWV, Paarl or Springbok Merlot or Saxenburg Merlot

HILARY'S MIDDLE EASTERN LAMB

Serves 8

3 racks of lamb

Marinade:
2 medium onions, finely chopped
2 Tbs (30 ml) minced garlic
3 Tbs (45 ml) lemon juice
½ cup (125 ml) honey
3 Tbs (45 ml) curry powder
1½ tsp (7 ml) cayenne pepper
2 tsp (10 ml) Coleman's mustard powder
2 tsp (10 ml) black pepper
2 tsp (10 ml) salt
1 cup (250 ml) olive oil

Combine ingredients.

1 cup (250 ml) Hoisin sauce

Place the lamb and marinade in plastic bag, tie and place in refrigerator 48 hours, turning occasionally. Remove lamb from marinade and let stand at room temperature 1 hour before cooking.

Brush with Hoisin sauce. Place lamb on rack in shallow roasting pan and roast in hot oven, 450°F (220°C), for 15-25 minutes for rare lamb or longer for a greater degree of doneness. Let rest 6-7 minutes before carving.

Hilary Isakow
Bloomfield Hills, Michigan

KWV, Paarl or Springbok Pinotage or Beyerskloof Pinotage

ISRAELI LAMB KEBABS

Serves 6

2 lbs (1 kg) cubed lamb
4 shallots, chopped
4 cloves garlic, crushed
1 Tbs (15 ml) freshly grated ginger
2 Tbs (30 ml) olive oil
juice of 1 lemon
1 tsp (5 ml) ground coriander
1 tsp (5 ml) salt
1 tsp (5 ml) freshly ground pepper
¼ cup (60 ml) chopped cilantro (dunia) or parsley
2 hot dried chilies
¼ cup (60 ml) olive oil

Sauté shallots, garlic, and ginger in 2 Tbs (30 ml) olive oil until soft. Combine lemon juice, coriander, salt, freshly ground pepper, cilantro or parsley and chilies in food processor until well blended and chilies are chopped. Add shallot mixture and blend. Add olive oil and blend until just mixed. Pour over lamb and marinade in refrigerator overnight.

Drain lamb cubes. Thread onto metal skewers or soaked bamboo skewers. Place on grill about 3" (7 cm) away from heat. Grill at moderate temperature 8 to 12 minutes or until desired doneness, turning and brushing with marinade every two minutes.

Serve over couscous with the following banana-raisin chutney:

1 lb (500 g) bananas, thinly sliced
3 onions, chopped
2 large cloves garlic, crushed
1 tsp (5 ml) salt
juice and grated rind of 1 orange
1½ cups (375 ml) raisins
½ tsp (3 ml) ground cumin
1 tsp (5 ml) ground cardamom
1 tsp (5 ml) coriander
pinch cayenne pepper
1 cup (250 ml) white wine vinegar
1 Tbs (15 ml) sugar, or to taste

Put all ingredients into a saucepan; bring to boil slowly, stirring occasionally. Reduce heat to very low and simmer 1 hour, stirring occasionally.

KWV, Paarl Roodeberg or Rust en Vrede Tinta Barocca

OSSO BUCCO

Serves 4-6

6 thick veal shanks—season with salt and pepper
4 Tbs (60 ml) olive oil
2 medium onions, diced
2 leeks, white part only, sliced
2 sticks celery, sliced thinly
10-12 baby carrots
1 tsp (5 ml) finely grated ginger
3 cloves garlic, crushed or finely chopped
1 tsp (5 ml) fresh thyme leaves or 1 tsp (5 ml) dried
2 fresh sage leaves or 1 tsp (5 ml) dried
2 bay leaves
few peppercorns
1 chicken bouillon cube
½ cup (125 ml) red wine (KWV Springbok Shiraz)
½ cup (125 ml) water
1 can baked beans (optional)

Heat oil in heavy saucepan. Add shanks and brown on both sides. Remove meat and place in ovenware dish. Add more olive oil to pan if necessary. Add onions, leeks, celery, carrots, ginger, garlic, herbs and sauté 5 minutes. Add crushed bouillon cube, wine and water. Pour mixture over meat in casserole*. Bake covered in a 350°F (180°C) for the first hour, uncover and bake until shanks are tender and browned.

*Add baked beans.

KWV, Paarl or Springbok Shiraz or Groot Constantia Estate Shiraz

PINEAPPLE, LAMB, AND GINGER CASSEROLE

Serves 6

1½ lbs (750 g) leg of lamb, cubed
2 onions, chopped
2 Tbs (30 ml) olive oil
2 cloves garlic
1 Tbs (15 ml) finely grated ginger
1 tsp (5 ml) ground ginger
½ lb (250 g) basmati rice
1 chicken bouillon cube combined with 1½ cups (375 ml) water
15 oz (475 g) can pineapple chunks, drained, reserving juice
3 Tbs (45 ml) soy sauce
stick cinnamon
2 oz (50 g) toasted pine nuts (optional)

Preheat oven to 350°F (180°C).

Fry onions in olive oil for a few minutes until limp. Add garlic, grated ginger, and ground ginger and cook another minute or two until fragrant. Remove from pan and set aside.

If necessary, add additional olive oil to pan. Heat and when hot, add lamb and stir to brown meat. Remove from heat. Add rice and onion/garlic mixture. Place mixture in large casserole dish.

In a pot, bring stock, pineapple juice and soy sauce to boil. Pour over lamb/rice mixture. Add cinnamon. Stir well, cover with lid or foil and place in oven. Cook for approximately 1 hour or until lamb and rice are tender and liquid has been absorbed. Fold in pineapple chunks and leave in oven additional few minutes to warm fruit. If desired, sprinkle with pine nuts before serving.

If re-heating add additional pineapple juice.

Marlene Segal
Johannesburg, South Africa

KWV, Paarl or Springbok Pinotage or Backsberg Estate Pinotage

ROAST BEEF WITH WINE SAUCE

Serves 8-10

3 lbs (1½ kg) piece of boneless beef sirloin strip (scotch fillet) or a whole tenderloin
3 tsp (15 ml) dry mustard powder
1½ tsp (7 ml) salt
2-3 tsp (10-15 ml) freshly ground green peppercorns
1 tsp (5 ml) ground black pepper
1 tsp (5 ml) garlic powder
1 tsp (5 ml) mixed dried herbs
3-4 Tbs (45-60 ml) olive oil
1 large onion, peeled and sliced

Rub meat well with mustard powder, salt, green peppercorns, black pepper, garlic powder and dried herbs. Rub with oil and cover with onion. Wrap in foil and refrigerate 24 hours. Roast in a 400°F (200°C) oven uncovered for about 20 minutes (rare), 25 minutes (pink in middle) on each side for a total of 40-50 minutes. Remove from pan and allow to rest on wooden board as you prepare sauce.

Pour excess fat off pan and leave onions. Add to the pan, 1 cup (250 ml) red wine (KWV Paarl or Springbok Pinotage), 1 cup (250 ml) water and 1 chicken or beef bouillon cube (crushed). Bring to the boil, scraping bottom of pan as you do so. Allow to reduce to 1 cup (250 ml). Strain and place in a smaller saucepan. Add 4 oz (125 g) of margarine or butter, whisking in a piece at a time until all is incorporated. Then remove from heat and continue to whisk to a sauce consistency and add ½ cup (125 ml) cream. Season to taste with salt and pepper.

If desired, add 1 or 2 tsp (5 or 10 ml) prepared horseradish or sautéed sliced mushrooms to the sauce or both.

Cathedral Cellar Triptych or Rust En Vrede Estate Wine

SPICY LAMB AND OKRA STEW

Serves 8

3-4 lb (1½-2 kg) stewing lamb
¼ lb (125 g) margarine
3 onions, coarsely diced
3-4 cloves garlic, crushed

salt, pepper and red pepper to taste
5 tomatoes, skinned and diced
1 lb (500 g) okra, fresh or canned (drained)

Heat a large saucepan on stove, spray with nonstick and brown meat. Remove from pot and set aside.

Melt margarine, add onions and garlic and brown lightly. Return meat to saucepan with tomatoes and season with salt, pepper and cayenne pepper (red pepper). Add 1 cup (250 ml) water and simmer over low heat for approximately 2 hours or until tender. Add okra about 20 minutes before serving.

Serve over rice, pasta or couscous.

KWV, Paarl, or Springbok Shiraz or Rust en Vrede Estate Shiraz

STIR FRY BEEF IN SWEET BEAN SAUCE

Serves 4

1 lb (500 g) beef sirloin tip, thinly sliced
1 Tbs (15 ml) soy sauce
2 Tbs (30 ml) wine (KWV Springbok Cabernet Sauvignon)
1 Tbs (15 ml) cornstarch
½ cup (125 ml) shredded green onion
2-3 Tbs (30-45 ml) oil

Shred green onion and place on a plate.

Seasoning Sauce:
1½ Tbs (23 ml) sweet bean sauce—tien mien jiang
1 Tbs (15 ml) soy sauce
2 Tbs (30 ml) water
1 Tbs (15 ml) sugar
½ Tbs (8 ml) sesame oil
salt and pepper to taste

Cut beef into strips and marinate with soy sauce, wine, and cornstarch for 20 minutes. Use high heat to heat 2 Tbs (30 ml) oil in the frying pan. Stir fry beef until it turns brown. Remove from frying pan. Add first four ingredients of seasoning sauce to pan and bring to boil. Return the beef and mix thoroughly. Add sesame oil. Season to taste with salt and pepper. Place on top of green onion and serve with steamed rice or rolled up in egg rolls.

KWV, Paarl or Springbok Cabernet Sauvignon or Neil Ellis Chardonnay

VEAL CHOPS WITH ROSEMARY AND OREGANO

Serves 4-6

4-6 veal chops

Marinade:
¼ cup (60 ml) olive oil
2 cloves garlic, crushed
juice of 1 lemon
the snipped-off leaves of 2 stems fresh rosemary
the snipped-off leaves of 2 stems fresh oregano
1 tsp (5 ml) salt
1 tsp (5 ml) freshly ground black pepper medley (red, green and black peppercorns)

Combine marinade ingredients in blender or food processor. Pour over veal chops and marinate for 30-60 minutes.

Grill 5 minutes each side—either in a hot nonstick pan or on the barbecue.

KWV, Paarl or Springbok Shiraz or Backsberg Estate Shiraz

VEAL ITALIENNE

Serves 4

1-lb (500 g) pkg veal scallopini
1 lb (500 g) sliced mushrooms
2 oz (50 g) butter or margarine
1 pkg frozen spinach, defrosted
1-2 Tbs (15-30 ml) olive oil

2 cloves garlic, crushed
mozzarella cheese
salt, pepper and flour
⅓ cup (80 ml) KWV Renasans Sherry
diced parsley for garnish

Brown mushrooms in butter or margarine. Cook spinach in oil with crushed garlic. Spread veal with spinach mixture. Sprinkle lightly with grated mozzarella cheese. Roll up and secure with toothpick. Season with salt, pepper and sprinkle lightly with flour. Brown veal in pan with mushrooms—add sherry. Remove from heat, sprinkle with diced parsley and serve immediately.

KWV, Paarl Roodeberg or Groot Constantia Merlot

MUSTARD SAUCE FOR TENDERLOIN

Combine a jar of mustard (of your choice) and an equal quantity of cream. Heat, but do not boil. Delicious served with tenderloin.

Desiree Blumenthal
Cincinnati, Ohio

Salads and Vegetarian Dishes

CHINESE CHICKEN SALAD

Serves 12

2 lbs (1 kg) chicken breasts—split, boned, skinned, trimmed and flattened
½ cup (125 ml) soy sauce
½ cup (125 ml) KWV Renasans Sherry
2 cloves garlic, crushed
4 oz (125 g) Chinese rice noodles (may use more)
½ cup (125 ml) cornstarch (cornflour)
½ cup (125 ml) flour
½ tsp (3 ml) salt
1 large head iceberg lettuce or napa cabbage
1 cup sliced green onions or scallions
¾ cup (200 ml) toasted slivered almonds
vegetable oil

Mix soy sauce, sherry and garlic to make marinade. Marinate chicken breasts in marinade. Cover and refrigerate several hours or overnight.

In skillet or wok, fry rice noodles in hot oil until they puff but do not brown. Drain well. They will stay fresh in an airtight container for days.

Mix cornstarch, flour and salt. Remove chicken from marinade and dip in cornstarch mixture. Fry chicken in 2" (5 cm) vegetable oil at 375°F (190°C) until brown and crispy. Drain. When cool, cut in bite-sized pieces.

Shred lettuce or cabbage.

To assemble, toss chicken, lettuce, scallions and almonds with enough dressing to coat well. Cover with rice noodles and toss together.

Dressing:
1 cup (250 ml) oil
¾ cup (200 ml) distilled white vinegar
½ cup (125 ml) sugar
2 Tbs (30 ml) soy sauce
½ tsp (3 ml) dry mustard
¼ tsp (1½ ml) pepper, freshly ground

Whisk to blend

If you do not wish to fry chicken, marinate as instructed and grill chicken. Omit step using cornflour.

Bari Holmes
Cincinnati, Ohio

KWV, Paarl or Springbok Chardonnay or De Wetshof Lesca Chardonnay

CUCUMBER AND COCONUT RAITA SALAD

Serves 6-8

2 English cucumbers, peeled and cubed
½ fresh coconut—reserve juice
2 green chilies, seeded and diced
2 cups (500 ml) yogurt
1 tsp (5 ml) salt
2 tsp (10 ml) vegetable oil
1 tsp (5 ml) mustard seeds

Cut cucumber into 1" (2.5 cm) cubes and place in a colander to drain.

Pare brown skin off coconut and cut flesh into cubes, reserving juice. Put coconut and chilies into food processor with 2-3 Tbs (30-45 ml) coconut milk and blend to puree. Transfer to serving bowl and stir in yogurt, drained cucumber cubes and salt.

Heat oil in a frying pan, and when hot, add mustard seeds. Cover and fry until they begin to spatter.

Stir seeds and oil into yogurt cucumber mixture and chill in refrigerator for 1 hour.

Serve chilled.

CURRY CHICKEN SALAD

Serves 10-12

6 chicken breasts, skinned, cooked and diced
1 cup (250 ml) nuts—peanuts, cashews or almonds
½ cup (125 ml) raisins
1 cup (250 ml) peas
1 can water chestnuts (optional)
1 can pineapple chunks, drained, reserving juice
1 cup (250 ml) mayonnaise
1 Tbs (15 ml) honey
1 tsp (5 ml) curry powder
1 tsp (5 ml) salt
8 oz (250 g) penne pasta, cooked al denté and drained
1 cup (250 ml) shredded nappa cabbage (chinese cabbage)

Combine chicken, nuts, raisins, peas, water chestnuts and pineapple chunks. Mix mayonnaise, honey, curry powder, salt and, if desired, a little bit of pineapple juice. Pour over chicken and mix in well. Fold in pasta and nappa cabbage.

KWV Chenin Blanc or Boschendal Estate Petit Pavillon

ELOISE'S NAPA SALAD

Serves 12

1 head Napa or Chinese cabbage, shredded
1 bunch green onions, sliced thinly, some tops included
½ cup (125 ml) sesame seeds
3 oz pkg (75 g) sliced almonds
⅓ cup (80 ml) sunflower seeds
1 pkg Ramen noodles—reserve the seasoning pkg. for another use

Dressing:
⅔ cup (160 ml) oil
2 Tbs (30 ml) soy sauce
½ cup (125 ml) sugar
⅓ cup (80 ml) vinegar

Combine cabbage and green onions and chill.

Spray the sesame seeds, almonds, sunflower seeds and ramen noodles with butter flavored spray and toast in a 350°F (180°C) oven. Cool.

Combine all dressing ingredients.

Toss dressing with cabbage, nuts, and noodles.

Eloise Schneider
Cincinnati, Ohio

KWV Paarl or Springbok Sauvignon Blanc or Groot Constantia Estate Sauvignon Blanc

EXOTIC LETTUCE, SUNDRIED TOMATO, AND GOAT CHEESE SALAD

The quantities in this salad will be left to your discretion. Use as little or as much of each ingredient as you wish.

Lettuce, 3-4 different kinds and radichio
avocado sliced and sprinkled with lemon juice
sundried tomatoes, diced
canned artichokes, drained and sliced
goat cheese, as prepared below
red and yellow peppers (halved, seeded and sliced)
pine nuts, toasted 1 Tbs (15 ml) per serving
(pine nuts can be toasted in the microwave, 100% power, 2-3 minutes)

Dressing:
1 cup (250 ml) balsamic vinegar
2 Tbs (30 ml) brown sugar
salt and pepper
½ cup (125 ml) olive oil
2-3 cloves garlic, crushed

Combine salad ingredients. Toss with dressing just before serving and garnish with slices of grilled goat cheese. The remaining salad dressing can be refrigerated and kept for other salads.

Grilled Goat Cheese:
Cut goat cheese into slices; coat each slice with lightly whisked egg white and then coat in dry bread crumbs; place on foil-lined baking sheet; spray cheese with olive oil-flavored spray or vegetable oil spray and place under broiler until crisp and golden on both sides. Lift with spatula and place on salad. Serve immediately. You may prepare the cheese earlier in the day and broil just before serving.

KWV, Paarl or Springbok Chardonnay or Weltevrede Chardonnay

GREEN BEAN SALAD

Serves 6-8

1 large onion, diced
2-3 Tbs (30-45 ml) olive oil
3-4 cloves garlic, crushed
2 skinned and diced tomatoes

½ cup (125 ml) tomato puree
salt and pepper to taste
1 x 10-oz (283 g) pkg frozen beans,
**   thawed and drained**

Sauté onion in olive oil until limp. Add garlic, tomatoes and tomato puree. Allow to simmer until thickened. Season to taste with salt and pepper and mix together with green beans.

MARINATED STEAK SALAD

Serves 6-8

2 lbs (1 kg) boneless sirloin steak—2" (5 cm) thick

Marinade:
¾ cup (200 ml) soy sauce
juice of ½ lemon
4 green onions, diced
2 cloves garlic, crushed
½ tsp (3 ml) grated gingerroot
½ tsp (3 ml) salt
½ tsp (3 ml) ground black pepper

Combine all marinade ingredients. Prick steaks well on both sides and pour marinade over. Refrigerate for up to two days, turning occasionally. Remove from marinade and grill or barbecue. Slice thinly on the diagonal.

Dressing:
⅓ cup (80 ml) olive or salad oil
1 Tbs (15 ml) mayonnaise
2 Tbs (30 ml) red wine vinegar
1 tsp (5 ml) sugar
6 cloves garlic, crushed
1 Tbs (15 ml) cavenders seasoning (Greek seasoning or lamb seasoning)
1 tsp (5 ml) freshly ground pepper

Combine all ingredients except oil in food processor. Slowly add olive oil in a slow stream until mixed thoroughly (add with motor running). Correct seasoning, if necessary.

6-8 new potatoes
1 green pepper, diced
1 red pepper, diced
1 can hearts of palm, drained and sliced
2 green onions
½ lb (250 g) sliced mushrooms

Boil new potatoes until tender.

Combine steak, potatoes, peppers, hearts of palm, green onions and mushrooms. Pour on the dressing and toss thoroughly. Serve at room temperature.

Cathedral Cellar Chardonnay or Neil Ellis Chardonnay

MARTIN'S SALAD

¼ head iceberg lettuce or napa (Chinese cabbage) cut in chunks
1 red cabbage, cut in chunks
1 bunch green onions, sliced
2 tomatoes, cut in chunks
broccoli flowerettes
1 banana, sliced thickly
3 slices pineapple, cut into chunks
3-oz can (75 g) tuna, drained
handful raisins

Use quantities you desire, but you must cut in chunks.

Combine all ingredients and mix with bottle of fat-free French dressing (or dressing of your choice).

Serve with toasted pita bread.

Martin Loon
Cincinnati, Ohio

KWV, Paarl Cape Riesling or Groot Constantia Estate Constantia Blanc

MIDDLE-EASTERN EGGPLANT SALAD

Serves 8-10

2 eggplant (aubergines), thinly sliced
olive oil
2 red peppers, roasted
1 leek, thinly sliced
1 small onion, chopped
3 cloves garlic, peeled and crushed

1½ Tbs (25 ml) lemon juice
½ cup (125 ml) chopped parsley
½ tsp (3 ml) ground cumin
1 tsp (5 ml) ground coriander
salt and black pepper

Sprinkle sliced eggplant liberally with salt and allow to stand for half and hour. Rinse well and pat dry. Brush with olive oil and place on a foil-lined baking sheet under oven broiler until nicely browned on each side. Cool. Cut into quarters, using scissors.

Roast red pepper until skin is blistered and charred, cool in plastic bag, skin, remove membrane, seed and slice in strips. Heat 1 Tbs (15 ml) olive oil in a pan and sauté leek and onion lightly. Combine with diced eggplant and roasted pepper.

Place garlic, lemon juice, 2-3 Tbs (30-45 ml) olive oil, parsley, cumin and coriander in blender. Combine with eggplant mixture and season to taste with salt and pepper.

Cathedral Cellar Sauvignon Blanc or Boschendal Sauvignon Blanc

ORIENTAL CHICKEN SALAD

Serves 6-8

2 whole chicken breasts, skinned, boned and split
bottled Italian dressing
head of Nappa cabbage, sliced thinly
bean sprouts
red and yellow peppers, cut into thin strips
½ lb (250 g) snow peas
½ cup (125 ml) toasted sesame seeds

Marinate chicken breasts in Italian dressing overnight in the refrigerator. Broil in oven or cook on barbecue. Cut in strips. Combine cooked chicken, cabbage, bean sprouts, peppers and snow peas. Just before serving, combine with the following dressing. Sprinkle with sesame seeds.

Dressing:
⅔ cup (160 ml) rice wine vinegar
¼ cup (60 ml) chili oil
⅓ cup (80 ml) vegetable oil
⅓ cup (80 ml) sesame oil
3 heaped tsp (20 ml) sugar
¼ cup (60 ml) soy sauce
3 cloves garlic, crushed
3" piece gingerroot, grated
1 tsp (5 ml) salt

Combine all ingredients in blender or food processor.

KWV, Paarl Chenin Blanc or Groot Constantia Weisser Riesling

SHARON'S SUMMER SALAD

Serves 12-14

Bibb lettuce and Spring mix (assorted salad greens)
1 avocado, diced
1 can artichoke hearts, drained
1 can mandarin oranges, drained
1 container raspberries
1 Granny Smith apple, diced
1 red delicious apple, diced
½ cup (125 ml) green olives
cherry tomatoes
English cucumber, diced
fresh asparagus (steam or microwave)
½ lb (250 g) chopped mushrooms
parsley
½ red onion, chopped

Dressing:
½ cup (125 ml) olive oil
¼ cup (60 ml) balsamic vinegar
1 envelope sweetener or 2 tsp (10 ml) sugar
½ cup (125 ml) orange juice
2 Tbs (30 ml) sour cream (nonfat) or plain yogurt
salt and freshly ground pepper to taste

Blend together.

Mix salad dressing with salad ingredients. May add cooked shrimp or crab meat.

Sharon Miller
Philadelphia, Pennsylvania

KWV, Paarl or Springbok Sauvignon Blanc

SPINACH AND RICE SALAD

Serves 8-10

1 cup fried brown rice or 1 pkg Rice-A-Roni, prepared as directed
2 avocados, cut into bite-sized pieces
1 grated hard-boiled egg
1 stick celery, diced
3 spring onions, diced
2 bunches washed spinach, torn into bite-sized pieces

Dressing:
½ cup (125 ml) oil
½ cup (125 ml) vinegar
4 Tbs (60 ml) sugar
4 Tbs (60 ml) mayonnaise
garlic (optional)
salt and pepper

Combine dressing ingredients until well blended.
Toss with salad ingredients.

Sally Kallmeyer
Johannesburg, South Africa

KWV, Paarl or Springbok Sauvignon Blanc

SPRING SALAD

Toss spring mix with the following dressing:

1 tsp (5 ml) sweet German mustard
⅓ cup (60 ml) olive oil
2 Tbs (30 ml) vinegar
1 Tbs (15 ml) maggi seasoning
1 Tbs (15 ml) freshly chopped chives or green onions
1 tsp (5 ml) chopped parsley
1 tsp (5 ml) chopped fresh dill or ½ tsp (3 ml) dry dill
1 Tbs (15 ml) sour cream

Combine all ingredients in jar and shake well.

KWV, Paarl or Springbok Sauvignon Blanc

SWORDFISH, AVOCADO AND SALSA SALAD WITH CORN CRISPS

Serves 8-10

2 lbs (1 kg) swordfish
tuna, halibut or salmon may be used—any leftover fish may be used

Fish may be poached in the following liquid or barbequed
⅔ cup (160 ml) white wine (KWV, Paarl, or Springbok Sauvignon Blanc)
⅔ cup (160 ml) fish stock or chicken stock
bay leaves, peppercorns, parsley
juice of 1 lemon
salt and freshly ground pepper

Bring all ingredients to boil in a large shallow saucepan. Add fish and continue to cook over moderate heat until fish is opaque. Cool, drain and flake fish coarsely.

Place fish on a bed of lettuce with sliced avocado and spoon over tomato salsa.

Tomato Salsa:
Place in blender or food processor until finely chopped:
1 red onion
2 cloves garlic
¾ cup (200 ml) cilantro
1 jalapeño pepper, seeded
1 tsp (5 ml) salt
1 Tbs (15 ml) lemon juice
1 tsp (5 ml) coarsely ground black pepper

Fold in 6-8 diced plum tomatoes or 2-3 large tomatoes and 1 Tbs (15 ml) olive oil. Add 1 can drained black beans or red kidney beans, 4 oz (125 g) feta cheese and ½ cup (125 ml) black olives, sliced.

Serve with the following corn chips:
1 cup (250 ml) cornmeal (preferably yellow)
1 tsp (5 ml) salt
½ tsp (3 ml) pepper
3 cups (750 ml) boiling water
2 Tbs (30 ml) butter
¼ cup (60 ml) Parmesan cheese

Combine cornmeal, salt and pepper. Bring water to boil and slowly add cornmeal, whisking constantly until thickened and smooth. Stir in butter and cheese. Drop spoonfuls onto greased tray and spread out thinly. Bake at 400°F (200°C) for 15-20 minutes until crisp. Turn oven off and leave chips to dry.

KWV, Paarl, or Springbok Sauvignon Blanc or Groot Constantia Estate Sauvignon Blanc

TORTELLINI SALAD

Serves 10-12

Dressing:
⅔ cup (160 ml) rice wine vinegar
½ cup (125 ml) soy sauce
2 Tbs (30 ml) freshly ground gingerroot
2 tsp (10 ml) minced garlic
1 tsp (5 ml) sugar
½ cup (125 ml) sesame oil
½ cup (125 ml) vegetable oil
¼ cup (60 ml) hot chili oil
1 Tbs (15 ml) honey

Blend dressing ingredients in food processor.

½ lb (250 g) or 10-oz (275 g) package, cheese-filled tortellini
1 lb (500 g) angel hair pasta
1 cup (250 ml) coarsely chopped green onion, including some tops
¼ cup (60 ml) chopped cilantro
1 cup (250 ml) coarsely chopped unsalted peanuts
1 small yellow pepper, thinly sliced
1 small red pepper, thinly sliced
1 English cucumber, sliced

Cook pasta and tortellini according to package directions until al dente. Drain, rinse quickly under cold running water and drain again. Transfer pasta and tortellini to a large bowl and add half of dressing and toss well. Cool to room temperature stirring occasionally to keep noodles separated.

Add all vegetables to pasta and add remaining dressing. May be kept in refrigerator overnight. Add peanuts shortly before serving.

Strips of barbecued chicken may be added to the salad.

KWV, Paarl or Springbok Chardonnay or Boschendal Estate Light Chardonnay

VEGETABLE AND HERB SALAD

Serves 10-12

1 cucumber, chopped
5 plum tomatoes, chopped
10 green onions, thinly sliced
1 small green pepper, finely chopped
1 Tbs (15 ml) parsley, chopped
1 Tbs (15 ml) cilantro (dunia) chopped
½ Tbs (7 ml) mint, chopped
black Greek olives, drained
1 cup (250 ml) thinly sliced carrots
1 cup (250 ml) frozen corn, cooked and drained

Dressing:
⅓ cup (80 ml) oil
6 Tbs (60 ml) red wine vinegar
4 cloves garlic, crushed
2 Tbs (30 ml) Cavenders (or any Greek seasonings or lamb seasoning)

Combine oil, red wine vinegar, garlic, and Greek seasoning. A few hours before serving, toss dressing with the vegetables.

Top the salad with the following drained yogurt balls or crumbled feta cheese or crumbled blue cheese.

4 cups (1 litre) plain yogurt
2 tsp (10 ml) salt
olive oil
coarsely ground black pepper
paprika

Mix salt and yogurt together. Line a colander with cheese cloth or a thick paper towel. Pour yogurt into lined colander and allow to drain for 48 hours. This gets rid of excess moisture. After 48 hours, chill the yogurt in the refrigerator and then roll into small balls. Store in jar covered with olive oil with a sprig of rosemary and 1-2 dried chile peppers.

When ready to eat, remove from oil, drain and roll in paprika.

KWV, Paarl or Springbok Sauvignon Blanc

WARM LOBSTER SALAD

This is per serving. The mushrooms and lobster must all be warm when assembling. Seasoned chicken livers dipped in flour and fried in hot oil (peri-peri oil) may be substituted for lobster.

1 portabella mushroom per serving
2 Tbs (30 ml) olive oil
1 oz (25 g) butter
4 oz (125 g) assorted mushrooms, sliced
1 clove garlic, crushed
½ tsp (3 ml) diced thyme
½ tsp (3 ml) diced oregano
salt and pepper to taste
lettuce of your choice
1 Tbs (15 ml) mayonnaise
1 steamed lobster tail per serving

Dressing:
¼ cup (60 ml) balsamic vinegar
1 tsp (5 ml) brown sugar
salt and pepper
1 Tbs (15 ml) olive oil
½ tsp (3 ml) Dijon mustard
2 cloves crushed garlic

Sauté whole portabella mushrooms in olive oil and butter. Set aside. Add assorted mushrooms, garlic and herbs and sauté until liquid has evaporated. Season to taste with salt and pepper.

Toss lettuce with dressing. Pile in center of plate. Place a portabella mushroom face down in center of lettuce. Spoon other mushrooms on top. Place dollop of mayonnaise over mushrooms and garnish with sliced lobster.

Can sprinkle a ring of finely diced red green, and yellow peppers around rim of plate.

Cathedral Cellar Sauvignon Blanc or Backsberg Estate Sauvignon Blanc

WILD RICE SALAD

Serves 12

Dressing:
½ cup (125 ml) sliced green onions
⅓ cup (80 ml) red wine vinegar
⅓ cup (80 ml) vegetable oil
⅓ cup (80 ml) olive oil
2 Tbs (30 ml) fresh parsley
2 cloves garlic
2 tsp (10 ml) dried basil
1 tsp (5 ml) dried dill
1 tsp (5 ml) salt
½ tsp (3 ml) pepper
½ tsp (3 ml) dried oregano
1½ tsp (7 ml) Dijon mustard

Combine all ingredients in food processor and blend.

1 cup (250 ml) wild rice
4 cups (1 L) vegetable broth or water
½ tsp (3 ml) salt
1 cup (250 ml) cooked white rice
½ cup (125 ml) flaked almonds
2 carrots, thinly sliced
2 sticks celery, thinly sliced
1 red pepper, diced
1 green pepper, diced
whole red onion, finely diced
1 stalk broccoli, sliced

Rinse wild rice well in a colander and allow to drain. In a large saucepan, bring vegetable broth or water and salt to a boil. Add wild rice, reduce heat and simmer covered approximately 35-40 minutes. Drain well and cool.

Toss wild rice and white rice, nuts, vegetables and dressing.

KWV, Paarl or Springbok Sauvignon Blanc or Saxenburg Sauvignon Blanc

BRINJAL AND MUSHROOM FLAN

Serves 8-10

1 large onion
1 lb (450 g) peeled eggplant (brinjal)
2 oz (50 g) butter plus 2 Tbs (30 ml) oil
½ lb (250 g) sliced mushrooms
½ pkg dry mushroom soup
1 cup (250 ml) sour cream
1 Tbs (15 ml) sherry
dash pepper
1 lb (489 g) pkg puff pastry
egg for brushing

Fry onions and cubed eggplant in butter and oil until eggplant softens. Add mushrooms and sauté for another 15-20 minutes. Stir in mushroom soup, sour cream, sherry and pepper. Line bottom and sides of 9" (23 cm) springform pan with puff pastry. Spoon filling into pan. Roll out remaining pastry, cut into strips and lay in crisscross fashion over filling. Brush with egg.

Bake at 400°F (200°C) for 40 minutes or until brown.

KWV, Paarl, Springbok Chardonnay or Boschendal Estate Chardonnay Light

FUSILLI PASTA WITH FETA CHEESE, OLIVES AND PINE NUTS

Serves 6-8

8 oz (250 g) fusilli pasta, cooked al dente (slightly chewy)
3 oz (90 g) basil and tomato feta cheese
10 kalamata olives, stoned, halved and quartered
1 Tbs (15 ml) olive oil
1 Tbs (15 ml) freshly chopped basil
¼ cup (60 ml) toasted pine nuts (place in microwave for 2-3 minutes to toast)
sundried tomatoes—finely diced

Cook pasta according to package directions and combine with remaining ingredients. Serve at room temperature.

KWV, Paarl Riesling or Groot Constantia Weisser Riesling

FUSILLI PASTA WITH MUSHROOMS AND ARTICHOKES

Serves 8

1-2 chopped onions
3 whole peppers—red, green and yellow—halved and sliced
1 Tbs (15 ml) oil
1 x 14-oz can (411 g) creamed mushroom soup
1 x 14-oz can (411 g) whole button mushrooms drained
1 x 14-oz can (411 g) artichokes, drained and halved
1 cup (250 ml) canned diced Italian tomatoes
1 lb (450 g) fusilli or penne pasta, cooked al dente
Parmesan cheese
fresh or dried basil

Sauté chopped onions and peppers in olive oil. When almost done (soft, not brown), add mushroom soup, mushrooms, and artichokes and cook 1-2 minutes. Add tomatoes and stir to blend with ingredients and cook a further minute.

In an ungreased 9" x 13" (22 cm x 32 cm) dish, alternate layers of pasta and sauce, finishing with a layer of sauce. Sprinkle liberally with Parmesan cheese and basil.

Bake at 350°F (180°C) for 20 minutes.

May be made 2 days in advance and refrigerated. Bake before serving. Do not freeze.

KWV, Paarl or Springbok Chardonnay or Boschendal Estate Chardonnay

GARDEN VEGETABLE ROULADE IN PHYLLO WITH SAFFRON CREAM AND PESTO SAUCE

Yield: 4-5 rolls

1 tsp (5 ml) freshly ground black pepper
4 shallots
6 cloves garlic, peeled
1 Tbs (15 ml) chopped parsley
4 oz (125 g) softened butter
1 lb pkg (500 g) phyllo pastry
1 cup (250 ml) dry bread crumbs
2 cups (500 ml) baby carrots
4 oz (125 g) snow peas
2 zucchini, thickly sliced
1 or 2 yellow squash, thickly sliced
½ leek, thinly sliced
1 red pepper, halved, seeded and sliced
1 large Portabella mushroom, sliced
1 onion, halved and sliced
salt and pepper
a few sprigs of thyme, sage and oregano, chopped (optional)

Combine black pepper, shallots, garlic, parsley, and butter in food processor. Set aside. Layer 2-3 sheets of phyllo, brushing with partially melted butter mixture in between each layer, and sprinkle lightly with bread crumbs. Mix vegetables together in a large bowl, season with salt and pepper to taste, and fold in chopped herbs, if desired. Place a pile of vegetables along the long side of the layered phyllo, tuck in ends and roll up. Place on a greased baking sheet. Repeat this whole process to make 4 or 5 phyllo rolls, using up the vegetables. Bake in a 450°F (230°C) oven for 15 minutes.

Saffron Cream Sauce:
See Grilled Salmon with Saffron Cream Sauce page 144, substituting vegetable for fish or chicken stock.

Pesto:

3 large garlic cloves, peeled   ½ cup pine nuts
2 cups (500 ml) lightly packed basil leaves   ¾ cup (200 ml) olive oil
½ cup (125 ml) grated Parmesan cheese

Process all pesto ingredients in food processor until mixture is well blended and smooth. Serve vegetable roulade sliced on a bed of saffron cream sauce that has been marbled with pesto sauce. For a buffet serve whole vegetable rolls with saffron cream sauce and pesto on the side. This dish cannot be frozen as the vegetables loose their crispness. However, it may be prepared the previous day and refrigerated until ready to bake. The saffron cream sauce and the pesto sauce may be prepared in advance and frozen or refrigerated until desired, at which stage, the saffron cream sauce would be reheated and the pesto brought to room temperature.

Cathedral Cellar Sauvignon Blanc or Groot Constantia Estate Sauvignon Blanc

GNOCCHI WITH TOMATO AND BASIL SAUCE

Serves 4-6

1 lb (½ kg) Idaho potatoes (2 large) cooked in jackets
2 egg yolks
¼ cup (60 ml) plus 2 Tbs (30 ml) grated Parmesan cheese
pinch nutmeg
½ tsp (3 ml) salt
1-1½ cups (250-375 ml) flour
1 small can tomatoes (plum, if available), undrained
¼ cup (65 ml) julienned fresh basil
2 Tbs (30 ml) olive oil

Peel potatoes. Transfer to a large mixer bowl and sieve. Make a well in center; add egg yolks, ¼ cup (60 ml) parmesan, nutmeg, and salt. Mix until smooth. Gradually mix enough flour into potato mixture until a smooth, stiff dough is formed.

On lightly floured surface, knead gently 5 minutes. Cut dough into quarters. Roll each piece into a rope about ¾" (2 cm) thick. Cut each rope into ¼" (¾ cm) thick slices. Place tines of a fork on top of each slice and quickly pull fork down toward you, flattening gnocchi into thin oblong shapes. Repeat with remaining dough. Heat a large pot of salted water to boiling point over high heat. Add gnocchi all at once; stir to prevent sticking. When gnocchi rise to the surface, cook 1 minute more. Drain. (Can be made ahead, cover and refrigerate up to 8 hours.)

Preheat broiler. Toss gnocchi with chopped canned tomatoes and juice, basil and olive oil. Transfer to a shallow baking dish. Sprinkle with remaining 2 Tbs (30 ml) Parmesan. Broil 4 inches from heat until cheese is browned (about 5 minutes).

Groot Constantia Estate or Backsberg Estate Sauvignon Blanc

GRILLED VEGGIE AND PASTA SALAD

Serves 10-12

1 red pepper, thickly sliced
1 yellow pepper, thickly sliced
1 medium zucchini, thickly sliced
1 red onion, thickly sliced
olive oil
freshly ground black pepper
1 pkg Ramen noodles (reserve seasoning for another use)
    or 5-oz can (150 g) chow mein noodles
8-oz (500 g) penne pasta
1 head Napa cabbage (Chinese cabbage), sliced thinly
bunch green onions

Dressing:
1 cup (250 ml) vegetable oil
¾ cup (200 ml) white vinegar
½ cup sugar (125 ml)
2 Tbs (30 ml) soy sauce
½ tsp (3 ml) dry mustard
1/4 tsp (1½ ml) freshly ground black pepper

Process all ingredients in blender or food processor. This will make more dressing than you may need.

To prepare grilled vegetables:
Brush peppers, onions and zucchini with olive oil and season with freshly ground black pepper. Place on hot grill and grill until done. When cool, cut into smaller pieces. May be prepared a day in advance.

If using Ramen noodles, crumble with your hands. Place noodles on a small baking sheet and bake in a 350°F (180°C) until golden, about 10-15 minutes, stirring once. (The noodles may be stored in an airtight container for two days or may be frozen.)

Cook pasta according to package directions. Drain and toss with 3 or 4 Tbs (45 or 60 ml) of dressing. This may be done early in the day.

To assemble salad, combine Napa cabbage, green onions, grilled vegetables and pasta and toss with sufficient dressing. Just before serving, sprinkle with Ramen noodles or chow mein noodles.

KWV, Paarl or Springbok Chardonnay or Backsberg Estate Chardonnay

KUGEL

Serves 12

8 oz (250 g) cream cheese
4 eggs beaten
4 oz (125 g) butter, melted
½ cup (125 ml) sugar
1 cup (250 ml) milk
12 oz (340 g) package noodles, cooked and drained

Beat cream cheese, eggs, melted butter, sugar and milk in mixer. Combine with cooked noodles. Place in greased dish 9" x 13" (22 x 32 cms).

Top with a handful of corn flakes and sprinkle with cinnamon and sugar. Bake at 350°F (180°C) for 1 hour.

Fern Spiegel
Cincinnati, Ohio

KWV Steen or Paarl Chenin Blanc

MUSHROOM RISOTTO

Serves 10-12

1 oz (25 g) dried oyster mushrooms
2 large onions, diced
½ cup (125 ml) olive oil
5-6 cloves garlic, minced
1½ lbs (3/4 kg) assorted mushrooms, roughly chopped
5 cups (1¼ litres) boiling water for stock
½ cup (125 ml) dry white wine
1 stick celery
2-3 carrots
1 bay leaf
2 vegetable bouillon cubes, crushed
1½ cups (375 ml) arborio rice (do not rinse)
4 ozs (125 g) butter or margarine
¼ tsp (1 ml) thyme
Parmesan cheese
Salt and pepper to taste

Pour boiling water over dried oyster mushrooms to cover and allow to soak for about 1 hour.

Prepare stock: Sauté onions in ¼ cup (60 ml) of the olive oil until translucent. Add garlic and cook another few minutes.

Add assorted chopped mushrooms (not oyster mushrooms) and sauté for another 10 minutes. Add boiling water and drained oyster mushrooms, wine, celery, carrots, bay leaf and bouillon cubes and allow to simmer for 35 minutes. Drain and reserve stock. Discard celery, carrots and bay leaf and set mushrooms aside.

In another saucepan, heat the remaining ¼ cup (60 ml) olive oil. Add rice and stir until it is well coated with the oil. Add the reserved stock which should be simmering, a ½ (125 ml) cup at a time, until each addition is thoroughly absorbed. Keep stirring risotto constantly whilst adding the stock and keep it simmering all the time—this process should take about 18-20 minutes. The last addition of stock should be stirred vigorously into the rice—this ensures a creamy consistency. Fold in mushrooms, stir in butter or margarine, thyme and parmesan cheese and if necessary, salt and pepper. Serve immediately.

You may add sautéed chicken, seafood or vegetables before serving.

Paarl Riesling or KWV Steen

213

ORZO WITH STIR FRY VEGGIES AND HERBS

Delicious served with any grilled chicken or fish.

Serves 12

1½ cups (375 ml) orzo (rice-shaped pasta), cooked according to package directions, then rinsed through with cold water to separate grains.
⅓-½ cup (80-125 ml) roasted garlic oil
1 large onion, cut in half lengthwise and then sliced
½ lb (250 g) sliced mushrooms
6 cloves garlic, crushed
1 red pepper, seeded and sliced into strips
1 yellow pepper, seeded and sliced into strips
1-2 zucchini, sliced into strips lengthwise
1 carrot, julienned (cut into very thin strips)
6-8 green asparagus, cut into pieces
1 cup (250 ml) broccoli flowerettes
½ lb (250 g) snow peas, left whole
1 Tbs (15 ml) dried Italian seasoning
    or combination of fresh herbs, such as basil, oregano, thyme, sage, parsley
salt, coarsely ground black pepper and garlic powder to taste

Using a large wok, heat roasted garlic oil and sauté onion until limp. Add mushrooms and continue to cook for another few minutes. Add garlic and remaining vegetables and herbs and stir fry for 3-4 minutes longer.

Season to taste with salt, pepper, and garlic powder, then toss with orzo to combine.

This can be made in advance and reheated in the microwave oven just until hot.

KWV, Paarl or Springbok Sauvignon Blanc

PASTA WITH ROASTED PEPPER SAUCE

Serves 8-10

1 lb penne pasta, prepared as directed on box
1 large red pepper
1 large green pepper
1 large yellow pepper
1 large leek, sliced
1 large onion, diced
2 Tbs (30 ml) olive oil plus 1 Tbs (15 ml) olive oil
2 heaped tsp roasted garlic*
1½ to 2 tsp (5-10 ml) salt
1 tsp (5 ml) freshly ground black pepper
14½-oz (411 g) can stewed tomatoes, preferably Italian-style
1 Tbs (15 ml) balsamic vinegar
1 tsp (5 ml) fresh garlic, chopped
4-6 basil leaves or 2 tsp (10 ml) dried basil
sliced canned mushrooms (optional), drained
sliced black olives (optional), drained
Parmesan shavings

Place peppers on a foil-lined baking sheet which has been sprayed with nonstick spray, and placed under broiler until charred and blistered on all sides. Place in a paper bag to cool.

Sauté leeks and onions in the 2 Tbs (30 ml) olive oil until transparent.

When peppers are cool, peel and discard membranes and seeds and place in the food processor with onions, leeks, roasted garlic, 1 Tbs (15 ml) olive oil, salt, pepper, stewed tomatoes, balsamic vinegar, fresh garlic and basil and process until smooth. Fold in mushrooms and olives, if using.

Serve on pasta and sprinkle with Parmesan shavings.

*To roast garlic: Preheat oven to 450°F (220°C). Cut small slice off the top and place in an ovenproof dish. Spray with cooking spray or sprinkle with a little olive oil. Bake uncovered for 15-20 minutes or until soft when squeezed. Cool.

KWV, Paarl or Springbok Chardonnay

PENNE PASTA WITH MUSHROOMS, ASPARAGUS, AND SUNDRIED TOMATO PESTO

Serves 8-10

1 lb (500 g) penne pasta
1 Tbs (15 ml) olive oil
1 lb (500 g) asparagus, steamed and diced
1 lb mushrooms (preferably portabella), washed and trimmed
2-3 Tbs (30-45 ml) roasted garlic olive oil
4-6 cloves garlic, crushed
½ tsp (3 ml) thyme
½ tsp (3 ml) oregano
½ tsp (3 ml) basil

Cook pasta al dente, drain and toss with 1 Tbs (15 ml) olive oil.

Marinate mushrooms in roasted garlic oil, olive oil, garlic, thyme, oregano and basil a couple of hours or overnight. Sprinkle with salt and freshly ground black pepper and grill on a foil lined pan under broiler. Slice and add to pasta with diced steamed asparagus and a few tablespoons of sundried tomato pesto. If you prefer a stronger garlic flavor, mix in some additional crushed garlic before serving.

SunDried Tomato Pesto:
3 oz (75 g) sundried tomatoes
½ cup (125 ml) pine nuts
¼ cup (60 ml) Parmesan cheese
½ cup (125 ml) olive oil
½ tsp (3 ml) salt
1 tsp (5 ml) freshly ground pepper

Pour boiling water over sundried tomatoes and allow to soften for ½ hour and then drain.

Place all above ingredients in food processor to blend to a paste. Keep refrigerated and toss a few tablespoons with pasta when required.

Cathedral Cellar Sauvignon Blanc or Neil Ellis Sauvignon Blanc

RATATOUILLE TORTE

Serves 10-12

3 Tbs (45 ml) olive oil
3 medium onions, diced
1 lb (500 g) sliced mushrooms
1 eggplant, peeled, quartered and sliced
4 zucchini (baby marrow), sliced
3 large ripe tomatoes, skinned and diced
2 cloves garlic, crushed (optional)
1 tsp (5 ml) coarsely ground black pepper
1 tsp (5 ml) salt
1 tsp (5 ml) each of dried oregano, basil, and parsley
1 vegetable or chicken bouillon cube, crushed
½ cup (125 ml) water
4 jumbo eggs
4 slices white or whole wheat bread, crusts removed, torn into small pieces
mozzarella and Parmesan cheese
goat cheese
pine nuts

Brown onions in oil. Add mushrooms, eggplant, zucchini (baby marrow), tomatoes, garlic, pepper, salt, herbs, bouillon cube and water. Simmer over gentle heat until vegetables are tender (about 15 minutes). Allow mixture to cool. Beat eggs just until blended and fold into vegetable mixture with bread.

Spray a 9" (22 cm) loose bottomed springform pan with nonstick spray. Sprinkle with a cup (250 ml) of dry bread crumbs. Spoon half vegetable mixture into pan. Sprinkle with mozzarella and Parmesan cheese. Top with remaining vegetable mixture. Top with a sprinkling of Parmesan cheese, goat cheese and pine nuts.

Bake at 400°F (200°C) for 25-30 minutes or until set. Allow to rest for 15 minutes before serving.

If you wish, you may line a springform pan with the following crust:

4 oz (125 g) butter
2 Tbs (30 ml) sugar
½ tsp vanilla
pinch salt

1 egg and 1 yolk
1¼ cup (300 ml) flour
1 tsp (5 ml) baking powder

Cream butter and sugar. Add vanilla, salt, egg and egg yolk. Lastly, add flour and baking powder. Press into pan which has been sprayed with nonstick spray and bake in a 350°F (180°C) oven for 20-25 minutes or until crust is nicely browned. Cool thoroughly. Place prepared ratatouille into cooled crust, sprinkle with goat cheese and pine nuts and bake as above.

Cathedral Cellar Chardonnay or Boschendal Estate Chardonnay Light

SPINACH GNOCCHI

Serves 8

10 oz (310 g) chopped fresh spinach or use 10 oz (310 g) frozen chopped spinach-defrosted and well drained
⅓ cup (80 ml) cottage cheese
½ cup (125 ml) ricotta cheese
2 egg whites
2 Tbs (30 ml) Parmesan cheese
½ cup (125 ml) all-purpose flour
½ tsp (3 ml) salt
¼ tsp (2 ml) pepper
sprinkling of freshly grated nutmeg

Wash spinach, drain well and chop in food processor. Combine with remaining ingredients and mix well. Drop by teaspoonsful into salted boiling water and poach, about 10 at a time, until they rise to the surface. Remove with a slotted spoon and place in a well-greased ovenware dish.

Sauce:
1 Tbs (15 ml) tomato puree
1 cup (250 ml) cream
salt and pepper to taste

2 Tbs (30 ml) Parmesan cheese
1 Tbs (15 g) butter

Whisk tomato puree and cream together until smooth. Season with salt and pepper to taste. Pour over gnocchi. Sprinkle with Parmesan and dot with butter. Bake in a 350°F (180°C) oven for about 20 minutes and until hot and sizzling.

KWV, Paarl or Springbok Sauvignon Blanc or Saxenburg Sauvignon Blanc

STELLA'S QUICK AND EASY PIZZA

Serves 4-6

1 store-bought pizza crust
Homemade salsa or pizza sauce
15-oz can (475 g) artichokes, drained
15-oz can (475 g) asparagus cuts, drained
1 red pepper, chopped
1 green pepper, chopped

1 cup (250 ml) mozzarella cheese
1 cup (250 ml) cheddar cheese
oregano
black pepper
black olives (optional)

Spread salsa or pizza sauce over pizza crust. Sprinkle remaining ingredients over sauce. Bake at 400°F (200°C) for 25-30 minutes.

Stella Glajchen
Johannesburg, South Africa

KWV, Paarl or Springbok Chardonnay or Weltevrede Estate Chardonnay

MIXED VEGETABLE GRILL

Use any selection of vegetables: assorted peppers, varieties of onions, zucchini, eggplant, summer squash.

Slice vegetables into thick slices.

Dressing:
½ cup (125 ml) olive oil
¼ cup (60 ml) fresh basil or 2 tsp (10 ml) dried basil
1 tsp (5 ml) greek seasoning (cavenders) or lamb seasoning
2 cloves garlic
2 Tbs (30 ml) soy sauce
1 Tbs (15 ml) red wine (KWV Springbok Pinotage)

Place all dressing ingredients in food processor and blend.

Marinate vegetables 4 hours or preferably overnight.

When ready to grill, place vegetables, cut side down, over medium-high heat, turning and brushing with marinade.

KWV, Paarl or Springbok Sauvignon Blanc or Saxenburg Sauvignon Blanc

VEGETARIAN LASAGNA

Make your own pasta as follows or use commercial, if you wish.

Serves 12

Pasta:
1½ cups (375 ml) flour
2 eggs
1 Tbs (15 ml) fresh or frozen chopped spinach

Place ingredients in food processor just until a dough is formed. Remove and knead on a lightly floured surface until smooth. Roll out paper thin or process with a pasta machine.

Lasagna:
4-6 eggplant (bringals) cut into rounds, sprinkled with salt and allowed to stand
½ cup (125 ml) olive oil
2 large onions, diced
2 leeks, sliced (white part only)
2 sticks celery, diced
1½ lb (750 g) assorted mushrooms, including portabella
2-3 cloves garlic, crushed
4 zucchini (baby marrow) sliced
2-3 carrots, grated
1 x 28-oz can (1 kg) whole peeled tomatoes
1 Tbs (15 ml) mixed herbs, freshly diced (basil, oregano, sage, thyme)
½ cup (125 ml) KWV Renasans Sherry
salt and freshly ground pepper to taste
1 lb (500 g) ricotta cheese
2 eggs
1 lb (500 g) mozzarella cheese, grated
Parmesan cheese

Rinse eggplant and pat dry.

Place oil in a large, wide saucepan, add onions, leeks and celery and brown lightly. Add mushrooms and cook another 15 minutes. Then add garlic, zucchini, eggplant, carrots, tomatoes (with juice), herbs and sherry. Simmer until vegetables are tender. Allow to cool. Season to taste with salt and pepper.

Combine ricotta with lightly beaten eggs and season with salt and pepper. Place vegetables, pasta, ricotta, mozzarella and a generous sprinkling of Parmesan in layers in the aforementioned order in a lasagna dish 9" x 13" (22 x 32 cms) that has been sprayed with nonstick. Bake in a 350°F (180°C) oven until hot and bubbling.

Allow to rest for 15-20 minutes before serving.

KWV, Paarl or Springbok Chardonnay

Desserts

PLATE PAINTING WITH CHOCOLATE GANACHE, SAUCES, AND FRUIT PUREES

Chocolate Plate and Creme Anglaise

Using a plastic squeeze bottle, pipe a ¾" (2 cm) thick ring of chocolate ganache around the outside of the plate. Pipe a ½" (1.25 cm) thick ring of creme anglaise then a ¼" (.75 cm) ring of milk chocolate ganache.

Draw a toothpick through the sauces in alternative directions, ½" (1.25 cm) apart. Draw the dark chocolate ganache toward the center of the plate and the milk chocolate ganache toward the top of the plate.

Place your dessert in the center of the plate.

Chocolate Fruit Puree Heart

Using a plastic squeeze bottle or a plastic bag filled with melted chocolate and with one corner snipped off, pipe a large heart on the top half of the serving platter. Allow the chocolate to set.

Using a squeeze bottle filled with fruit puree, carefully fill in the heart making sure to stay inside the lines.

Place the dessert at the bottom of the heart.

Creme Anglaise Fruit Puree Plate

Place ½ cup (125 ml) of creme anglaise onto a plate. Tilt the plate to cover the entire surface. Using one of two fruit purees in separate squeeze bottles, pipe alternating dots around the edge of the creme anglaise. Draw a toothpick through the dots around the plate to form heart designs.

Creme Anglaise:

1 cup (250 ml) cream
1 cup (250 ml) milk
5 egg yolks

1½ Tbs (20 ml) cornstarch
1 heaped Tbs (15-17 ml) sugar
1 tsp (5 ml) vanilla

Scald cream and milk in the top of a double boiler. Beat egg yolks, cornstarch and sugar until thick and creamy. Add vanilla and slowly add scalded cream and milk beating all the while as you do so. Return this mixture into the top of the double boiler and cook, stirring all the time with a wooden spoon until the mixture thickens. Do not overcook as it will curdle.

Chocolate Ganache:

½ cup (125 ml) cream
1 tsp (5 ml) vanilla
11 oz (275 g) semi-sweet chocolate, milk or white coarsely diced

Scald cream and vanilla. Remove from heat and pour over chocolate and stir until smooth. Cool until thick enough to use.

BANANAS FOSTER WITH GINGER AND PISTACHIO NUTS

Serves 4

4 large firm under ripe bananas—halved and sliced lengthwise
2 oz (60 g) butter
½ tsp (3 ml) finely grated ginger
rind of 1 orange, finely grated
1 cup (250 ml) brown sugar
juice of 1 orange
juice of 1 lemon
chopped pistachio nuts
6 Tbs (90 ml) KWV 10-Year-Old Brandy

In a large 12" (30 cm) skillet over medium-high heat add butter, ginger, and orange rind. When butter begins to bubble, add sugar and cook 1-2 minutes, stirring constantly.

Add bananas, cut side down. Add orange juice and lemon juice and sauté 1 minute. Carefully turn over and cook another minute until sauce begins to caramelize.

Transfer bananas to warm platter. Sprinkle with pistachio nuts. Return pan to medium-high heat. Add brandy. As soon as liquor is hot, ignite with a match. Immediately pour sauce over bananas.

Serve sauce spooned over vanilla ice cream or top with whipped cream.

KWV Tawny Port

BREAD PUDDING

Serves 6

½ loaf fresh sliced white bread
1 Tbs (15 ml) smooth apricot jam
¼ lb (125 g) butter or margarine, melted
3 large eggs

2½ cups (625 ml) milk
sugar to taste—2-3 Tbs (30-45 ml)
1 tsp (5 ml) vanilla essence

Cut crusts off bread and cut slices into small squares. Place jam in ungreased dish, 10" x 6½" x 2" (25 x 16 x 5 cm) and place squares of bread over jam. Pour melted butter over bread. Beat together eggs, milk, sugar and vanilla and pour over bread. Place small dabs of butter over mixture.

This dish must be placed into a larger container filled with an inch (2 cm) of hot water and baked at 350°F (180°C) for approximately 30 minutes.

Pauline Greek
Cape Town, South Africa

KWV 1975 Muscadel

CHOCOLATE IN PHYLLO

1 pkg phyllo
melted butter

Chocolate filling:
1 lb (500 g) dark chocolate, coarsely chopped
1 cup (250 ml) cream

Coarsely chop chocolate. Heat cream to boiling, pour over chocolate, and stir until melted and smooth. Cool and roll into fingers—approx. 2" (5 cm) long.

Vanilla sauce:
Beat 3 egg yolks with 2 Tbs (30 ml) sugar. Slowly beat in 1 cup (250 ml) scalded cream; then place mixture in top of double boiler and cook, stirring constantly, until thickened. Remove from heat and add 1 tsp (5 ml) vanilla.

Raspberry sauce:
20 oz (550 g) frozen raspberries, thawed
⅓ cup (80 ml) superfine sugar
3 Tbs (45 ml) raspberry liqueur

or

Tangerine sauce:
20 oz (550 g) canned mandarins, drained
⅓ cup (80 ml) super fine sugar
3 Tbs (45 ml) KWV Van der Hum Liqueur

To prepare either sauce, place all ingredients in food processor and puree. Strain the raspberry sauce to remove the seeds.

Prepare phyllo:
Stack 6 sheets of phyllo, brushing lightly with melted butter between each layer. Cut into 4" (10 cm) squares. Place a chocolate finger in each one, fold over sides and roll up. Brush top with melted butter and bake in a 350°F (180°C) oven for 10-15 minutes or until light golden brown.

Place piping hot on a plate with vanilla sauce and raspberry or tangerine puree which you can place in a plastic squeeze bottle. Pipe dots of either puree all around the edge of the vanilla sauce and then take a toothpick and draw through the dots to form a heart.

KWV or Paarl VSOP Brandy

CHOCOLATE MOUSSE MERINGUE

Serves 12

5 egg whites
pinch cream of tartar
1¼ cups (250 g) sugar
1 tsp (15 ml) vanilla
1 cup (200 g) icing sugar (powdered sugar)
¼ cup (60 ml) cocoa
1 tsp (15 ml) cinnamon

Beat egg whites and cream of tartar until stiff, gradually adding sugar and continue to beat until stiff and shiny. Beat in vanilla.

Sift icing sugar, cocoa and cinnamon together and fold into mixture.

Line a 12" x 17" (32 x 44 cm) pan with foil, spray with nonstick spray, spread mixture evenly into pan and bake at 350°F (180°C) for 40 minutes. When removing from oven, cut meringue into half lengthwise. Cool.

Filling:
5 egg yolks
1 cup (250 ml) cream
1-5 oz (147 ml) can evaporated milk
2 Tbs (30 ml) sugar
2 egg whites
10 oz (283 g) raspberry-flavored chocolate chips or plain chocolate chips
1 cup (250 ml) nondairy creamer or cream, whipped

Combine egg yolks, cream, evaporated milk, sugar, and chocolate and cook in microwave for 4½-5 minutes on 50% power, whisking every 30 seconds until thickened or use a double boiler, whisking mixture constantly until thickened. Cool. Whisk egg whites until stiff. Combine with nondairy creamer or cream and then fold into chocolate mixture.

For parve dessert, substitute nondairy creamer instead of cream and evaporated milk.

Sandwich meringue layers together with filling, leaving some to frost top and sides. If you have any trimmings or crumbs from the meringue, crush and press onto sides. Decorate top with chocolate curls and dust lightly with powdered sugar just before serving.

KWV or Paarl VSOP Brandy

CHOCOLATE RASPBERRY CREME BRULEE

Sinfully rich but delicious!

Serves 12

5 cups (1.25 L) whipping cream
½ cup (125 ml) sugar
1½ lbs (750 g) semi-sweet chocolate chips or coarsely diced chocolate
8 egg yolks
sugar
raspberries

Using a 2-qt (2 L) ovenware dish, layer raspberries at the bottom of the dish.

Combine cream and sugar in a double boiler over simmering water. Stir until sugar is dissolved. Add chocolate and stir until melted. Set aside.

Beat egg yolks in mixer until thick and creamy (about 5 minutes). Add chocolate cream mixture. Pour over raspberries. Place dish into a roasting pan and fill pan with hot water until halfway up sides of dish. Bake at 350°F (180°C) for 50 minutes until knife inserted comes out clean. Remove dish from pan and cool. Chill.

When cold, sprinkle sugar to cover over custard. Broil directly under broiler until caramelizes*. Refrigerate until serving. May be made a day in advance and kept refrigerated. Decorate with fresh raspberries and whipped cream.

*You may use a blowtorch for this.

KWV, Paarl Ruby Port

CITRUS FLOATING ISLAND

Serves 12

Meringue:
1 Tbs (15 ml) unflavored gelatin
¼ cup (60 ml) cold water
½ cup (125 ml) lemon juice
4 egg whites
1½ cups (375 ml) sugar
1 tsp (5 ml) finely grated lemon rind

Custard:
2 cups (500 ml) milk
½ cup (125 ml) cream
4 egg yolks
2 Tbs (30 ml) sugar
1 Tbs (15 ml) cornstarch
finely grated rind of 1 orange

Method:
Soften gelatin in cold water. Add lemon juice and heat gently until gelatin has thoroughly dissolved (this can be done in the microwave but be sure it does not boil over). Beat egg whites until stiff. Gradually add sugar and continue to beat until very stiff and shiny. Beat in lemon rind. Fold in cooled gelatin mixture. Pipe into 12 swirls on foil-lined tray which has been sprayed with nonstick and refrigerate until set—a couple of hours or overnight.

Prepare custard:
Scald milk and cream in the top of a double boiler. Beat the egg yolks and sugar until light and creamy, then add cornstarch and orange rind and beat until blended. Slowly add the scalded mixture to the egg yolks, beating constantly as you do so. Return this mixture to the double boiler and cook until thickened, stirring constantly with a whisk.

To serve:
Spoon the custard into a serving dish. Lift the meringues with a spatula and place on top of the custard. Garnish with strips of julienned orange and lemon rind.

KWV Van der Hum Liqueur

COULDN'T BE SIMPLER MANGO ICE CREAM

Serves 12-14

½ **gallon (1.89 litres) vanilla ice cream**
1 x 2 lbs (1 kg) mangoes, drained and pureed or fresh pureed mangoes
2 Tbs (30 ml) KWV Van der Hum Liqueur

Soften ice cream slightly. Mix in mango and liqueur. Pour into mold and freeze.

Unmold and serve.

KWV Noble Late Harvest

2-TONE CREME BRULEE CAKE

Serves 10-12

Cake:
6 eggs, separated
¾ cup sugar (200 ml)
1 tsp (5 ml) vanilla
2 Tbs (30 ml) cocoa
2 Tbs (30 ml) cornstarch

Beat egg yolks and sugar until light and fluffy. Beat in vanilla and then fold in sifted cocoa and cornstarch. Lastly fold in stiffly beaten egg whites.

Pour into a 12" x 17½" (31 x 44 cm) nonstick baking sheet which has also been sprayed well with nonstick spray and bake at 350°F (180°C) oven for 15-20 minutes. Allow to cool in pan pushing gently away from edges to make sure it does not stick (not likely).

When cool, center into a 10" or 12" (25 x 30 cm) springform pan which has been sprayed with nonstick spray. Press gently into pan and cut off edges that overlap, using them to fill in on the sides where necessary.

Sprinkle bottom of cake with fresh raspberries and prepare the creme brulee as follows.

4 cups (1 L) cream
10 egg yolks
4 Tbs (60 ml) sugar
10 oz (283 g) raspberry flavored chocolate chips or plain chocolate

Scald cream in top of double boiler. Beat egg yolks and sugar until thick and creamy. Slowly add scalded cream beating continually as you do so. Return half of the mixture to the top of double boiler and cook stirring constantly with a wooden spoon until mixture thickens. Do not overcook as it will curdle. Pour this half into a bowl and stir in raspberry-flavored chocolate chips or plain chocolate chips. Allow to cool while you prepare the second half of the creme brulee mixture as above, cooking until thickened on top of double boiler. Pour into bowl and allow to cool. Spoon the chocolate-flavored creme brulee over the raspberries and then gently spoon the vanilla custard over the chocolate custard. Allow to set in refrigerator overnight. Trim edges of the cake so that they are totally level with the creme brulee and cover edges of cake with foil to prevent burning. Cover the custard with sugar so that you cannot see through it and place directly under broiler until it caramelizes.*Watch carefully that it does not burn.

*This can be done with a blowtorch.

KWV Noble Late Harvest or KWV Van der Hum Liqueur

CREPES CALYPSO

Yield: 25

Batter:
1 cup (250 ml) flour
4 eggs
2 cups (500 ml) milk
pinch salt
oil for frying

Filling:
1 20-oz (567 g) can pineapple chunks
2 Tbs (30 ml) KWV 10-Year-Old Brandy
1 Tbs (15 ml) KWV 1975 Red Muscadel

Sauce:
4 oz (125 g) chocolate
6 Tbs (75 g) butter
1 cup (250 ml) cream
1 tsp (5 ml) vanilla

To prepare batter, beat all ingredients together until smooth. Heat oil in a small pan and pour in small amount of batter. Rotate to cover pan evenly. Fry quickly until crisp and golden. Remove onto a clean cloth. When cool, stack one on top of another.

Fill each crepe with chunks which have been marinated in brandy and muscadel. To serve, pour over hot chocolate sauce and sprinkle with flaked toasted almonds.

To prepare sauce, melt chocolate and butter in double boiler. Stir in cream and vanilla.

KWV 10-Year-Old Brandy

CROISSANT BREAD PUDDING WITH BRANDY CREAM SAUCE

Serves 10-12

8 plain croissants or 8 chocolate croissants, broken into pieces
½-¾ cup (125-180 ml) raisins or chopped figs or a mixture of both
3 eggs
¾ cup (200 ml) sugar
1 cup (250 ml) milk
1 cup (250 ml) cream
2 Tbs (30 ml) KWV, Paarl VSOP or KWV 10-Year-Old Brandy
¼ cup (60 ml) butter, melted
1 tsp (5 ml) cinnamon
1 tsp (5 ml) nutmeg
1 tsp (5 ml) vanilla essence
pinch of salt
2 oz (50 g) butter
1 Tbs (15 ml) cinnamon sugar

Bourbon cream sauce:
2 oz (50 g) butter
1 cup (250 ml) brown sugar
½ cup (125 ml) water
½ cup (125 ml) cream
1 tsp (5 ml) vanilla
2 Tbs (30 ml) cornstarch, mixed to a paste with cold water
2-3 Tbs (30-45 ml) KWV VSOP or 10-Year-Old Brandy

Preheat oven to 350°F (180°C).

Grease a 13" x 9" (23 x 32 cm) or 9" x 11" (22 x 28 cm) casserole dish. Place half the croissants in the dish; sprinkle with raisins and/or figs and then top with remaining croissants. Beat the eggs until light, gradually adding the sugar until thick. Whisk in milk, cream, brandy, melted butter, cinnamon, nutmeg, vanilla and salt. Pour mixture over the croissants and leave to absorb in the refrigerator for an hour or so. This dish may be prepared to this point a day in advance. Cover and refrigerate.

Before baking, bring to room temperature. Dot with butter and sprinkle with cinnamon and sugar and bake for 40 minutes and then increase heat to 400°F (200°C) and bake until top is brown and crispy. Serve immediately with sauce.

Sauce:
In a small saucepan, combine butter, brown sugar and water and stir until boiling and sugar has dissolved. Add cream, vanilla and cornstarch paste and stir until thickened. Lastly, add brandy.

Sauce can be made a few days in advance and heated before serving.

KWV 10-Year-Old Brandy or KWV, or Paarl Ruby Port

DIVINE BAKED CARAMEL APPLES

Ingredients:
5-6 Granny Smith apples
thinly peeled rind of 1 lemon
juice of 1 lemon
sultanas (golden raisins)—plumped (do this by covering with boiling water, strain
off and dry on absorbent paper)

Caramel sauce:
4 oz (125 g) butter
1 cup (250 ml) tightly packed brown sugar
¾ cup (200 ml) boiling water
½ cup (125 ml) cream
2 tsp (10 ml) cornstarch/cornflour mixed to a paste with a little cold water

Method:
Core apples. Place in an ovenware dish and sprinkle the inside with lemon juice and place a few of the plumped raisins in each and then stuff with a small roll of the lemon rind.

Combine sauce ingredients in a small saucepan and heat until butter has melted and sauce has thickened. (This can also be done in the microwave.) Pour sauce over and around apples and bake in a 350°F (180°C) oven for 1-1½ hours, basting occasionally with the sauce. Serve warm with vanilla ice cream.

KWV Noble Late Harvest or KWV or Paarl Tawny Port

FROZEN LEMON MERINGUE

For kosher households, this is a wonderful parve dessert by substituting nondairy cream-er whipped topping for the cream.

Serves 12

9 egg whites
½ tsp (2 ml) cream of tartar
2 cups (500 ml) sugar
½ tsp (2 ml) grated lemon rind
1½ Tbs (20 ml) cornstarch
3 cups (750 ml) walnuts and pecans, coarsely chopped

Preheat oven to 325°F (160°C) and line two baking sheets 15" x 10" (38 x 25 cm) or one 28" x 40" (71 x 102 cm) with foil and spray well with nonstick cooking spray.

Beat egg whites and cream of tartar until soft peaks form. Gradually add sugar and beat until stiff and shiny. Beat in lemon rind. Combine nuts and cornstarch and fold into egg white mixture. Bake for 40 minutes or until crisp and golden. When cool, cut each meringue into half lengthwise. Stack the four layers of meringue with filling on a large piece of foil on a baking sheet so that you can wrap it completely when assembled and can slide it from the tray into the freezer. The foil also serves to hold the dessert in shape as sometimes the lemon filling is fairly runny.

Spread the following filling between layers and spread on outside of meringue.

Freeze.

This dessert should be served direct from the freezer. Decorate with lemon twists and mint sprigs.

Filling:
9 egg yolks
1 cup (250 ml) sugar
grated rind of 1 lemon
⅔ cup (300 ml) lemon juice
3 cups (750 ml) cream

Put egg yolks in double boiler with sugar, lemon rind and juice and whisk constantly, cooking until thickened. Allow to cool, whisking occasionally while cooling. Fold in whipped cream.

KWV 10-Year-Old Brandy

GRILLED FRUIT WITH MANGO OR PASSION FRUIT CREAM

Papayas—peeled, cut in half and seeds removed
Mango—peeled and slice thickly, lengthwise
Pineapple—peeled and sliced into fingers lengthwise
or fruits of your choice; e.g., bananas, peaches, nectarines, plums,
**   grapefruit, or oranges**
1 cup (250 ml) powdered sugar combined with 1 tsp (5 ml) ground cinnamon

Sprinkle fruit generously with powdered sugar mixture. Place fruit on grill over medium heat, turning occasionally and sprinkling with sugar mixture until fruit coating is glazed (approximately 5 minutes), removing pieces to platter as it browns.

To do under broiler, line a baking sheet with foil and spray with nonstick cooking spray. Place fruit on foil-lined pan and cook under broiler.

Beat 1 cup (250 ml) cream until thick. Fold in pureed mango or passion fruit. Serve with grilled fruit.

Can flame the fruit with KWV Van der Hum Liqueur.

KWV Noble Late Harvest

HAWAIIAN GRILLED FRUIT WITH COCONUT VANILLA SAUCE

1 medium pineapple and 2 papayas, peeled, cut in quarters lengthwise and seeds
    removed and 2 or 3 mangoes, peeled and sliced
4 bananas, firm and slightly underripe
½ cup (125 ml) coconut milk
½ cup (125 ml) cream
3 large egg yolks
2 Tbs (30 ml) sugar
2 Tbs (30 ml) fresh lemon juice
powdered sugar (icing sugar)
mint sprigs

Place coconut milk and cream in double boiler and cook over moderate heat until scalded (small bubbles form around edges of saucepan).

In a small bowl, beat yolks and sugar until thick and pale, about 5 minutes. Whisk the hot coconut milk into egg yolks. Return mixture to double boiler and cook stirring constantly until the custard just starts to thicken.

Trim off the top and bottom of the pineapple, slice off skin and remove eyes. Cut pineapple into ¼" (1 cm) thick crosswise slices and cut out core. Cut bananas in half lengthwise and then in half crosswise. In a small bowl, combine bananas and lemon juice. Line a baking sheet with foil. Spray well with nonstick cooking spray. Sprinkle fruit thickly with powdered sugar and place directly under grill and broil about 5 minutes until browned and bubbly (watch carefully), sprinkling once more with powdered sugar and removing fruit from broiler as it browns.

Arrange fruit on platter, spooning any juices over fruit. Pour sauce into plastic bag, snip a tiny hole in one corner and drizzle sauce in zigzag pattern over fruit or surround fruit with sauce.

Sauce may be prepared a day ahead and refrigerated. Fruit must be done just before serving.

KWV Van der Hum Liqueur

HILARY'S CHEESE CAKE SOUFFLÉ

Serves 8-10

Filling:
16 oz (500 g) cream cheese (Philadelphia)
3 eggs
⅔ cup (150 ml) sugar

Beat cream cheese until light and creamy. Add eggs, one at a time, beating thoroughly. Add sugar and beat until smooth. Pour mixture into a 2 qt (2 L) casserole that has been lined with plastic wrap. (This makes it easy to remove.) Cover and freeze.

Batter:
½ lb (250 g) butter, melted
½ cup (125 ml) sugar
2 eggs
2 tsp (10 ml) baking powder
1 cup (250 ml) flour
¼ tsp (1 ml) salt
¼ cup (60 ml) milk
1 tsp (5 ml) vanilla

Blend all ingredients for batter.

Pour half the batter into buttered 2-qt (2 L) casserole. Place frozen cream cheese mixture on top and pour over remaining batter. Sprinkle with cinnamon and sugar. Bake at 300°F (150°C) for about 45-60 minutes until set.

May be prepared a day in advance and reheated. Freezes well. Ideal for a brunch.

Hilary Isakow
Bloomfield Hills, Michigan

KWV Noble Late Harvest

KADAYIF WITH CUSTARD

Lesley attends a gourmet Dinner Group which meets every few months to share an ethnic meal. Melanie Minson, who is of Armenian descent, prepared a wonderful Armenian meal. This dessert is delicious and it is from an Armenian cookbook which her late mother compiled.

Serves 12

1 lb (½ kg) kadayif (shredded phyllo)
¾ lb (375 g) butter, melted
½ cup (125 ml) cornstarch
2 cups (500 ml) whipping cream
2 cups (500 ml) half and half
2 cups (500 ml) milk

Syrup:
1 tsp (5 ml) lemon juice
3 cups (750 ml) sugar
2 cups (500 ml) water
1 Tbs (15 ml) KWV Van der Hum Liqueur

Pull the shredded phyllo apart. Pour butter over kadayif and blend thoroughly. Put three quarters into bottom of 9 x 13 x 2½" (23 x 32 x 7 cms) ovenproof dish and press kadayif up sides of dish as well. Make custard by dissolving cornstarch in milk, add whipping cream and half and half, and cook slowly over medium heat until it comes to a boil and thickens. Spread custard over kadayif that has been pressed into pan. Top lightly with remaining kadayif clear to edges of pan. Bake at 375°F (190°C) until golden brown on top and bottom. If top browns too rapidly, cover lightly with foil, approximately 35 minutes.

After removing kadayif from oven, pour cooled syrup evenly over it. (To make syrup, combine sugar, water and lemon juice and cook for 10 minutes.) Add liquer.

To microwave custard: Dissolve cornstarch in milk, add whipping cream and half and half. Cook 17-20 minutes on 100% power whisking every 2 minutes for the first 12 minutes and then every minute for the remaining 5-8 minutes.

This dessert is best served warm and can be heated in the microwave on full power for 3-5 minutes.

Melanie Minson
Cincinnati, Ohio

KWV 10-Year-Old Brandy or KWV or Paarl Tawny Port

KWV VAN DER HUM CREPE DELIGHT

We created this delicious dessert especially for KWV

Serves 12

Batter:
1 cup (250 ml) flour
4 eggs
2 cups (500 ml) milk
pinch salt
oil for frying

Filling:
1 sponge cake or pound cake, cut into fingers
4 egg yolks
2 Tbs (30 ml) sugar
2 cups (500 ml) scalded milk
1 tsp vanilla
2 Tbs (30 ml) KWV Van der Hum Liqueur

Sauce:
½ cup (125 ml) brown sugar
½ cup (125 ml) water
juice of 2 oranges
juice of 1 lemon
1 Tbs (15 ml) butter
2 Tbs (30 ml) KWV 10-Year-Old Brandy
2 Tbs (30 ml) KWV Van der Hum Liqueur

To prepare batter, beat all ingredients together until smooth. Heat oil in a small pan and pour in small amount of batter. Rotate to cover pan evenly. Fry quickly until crisp and golden. Remove onto a clean cloth. When cool, stack one on top of another.

To prepare filling, beat egg yolks and sugar until light and creamy. Add scalded milk, beating the entire time as you do. Place in a double boiler and cook, stirring constantly until very slightly thickened. Remove from heat. Add vanilla and liqueur. Soak cake fingers in this custard.

To prepare sauce, mix all ingredients for sauce together. Boil.

Place a finger of custard soaked cake on each crepe and roll up. Place in greased ovenproof dish and pour sauce over crepes. Bake in a 400°F (200°C) oven for 20-25 minutes or until hot or bubbling. Serve piping hot with whipped cream or ice cream.

You may substitute boudoir biscuits (lady fingers) for the sponge cake.

LOKSHEN PUDDING

Serves 8-10

½ lb (250 g) medium lokshen noodles
4 large eggs
¼ lb (125 g) butter or margarine
3 cups (750 ml) milk
2 Tbs (30 ml) seedless raisins (optional)
¾ cup (200 ml) sugar (to taste)
1 Tbs (15 ml) vanilla essence

Boil lokshen noodles according to instructions on package. Rinse with cold water. Melt butter and gently fold into lokshen. Beat eggs, milk, sugar add vanilla essence and combine with lokshen. Fold in raisins. Pour into greased 9" (22 cm) square ovenware dish.

Place a container of hot water on a shelf below the pudding and bake at 350°F (180°C) 40-45 minutes.

For richer pudding, add ¼ lb (125 g) softened cream cheese to lokshen mixture.

Pauline Greek,
Cape Town, South Africa

KWV 1975 Muscadel or Kwv or Paarl Tawny Port

MARTIN'S TROPICAL FRUIT SMOOTHIE

Serves 1

Mix the following in a blender:

2 bananas
2 scoops lowfat frozen yogurt or sherbert, flavor of your choice
1 cup orange juice
pulp of 1 passion fruit, if available

Pour into glass and serve immediately.

Martin Loon
Cincinnati, Ohio

PARVE APPLE TART

Serves 8-10

1 can unsweetened apples, drained
1 large Granny Smith apple, peeled and thinly sliced
juice of 1 lemon
handful of raisins
cinnamon and sugar
2 eggs
1 cup (250 ml) sugar
¾ cup (200 ml) oil
1 tsp (5 ml) vanilla
1 cup (250 ml) flour
1 tsp (5 ml) baking powder

Combine canned and fresh apples. Place in a 10" (25 cm) greased ovenware dish, sprinkle with lemon juice and raisins and the cinnamon and sugar, about 2-3 Tbs (30-45 ml).

Beat eggs and sugar very well. Beat in oil and vanilla and then beat in sifted flour and baking powder. Pour over apples and bake in a 325°F (160°C) oven 45 minutes to 1 hour.

Serve with custard, whipped cream or ice cream or nondairy whipped topping.

For Thanksgiving use the following filling:

Combine 1½ lbs (½ kg) cranberries, coarsely chopped
1¼ cups (300 ml) sugar
juice and rind of 1 orange
½ tsp (3 ml) cinnamon
2 peeled and sliced or diced Granny Smith apples
2 Tbs (30 ml) cornstarch

Top with the same batter and bake as instructed.

KWV or Paarl Ruby Port

PAVLOVA

Serves 10-12

6 egg whites
pinch salt
1½ cups (375 ml) superfine (castor) sugar
2 Tbs (30 ml) cornstarch (cornflour)
2 tsp (10 ml) lemon juice
extra cornflour (cornstarch)

Cut 9" (23 cm) circle from a piece of parchment paper. Place on greased oven tray and spray with nonstick spray and dust with extra cornstarch (cornflour). Shake off excess.

Beat egg whites with salt until soft peaks form. Add sugar gradually, beating well after each addition until stiff and shiny. Lightly fold in cornstarch (cornflour) and lemon juice. Spread in a thick, even layer over prepared circle. Bake at 300°F (150°C) one hour and then 100°C (50°C) for 4-5 hours. Then turn oven off and leave until completely cooled.

Fill with whipped cream and fresh fruit (strawberries, kiwi, mangoes, or fruit of your choice.)

KWV Noble Late Harvest

PINEAPPLE-APPLE MOLDS WITH VANILLA SAUCE

Virtually a fat-free dessert but without losing any flavor. It's delicious!

Serves 4-6

Carmelized apples:
3 large Granny Smith apples
½ cup (125 ml) sugar
Nonstick spray—preferably butter flavored

Fruit filling:
1 fresh pineapple, core removed and cut into cubes or use 1 can pineapple chunk
    in its own juice—drain and reserve juice.
2 Granny Smith apples, peeled and cubed
2 Tbs (30 ml) reserved pineapple juice
2 Tbs (30 ml) sugar or artificial sweetener to taste
1 Tbs (15 ml) pancake syrup
1 tsp (5 ml) cinnamon
1 tsp (5 ml) vanilla
1 tsp (5 ml) cornstarch mixed to a paste with pineapple juice

Vanilla Sauce:
2 cups (500 ml) skimmed milk
2 eggs
artificial sweetener to taste [about 2-3 tsp (5-10 ml)]
2 heaped tsp (10 ml) cornstarch (cornflour)
1 tsp (5 ml) vanilla

Preheat the broiler. Line a baking sheet with foil and spray with nonstick spray. Core and peel the apples. Cut the apples in half vertically, cutting through the hole. Cut the halves into very thin slices and arrange on the foil-lined pan. Sprinkle with the sugar and then spray again with spray. Place 2" (5 cm) from the heat and broil until apples are golden and caramelized. Allow to cool enough to handle.

Using 5 to 6 ramekins, spray them with nonstick spray. Place apple at the bottom of each mold and then line the sides with overlapping apple slices, leaving the caramelized side against the mold (so that when you unmold it, the caramelized side will be on the outside).

Prepare the fruit filling:
Squeeze the excess juice out of the cubed pineapple and reserve. Spray a medium-sized skillet with nonstick. Heat and add pineapple. Cook until pineapple browns a little, then add cubed apple and allow to brown a little as well. Add reserved pineapple juice, sugar, or sweetener, pancake syrup, cinnamon and vanilla and continue to cook on medium-low heat until apple is tender. Stir in cornstarch to thicken. Divide this fruit mixture evenly between the apple-lined ramekins. Press down with back of spoon and then turn the apple slices over to enclose the filling.

Cover each with plastic wrap and refrigerate until needed. It may be prepared to this point and refrigerated for 2-3 days in advance.

Vanilla sauce:
2 eggs
2 cups plus 2 Tbs (530 ml) skimmed milk
2 tsp (10 ml) cornstarch
2-3 Tbs (30-45 ml) sugar
or 1½-2 tsp (7-10 ml) powdered sweetener
1 tsp (5 ml) vanilla

Mix cornstarch with 2 Tbs (30 ml) cold milk. Beat eggs slightly. Add cornstarch mixture and blend. Boil milk and sugar (or sweetener) together. Stir into egg yolk mixture, stirring constantly until thickened. If necessary, microwave on medium 2-3 minutes longer to thicken more or return to stove. Add vanilla.

Final preparation:
Heat ramekins in microwave, turn out onto serving platter and spoon vanilla sauce around the mold. Serve immediately. Can also serve with frozen vanilla yogurt sprinkled with cinnamon.

KWV Noble Late Harvest or KWV Paarl Tawny Port

PRALINE CRUSTED CHOCOLATE MOUSSE

Excellent as a parve dessert.

Serves 8-10

Crust:
1½ cups (375 ml) hazelnuts or macadamia nuts, toasted*
1¼ cups (375 ml) sugar
3 oz (75 g) melted butter or margarine
4 Tbs (60 ml) flour

Preheat oven to 350°F (180°C). Place sugar in large saucepan over medium heat and stir until sugar starts to melt and is lumpy; then turn to low heat and continue stirring until sugar is melted and lumps go away. Remove from heat and quickly stir in nuts and pour onto foil-lined pan which has been sprayed with nonstick cooking spray. Allow to cool and harden. Break up and place in food processor and chop finely. Add melted butter and flour and process just to blend. Turn mixture into a 10" (25 cm) loose bottom springform pan. Press down well onto bottom of pan only and bake 15-20 minutes. After removing from oven, allow to cool.

*Nuts may be toasted by placing on a plate in microwave and cook on high power (100%) for 2 to 3 minutes.

Filling:
½ cup (125 ml) sugar
2 Tbs (30 ml) water
4 eggs, separated
1 cup (250 ml) cream or non-dairy creamer
1 lb (500 g) chocolate
1 oz (30 g) margarine or butter
1 Tbs (15 ml) KWV 10-Year-Old Brandy or KWV Van der Hum Liqueur

Boil sugar and water on high heat until it comes to a boil. Turn to low and boil for 1 ¼ to 2 minutes or until mixture spins a thread when dropped from a spoon. Beat yolks until thick and creamy.

Turn beaters to low and pour syrup in a slow stream onto yolks while beating continuously. Pour syrup away from sides of bowl into middle of bowl (if it touches the side of the dish, it will harden).

Melt chocolate and margarine in microwave on 30% power. Add Van der Hum or brandy. Pour onto egg mixture and continue beating until mixture is well combined. Beat egg whites until stiff. Beat nondairy creamer or cream until thick. Mix whites and nondairy creamer together and fold into chocolate mixture. Pour over crust and allow to set. May be frozen—defrost in refrigerator. Decorate with chocolate curls. Just before serving, dust with powdered sugar.

KWV 10-Year-Old Brandy or KWV Van der Hum Liqueur

TIRAMISU

Serves 12

12 oz (300 g) pound cake (may use store-bought)
⅓ cup (80 ml) expresso or strong coffee mixed with 2 Tbs (30 ml)
   KWV or Paarl VSOP Brandy
6 oz (175 g) dark chocolate
½ cup (125 ml) cream
1 Tbs (15 ml) additional Kahlua or KWV or Paarl VSOP Brandy
5 yolks
½ cup (125 ml) sugar
1 cup (250 ml) milk
1 lb (500 g) Marscapone cheese at room temperature

Slice pound cake. Place one layer in bottom of glass trifle bowl. Brush with coffee and Kahlua mixture.

Prepare chocolate ganache:
Place coarsely chopped chocolate in bowl. Heat cream in saucepan. Pour cream over chocolate and stir until smooth and melted. Add additional Tbs (15 ml) of Kahlua. Beat yolks with sugar until thick and creamy. In double boiler, scald milk. Whisk hot milk into egg yolks. Return mixture to top of double boiler and cook over moderate heat, stirring constantly until custard just starts to thicken and coats the back of a wooden spoon, approximately 3-5 minutes. Allow to cool and then whisk in softened Marscapone cheese. Leave in refrigerator until ready to use.

Pour layer of chocolate ganache over pound cake. Allow ganache to set in refrigerator for a few minutes and then pour a layer of custard over chocolate ganache. Continue in this manner until all ingredients have been used up; coffee brushed pound cake, ganache, custard. Cover and allow to set in refrigerator, preferably overnight.

When ready to serve, dust with sifted chocolate drinking powder or cocoa.

This dessert can be frozen. Defrost in refrigerator before serving.

KWV 10-Year-Old Brandy

VERY BERRY SALAD

Strawberries
Blueberries
Raspberries
Blackberries
1-2 cans drained lychees
Sprigs of mint for garnish

Carefully combine fruits gently so as not to squash the berries. Place in a glass bowl and garnish with sprigs of mint.

This is particularly good served with chocolate mousse. Very refreshing too!

KWV Noble Late Harvest

CITRUS PEEL AND CANDIED GINGER

Place ½ cup (125 ml) sugar in pan. Add 1/4 cup (60 ml) water. Stir constantly without boiling until sugar is dissolved. Bring to rapid boil and cook uncovered until light golden brown.

Add strips of rind and simmer about 5 minutes. Remove rind from syrup to tray to cool before using. Roll in sugar whilst still sticky.

Use for decoration.

Candied Ginger:
Peel and slice gingerroot into rounds. Boil with equal amounts of sugar and water over gentle heat until ginger is translucent. Drain and cool. Roll in sugar or refrigerate ginger in syrup in jars. The syrup is good used in gingerbreads et cetera.

Cakes and Tarts

CHOCOLATE DECORATIONS

To make a chocolate rose you will need a few plastic bowls (a little deeper than a saucer) which must be lined with plastic wrap. Prepare foil petals by cutting heavy duty foil into a triangle shape with rounded corners and bend up slightly to resemble a petal.

Melt dark, milk or white chocolate either in a double boiler over simmering water or in the microwave. Always melt chocolate on 30% power for 5-7 minutes or as long as necessary, depending on the amount of chocolate you use. Each rose uses about 2 oz (60 g) chocolate for the petals.

Coat the petals on the shiny side of the foil with chocolate, allowing excess to drip off and place on a foil-lined tray. When the tray is full, place in refrigerator to set. Remove and carefully peel off foil. You will need 10-12 petals for each rose.

To make the center of the rose, mix chocolate clay as follows:
1 cup melted chocolate with 1-2 Tbs (15-30 ml) light corn syrup just until combined to form consistency of clay. Wrap in waxed paper and allow to set a couple of hours or overnight. Break off pieces the size of a walnut, knead slightly in your hand until it softens and forms into a ball. Then roll out between 2 pieces of plastic wrap to an oval shape. Remove the wrap and roll up into a cone shape to resemble the center of a rose, pinching the bottom together to secure the shape. Place on a sheet of waxed paper to dry.

To assemble the rose, spoon some melted chocolate into the base of the plastic-lined bowl. Arrange the petals in layers, working from the outside in and pressing into the melted chocolate. Place one of the prepared centers in the middle and allow to set. Pull rose out with the plastic wrap and peel off. These roses can be stored in the refrigerator or freezer for use when desired. Surround with chocolate leaves made by melting chocolate and spreading on the back of washed and dried lemon or rose leaves. Allow to set, peel off leaves carefully.

Two-Tone Chocolate Bands or Lace to Wrap Around Cakes or Desserts
Measure the height and circumference or your cake or dessert. Cut acetate, plastic mylar, or parchment paper into strips the same height and circumference. (You might need to use two strips.) Place these strips onto a large baking sheet. Melt the chocolate [about 2 oz (60 g)] on 30% power for 3-5 minutes and pour into a high quality plastic bag. Snip a tiny bit off the one bottom corner of the bag with a sharp scissors and pipe a crosshatch or lacey design on each of the strips. Allow to set.

Melt the dark chocolate [about 4 oz (125 g)] on 30% power for 5-7 minutes. Using an offset metal spatula, spread the dark chocolate to completely cover the design and make sure to go slightly over the edges, making sure that the ends are well covered. Allow to set until the chocolate has lost its shine but has not hardened as you must be able to wrap it around the cake. Place the strip gently, chocolate side against the cake, and gently wrap around the outside of the cake. Repeat with the second strip, making sure that the ends do not overlap but just meet. Refrigerate until the bands are set and peel off the paper or mylar.

To make chocolate lace, just make a lacy pattern on your parchment or mylar and before it sets, wrap around cake as described above.

ALMOND CHOCOLATE LAYER CAKE

This would be a great Passover dessert.

Serves 10-12

Almond soufflé:
8 egg yolks
1 cup (250 ml) sugar
6 oz (175 g) butter, melted
6 oz (175 g) ground almonds (almond meal)—3 small packages
½ tsp (3 ml) almond extract
4 egg whites, stiffly beaten

Beat egg yolks and sugar until light and fluffy. Beat in melted butter and almond extract. Fold in almond meal and lastly fold in stiffly beaten egg whites. Grease or spray two 9" (22 cm) round layer pans, line with paper and spray again. Pour mixture evenly into the two pans and bake in a 325°F (160°C) oven for 26 to 28 minutes. Turn out onto a sheet of foil which has been sprayed with nonstick. Peel off paper and allow to cool.

Flourless chocolate cake layer:
8 oz (250 g) dark chocolate, coarsely chopped
6 oz (175 g) butter
8 egg yolks
1 cup (250 ml) sugar
4 egg whites
1 tsp (5 ml) vanilla or KWV Van der Hum Liqueur

Melt chocolate and butter together. In the meantime, beat egg yolks and sugar until light and fluffy. Add vanilla or liqueur. Add chocolate butter mixture and blend well. Beat egg whites stiffly and fold in a quarter of the egg whites into the chocolate mixture. Continue to fold in the balance of the egg whites using an up and over motion as gently as possible.

Grease or spray two 9" (22 cm) layer pans, lined with paper and spray again. Pour mixture evenly into the two pans and bake in a 325°F (160°C) oven for 26-28 minutes. Turn out onto a sheet of foil, peel paper off, and allow to cool.

Orange buttercream:
⅔ cup (160 ml) sugar
⅓ cup (80 ml) orange juice
4 egg yolks, slightly beaten
grated rind of 1 orange
2 Tbs (30 ml) KWV Van der Hum Liqueur
1 cup (250 g) butter, at room temperature

Combine sugar and orange juice in a heavy saucepan and stir until boiling. Beat egg yolks with a whisk until blended. Slowly add boiling mixture to egg yolks, beating constantly as you do so. Return mixture to saucepan and bring to boil over gentle heat, whisking constantly until thickened (approximately 1-2 minutes). Remove from heat and add orange rind and liqueur. Beat butter until creamy and gradually add cooled sugar mixture.

Chocolate ganache:
8 oz (250 g) dark chocolate, coarsely chopped
1 cup (250 ml) heavy cream or whipping cream
3 Tbs (75 g) butter
(Can add Van der Hum Liqueur.)

Combine chocolate, cream and butter in a saucepan and stir over gentle heat until chocolate has melted. Remove from heat and place saucepan in a larger container filled with ice water and stir occasionally until mixture has cooled. Place in refrigerator until nicely thickened for spreading.

To assemble:
Place layer of chocolate cake on a cardboard round or on a large foil-lined baking sheet. Spread with half the ganache, then a layer of almond soufflé, 1/2 cup (125 ml) orange buttercream and repeat process, reserving 1 cup (250 ml) buttercream to frost sides and top of cake.

Decorate with dark chocolate curls and just before serving, dust the curls lightly with powdered sugar.

In the photograph we have this cake surrounded with the white and dark chocolate band, as described in chocolate decorations on page 251.

ALMOND GINGER TART

Serves 10-12

Pastry:
2 cups (500 ml) flour
1 tsp (5 ml) baking powder
pinch salt
2 Tbs (30 ml) sugar
4 oz (125 g) butter
3 egg yolks, mixed with a little cold water
apricot jam

Combine flour, baking powder, salt and sugar in food processor. Add butter and blend with egg yolk mixture to form a smooth dough. Line a 12" (27.5 cm) pie dish or loose bottom pan thinly with pastry. Prick all over and spread thinly with apricot jam.

Filling:
8 oz (250 g) butter
¾ cup (200 ml) sugar
4 eggs
8 oz (225 g) ground almonds
2 cups (500 ml) leftover cake crumbs (or use bought plain cake and put in blender or food processor to crumble)
2 tsp (10 ml) almond essence
½ cup (125 ml) chopped crystallized or preserved ginger

Cream butter and sugar. Add eggs and the rest of the ingredients and mix well. Fill tart shell with filling and bake at 375°F (190°C) until golden brown, approximately 20-25 minutes. When cool, spread with the following.

Icing:
1 cup (50 ml) icing sugar
3 Tbs (45 ml) warm water or lemon juice

Mix icing sugar and water until smooth and glossy and spreadable. It should coat the back of a wooden spoon evenly. If too thick, add a few drops warm water; if too thin, add a little more icing sugar.

Spread over cake and sprinkle round edge with toasted almonds and slices of ginger.

(If you wish, you may omit ginger.)

APPLE CAKE DELUXE

Serves 12

4 large Granny Smith apples, peeled, cored, and thinly sliced
2 cups (500 ml) sugar
cinnamon and sugar
3 cups (750 ml) flour
3 tsp (15 ml) baking powder
1 tsp (5 ml) salt
1 cup (250 ml) oil
4 eggs
¾ cup (200 ml) orange juice or apple juice
1 Tbs (15 ml) vanilla

Grease bundt (chiffon) pan. Sprinkle apples liberally with additional sugar and cinnamon. Set aside.

Sift remaining dry ingredients. Make a well in center of dry ingredients. Add eggs, oil, orange juice and vanilla. Beat until well blended.

Spoon ⅓ of batter into pan. Top with half of drained apples. Spoon over another ⅓ of batter. Spoon over remaining drained apples and top with remaining batter. Smooth over top and bake at 350°F (180°C) for 1¼ hours.

Ethel Grayce
Cincinnati, Ohio

APRICOT CUSTARD TART

Serves 10-12

Tart dough:
4 oz (125 g) butter
2 Tbs (30 ml) sugar
1 egg
1¼ cup (300 ml) flour
1 tsp (5 ml) baking powder
1 tsp (5 ml) vanilla

Cream butter and sugar. Add egg, sifted flour, baking powder and vanilla. Blend to a dough. If necessary, refrigerate before using. Roll out dough and press onto bottom and halfway up side of 9" (23 cm) springform pan. Place a sheet of foil or waxproof paper over the dough and fill the shell with dried beans.

Bake in a 350°F (180°C) oven 10-15 minutes. Remove beans and paper and bake for a further 15 minutes or until golden brown. Cool.

Filling:
2 x 5.5-oz cans (165 g) apricot nectar
4 egg yolks
½ cup (125 ml) sugar
1 Tbs (15 ml) cornstarch mixed to a paste with a little cold water
1 cup (250 ml) cream, whipped

Place apricot nectar, egg yolks, and sugar in a double boiler and whisk until thickened. Add cornstarch and cook a little longer. Cool thoroughly in refrigerator. When cold, fold in whipped cream.

Topping:
2 cans apricots, drained
1 cup (250 ml) apricot jam (preserves)

To complete tart, spoon custard filling into baked shell, top with apricots, cut side down. Boil together jam and lemon juice, cool and brush over apricots.

AUNTIE CELIE'S CHOCOLATE CREAM SWISS ROLL

Serves 8-10

4 eggs, separated
½ cup (125 ml) sugar
2 Tbs (30 ml) cocoa
2 Tbs (30 ml) cornstarch
1 tsp (5 ml) baking powder

Beat yolks and sugar. Add sifted cocoa, cornstarch, and baking powder. Lastly, fold in stiffly beaten egg whites.

Bake 7-10 minutes at 350°F (180°C) in a jelly roll pan. Turn onto damp cloth that has been sprinkled with sugar and roll up. Allow to cool, unroll, fill with cream filling and roll up again. Dust with powdered sugar before serving.

Cream filling:
Whip ½ pint (250 ml) cream. Add 1 Tbs (15 ml) castor sugar (superfine) and coffee, if desired.

(Can add 1-2 Tbs (15-30 ml) Van der Hum Liqueur.)

AUNTIE CELIE'S YOGURT CAKE

Serves 6-8

4 oz (125 g) butter
¾ cup (200 ml) sugar
2 egg yolks
½ tsp (2 ml) baking soda
½ cup (125 ml) plain yogurt
½ tsp (2 ml) baking powder

1 cup (250 ml) cake flour (rounded)
pinch of salt
3 egg whites, stiffly beaten
1 tsp (5 ml) vanilla essence
2 oz (60 g) dark chocolate
2 Tbs (30 ml) milk

Cream butter and sugar. Beat in egg yolks. Dissolve baking soda in yogurt and add to creamed mixture with remaining dry ingredients. Lastly fold in egg whites and vanilla.

Pour into 8" (20 cm) springform pan. Melt chocolate and milk in microwave on 30% power for 2½ minutes. Stir until smooth. Drizzle over cake. Bake at 350°F (180°C) for 40 minutes. Remove from oven and pour over the topping.

Topping:
4 Tbs (60 g) butter
½ cup (125 ml) sugar
3 Tbs (45 ml) cream

½ cup (125 ml) coconut
½ tsp (3 ml) vanilla

Boil butter, sugar and cream for 2 minutes. Remove from heat. Add coconut and vanilla. Spread over baked cake and place under broiler for a few minutes.

BANANA GINGER CAKE

Serves 12

1-1½ cups (250-375 ml) chopped stem or glace ginger
3 cups (750 ml) flour
½ lb (250 g) butter
1½ cups (375 ml) sugar
4 eggs
1½ cups (375 ml) ripe mashed bananas
1 tsp (5 ml) vanilla
3 tsp (15 ml) ground ginger
2 tsp (10 ml) baking soda (bicarb)
pinch salt
1 cup (250 ml) buttermilk

Preheat oven to 350°F (180°C). Spray a 10" (25 cm) bundt pan with nonstick spray. Toss stem ginger with ½ cup of the measured flour (125 ml) and set aside.

Cream butter and sugar well. Add eggs, one at a time, beating well after each addition. Add bananas and vanilla. Sift remaining dry ingredients and add alternately with buttermilk. Fold in floured ginger. Pour into prepared pan and bake approximately 1 hour. Invert onto cooling rack.

To serve: Dust lightly with sifted powdered (icing) sugar.

This cake can also be baked in two loaf pans as it freezes exceptionally well. In this case, it need only be baked for 40-45 minutes.

BEST EVER CHOCOLATE CAKE WITH CARAMEL FROSTING

Serves 12

Cake:
6 oz (175 g) butter
1½ cups (375 ml) sugar
2 Tbs (30 ml) cocoa
2½ cups (625 ml) flour
2 tsp (10 ml) baking powder
1 tsp (5 ml) baking soda (bicarb)
4 eggs
1½ cups (375 ml) buttermilk
1 tsp (5 ml) vanilla
6 oz (180 g) semi-sweet chocolate, melted

Cream butter and sugar. Sift dry ingredients. Add eggs, buttermilk, vanilla, melted chocolate, and sifted dry ingredients to creamed butter. Beat in food mixer 3-4 minutes, scraping the bottom and sides of the bowl so that the ingredients are well blended. Divide mixture evenly between two pans, 9" (23 cm) round and 2" (5 cm) deep, or two 9" (23 cm) square pans, greased and floured or sprayed with nonstick spray. Bake in a 350°F (180°C) oven for 30-35 minutes. Turn out onto racks to cool.

Caramel frosting:
1 can condensed milk
1½ oz (35 g) butter
1 Tbs (15 ml) syrup or honey*
2 oz (60 g) dark chocolate

Place all ingredients in double boiler and cook stirring constantly until thickened. Cool.

This mixture can also be cooked in microwave for 3 minutes on 100% power, then 50% power, stirring every minute until thickened.

Sandwich cake together with half of this mixture. Spread remaining mixture over top and allow to drip down sides. Pour over chocolate glaze and allow to drip down sides.

Glaze:
4 Tbs (6 ml) butter
½ cup (125 ml) syrup
¼ cup (60 ml) hot water
12 oz (360 g) semi-sweet chocolate chips

Combine butter, syrup, and hot water in a saucepan. Bring to a boil and stir in chocolate chips until melted and smooth.

*It is always a good tip to remember to spray your utensil with nonstick spray and the syrup will pour out easily.

CARAMEL APPLE KUCHEN

Serves 12

1¼ cups (310 ml) flour
¼ cup (60 ml) sugar
2 tsp (10 ml) baking powder
pinch salt
4 oz (125 g) butter
1 egg beaten
¼ cup (60 ml) milk
1 tsp (5 ml) vanilla
4 Granny Smith apples, peeled and sliced
1 Tbs (15 ml) each of flaked almonds, sultanas (golden raisins) raisins, combined cinnamon and sugar

Blend flour, sugar, baking powder and salt in food processor. Add cut up butter and process until well blended. Combine egg, milk, and vanilla and add to flour mixture in bowl and blend until smooth. Allow dough to rest in refrigerator for 15 minutes. Spread mixture with floured hands, as it is a very sticky dough, evenly into a 12" (27.5 cm) loose bottomed flan pan.

Arrange apple slices, overlapping in parallel rows over the batter. Mix almonds, sultanas, raisins, cinnamon and sugar and place between rows of apples. Bake in a 350°F (180°C) oven for 30-40 minutes.

Topping:
¾ cup (200 ml) cream
2 Tbs (50 g) butter
1 cup (250 ml) powdered (icing) sugar

Boil topping ingredients together for 10 minutes. Allow to cool a little and pour over cake after removing from oven.

Serve at room temperature. Delicious served with whipped cream.

CARAMEL FUDGE CHEESECAKE

Serves 10-12

Crust:
1½ cups (375 ml) crushed vanilla wafers or marie biscuits
4 oz (125 g) butter or margarine, melted

Process together in food processor and press into 9" (23 cm) springform pan.

Cheese filling:
1½ lb (750 g) cream cheese (Philadelphia style)
¾ cup (180 ml) sugar
1 tsp (5 ml) grated lemon rind
3 eggs
1 cup (250 ml) sour cream

Cream cheese and sugar. Add lemon rind, eggs, and lastly fold in sour cream.

Caramel:
14 oz can (430 g) condensed milk
2 Tbs (30 ml) butter
2 Tbs (30 ml) golden syrup

Combine ingredients and microwave on high 3 minutes and then microwave on medium 3 minutes. Fold in ½ cup (125 ml) chopped walnuts. (optional)

To do on stove top: Combine ingredients in pot over medium heat until boiling. Allow to simmer over low heat for 5 minutes.

Pour half cheese mixture in prepared pan. Pour caramel on top of cheese and cover with balance of cheese mixture. Bake at 350°F (180°C) for 15 minutes. Turn oven to 300°F (150°C) and bake further 45 minutes. Turn off completely and leave in oven for a further hour. Top with either of the following:

Chocolate glaze (optional):
½ cup (125 ml) cup whipping cream
2 Tbs (30 ml) plus 2 tsp (10 ml) Van der Hum (orange-flavored liqueur)
11 oz (275 g) semi-sweet chocolate

Scald cream with Van der Hum. Remove from heat. Add chocolate and mix until smooth. Cool glaze until thick enough to spread. Pour over cake.

Caramel topping (optional):
3 Tbs (45 ml) water
½ cup (125 ml) sugar

Combine water and sugar in heavy saucepan. Cook over medium heat, stirring constantly until sugar is dissolved. Turn to high heat and cook until mixture turns a rich brown.

Both glazes are optional. We prefer it without any glaze as we feel it is rich enough as it is.

CHOCOLATE GLAZED BANANA CAKE

Serves 10-12

3 cups (750 ml) flour
2 tsp (10 ml) baking soda (bicarbonate of soda)
1 tsp (5 ml) baking powder
pinch salt
1½ cups (375 ml) sugar
4 eggs
1 cup (250 ml) oil
1 tsp (5 ml) vanilla
1½ cups (375 ml) very ripe bananas, mashed (about 3 large)
1 cup (250 ml) orange juice

Preheat oven to 350°F (180°C). Spray a 10" (25 cm) bundt pan with nonstick spray.

Sift dry ingredients—make a well in the center and add eggs, oil, vanilla, bananas, and orange juice. Beat until well blended. Pour into pan and bake approximately 1 hour—check for doneness after 1 hour—it may require a further 5-10 minutes baking time.

Pour the following glaze over cooled cake.

Glaze:
4 oz (125 g) butter
3 Tbs (45 ml) cocoa
2 egg whites
1 envelope Choc-O-Bake (optional)
3 cups (750 ml) powdered sugar
1 tsp (5 ml) vanilla

Melt butter with cocoa.
Mix 2 unbeaten egg whites with powdered sugar and if using, add Choc-O-Bake.
Add to melted butter mixture and cook over low heat until slightly thickened.
If glaze gets too thick, heat slightly until required consistency.

The Choc-O-Bake adds a really intense flavor.

CHOCOLATE MARSCAPONE TORTE

Serves 8-10

Cake:
4 eggs
1 cup (250 ml) sugar
1 tsp (5 ml) vanilla
pinch salt
2 Tbs (30 ml) cocoa

1 cup (250 ml) flour
3 oz (75 g) butter
½ cup (125 ml) milk
2 tsp (10 ml) baking powder

Chocolate Filling:
1 cup (250 ml) cream
¼ cup (60 ml) powdered (icing) sugar
1 Tbs (15 ml) cocoa
1 Tbs (15 ml) drinking chocolate
1 tsp (5 ml) vanilla
½ tsp (3 ml) instant coffee dissolved in 1 Tbs (15 ml) boiling water

Marscapone filling:
1½ cups (375 ml) cream, whipped stiffly
¼ cup (60 ml) powdered (icing) sugar

1 tsp (5 ml) vanilla
8 oz (250 g) marscapone cheese

Preheat oven to 400°F (200°C).

Cake Method: Beat eggs and sugar until very light and creamy. Beat in vanilla. Sift salt, cocoa, and flour together and set aside. Bring butter and milk to a boil together in a small saucepan. Add alternatively to egg mixture with the sifted dry ingredients. Lastly fold in baking powder. Pour mixture evenly into three 8" (20 cm) pans and bake for 12-15 minutes.

Chocolate filling: Beat cream and powdered sugar together until stiff. Fold in sifted cocoa and drinking chocolate. Lastly add vanilla and dissolved coffee.

Marscapone filling: Blend all ingredients together gently with a spatula.

Chocolate band: Cut a strip of wax paper or mylar sheeting 24" (62 cm) long and 4¼" (11 cm) wide. Place shiny side up on a large sheet of foil and cover with melted chocolate. Allow to set at room temperature but not harden.

To assemble cake: Alternate a layer of chocolate filling and marscapone filling between the three layers beginning and ending with the marscapone. Gently press the chocolate band around the side of the torte. Refrigerate until set and peel off the mylar or wax paper.

Dust the top of the cake with a mixture of 1 Tbs (15 ml) cocoa and 1 Tbs (15 ml) drinking chocolate mixed together.

CHOCOLATE PECAN PIE

Serves 8-10

Pastry:
1 cup (250 ml) flour
½ cup (125 ml) sugar
¼ cup (60 ml) cocoa powder
pinch salt
½ cup (125 g) butter

Combine ingredients in food processor to form dough. Press into a lightly greased 9" (23 cm) springform pan. Bake in 350°F (180°C) oven for 10-15 minutes. Cool and fill.

Filling:
4 eggs
1 cup (250 ml) brown sugar
⅓ cup (80 ml) melted butter
1 cup (250 ml) light corn syrup
4 oz (125 g) melted chocolate
½ tsp (3 ml) vanilla
1⅓ cup (300 ml) toasted pecans

Beat eggs. Add sugar and continue beating. Stir in melted butter, corn syrup, melted chocolate, and vanilla. Place pecans on bottom of crust and pour filling over. Bake at 350°F (180°C) for 45 minutes. When chilled, spread with fudge glaze (optional). This pie is very rich even without the glaze.

Glaze:
½ cup (125 ml) whipping cream
2 Tbs (30 ml) KWV Van der Hum Liqueur
11 oz (325 g) semi-sweet chocolate

Scald cream with liqueur. Remove from heat. Add chocolate and mix until smooth. Cool glaze until thick enough to spread.

CHOCOLATE RASPBERRY DACQUOISE TORTE

This would make a wonderful American wedding cakes as well as a spectacular Passover dessert—substitute potato starch for the cornstarch in the Dacquoise.

Serves 12

Flourless Chocolate Cake Layer:
8 oz (250 g) dark chocolate, coarsely chopped
6 oz (175 g) butter
8 egg yolks
1 cup (250 ml) sugar
4 egg whites
1 tsp (5 ml) vanilla

Melt chocolate and butter together. In the meantime, beat egg yolks and sugar until light and fluffy. Add vanilla. Add chocolate butter mixture and blend well. Beat egg whites stiffly and fold in a quarter of the egg whites into the chocolate mixture. Continue to fold in the balance of the egg whites using an up and over motion as gently as possible.

Grease or spray two 9" (22 cm) round layer pans, lined with paper and spray again.

Pour mixture evenly into the two pans and bake in a 325°F (160°C) oven for 26-28 minutes. Turn out onto a sheet of foil, peel paper off and allow to cool.

Hazelnut Dacquoise:
2 cups (500 ml) hazelnuts (filberts)—toasted
2 Tbs (30 ml) cornstarch (cornflour)
6 egg whites
1 cup (250 ml) sugar

Preheat oven to 300°F (150°C). Grease two 9" (22 cm) pans with nonstick. Line with waxed paper and spray again with nonstick. Toast hazelnuts in microwave on 100% power for 3-5 minutes. Place nuts in food processor and blend until fine but not oily. Combine nuts and cornstarch.

Beat egg whites until stiff. Gradually add sugar and continue to beat until very stiff. Fold in nut/cornstarch mixture. Bake 40-45 minutes.

Mocha Chocolate Buttercream:
⅔ cup (180 ml) sugar
¼ cup (60 ml) water
2 tsp (10 ml) instant coffee
4 egg yolks, lightly beaten
1 lb (500g) butter
1 tsp (5 ml) vanilla
4 oz (125 g) dark chocolate, melted (place in microwave safe bowl
    on 30% power for 3-5 minutes)

Combine sugar, water and coffee in a heavy saucepan and cook over high heat until mixture boils. Gradually pour this boiling mixture onto the beaten egg yolks, whisking continually as you do so. Return this mixture to the saucepan and cook over gentle heat whisking all the time until mixture thickens, 1-2 minutes. Remove from heat and cool to room temperature.

Beat butter in food mixer until creamy. Add cooled sugar mixture, beating until combined. Add vanilla and melted cooled chocolate and beat in. If necessary, cool in refrigerator until of spreading consistency.

Chocolate Ganache:
8 oz (250 g) dark chocolate, coarsely chopped
1 cup (250 ml) cream
2 oz (50 g) butter

Combine chocolate, cream and butter in saucepan over gentle heat and stir until melted. Cool and place in refrigerator, stirring occasionally until required consistency is attained.

To assemble:
10-oz pkg (300 g) frozen raspberries, thawed
10 or 12" (25-27.5 cm) cardboard round

Place layer of flourless chocolate cake on cardboard round or on a large foil-lined baking sheet. Spread with raspberries, spooning a little of the juice over to soak into the cake. Spread half the ganache over then a layer of hazelnut dacquoise, ½ cup (125 ml) buttercream and repeat process, reserving 1 cup (250 ml) buttercream to frost sides and top of cake. Cover lightly and refrigerate at least 6 hours before serving.

This cake freezes extremely well.

CHOCOLATE RASPBERRY PYRAMID OR SLICE

Serves 8-10

9 eggs, separated
1¾ cups (300 ml) sugar
1 tsp (5 ml) vanilla

3 Tbs (45 ml) heaped, cocoa
3 Tbs (45 ml) heaped, cornstarch
1 pkg frozen raspberries, drained well,
reserving juice

Beat yolks with sugar until light and creamy. Add vanilla. Add sifted cocoa and cornstarch. Lastly fold in stiffly beaten egg whites. Bake in 2 x 13" x 9" (23 x 32 cm) jelly roll pans which have been sprayed very well with nonstick at 350°F (180°C) for 20 minutes until springs back when lightly touched. (Even if using nonstick pan, it is still necessary to spray with cooking spray.) Turn out onto cloth. When cool, cut lengthwise into three even strips. Sprinkle lightly with juice drained from raspberries. Raspberry liqueur may be added to the juice, if desired.

Filling:
1 pt (½ L) whipping cream
12 oz (300 g) white chocolate

In saucepan, scald cream. Pour over chocolate and stir until chocolate has totally melted. Leave in refrigerator overnight. When ready to use, beat until thick. Add very well-drained raspberries and streak with a knife. Do not mix in completely.

To assemble: Place three strips of cake on foil, side by side; cover with some of filling and place remaining strips of cake on top. Spread with more filling, then place a row of raspberries along the center. Place your hands underneath the foil and lift the two sides, pressing together to form a pyramid. Allow to set in freezer. Pour over glaze.

Alternate method: raspberry slice: Cut each jelly roll in half lengthwise. Put one strip on foil. Spread with some filling and raspberries. Cover with second slice of cake and repeat process using 4 layers of cake. Set in freezer. Pour over glaze.

Glaze: Combine 1 egg white and 1½ cups (375 ml) powdered sugar until smooth. In small saucepan, melt 4 oz (125 g) butter and 2 Tbs (30 ml) cocoa. Bring to boil. Remove from heat and quickly stir in egg white mixture stirring constantly until smooth and shiny. Allow to cool completely before pouring over cake. If mixture is still too runny, add additional tablespoon (15 ml) or two (30 ml) of powdered sugar.

After cake is glazed, drizzle with white chocolate. Melt high quality white chocolate in double boiler or in microwave.

To make parve ganache: Melt together 1 lb (500 g) dark chocolate with 1¾ cups (375 ml) nondairy creamer in microwave for 4 minutes on 50% power. Stir until smooth. Beat nondairy creamer and spread on first layer. Drizzle with cooled ganache. Dot with raspberries.

COCONUT BAVARIAN CREAM PIE WITH CHOCOLATE SAUCE

Serves 8-10

Crush vanilla wafers or marie biscuits in food processor. Blend 2 heaped cups (500 ml) crushed cookies and 4 oz (125 g) melted butter. Pat into sides and bottom of 9" (22 cm) loose bottomed pan. Bake at 350°F (180°C) for 10 minutes. Cool.

Filling:
1 Tbs (15 ml) gelatin mixed with 1/4 cup (60 ml) cold water
¼ cup (60 ml) boiling water
3 eggs, separated
1 cup (250 ml) sugar, divided
1¼ cups (300 ml) milk
pinch salt
1½ tsp (7 ml) vanilla
1 cup (250 ml) cream
¼ tsp (2 ml) cream of tartar
Toasted coconut to garnish—to toast coconut, place in 350°F (180°C) oven for 5-10 minutes until brown

Beat yolks with ½ cup (125 ml) sugar until creamy and lemon colored. Scald milk and salt in double boiler. Remove from heat and pour slowly into beaten egg yolks, beating continually as you do so. Return this mixture to double boiler and bring to the boil whisking constantly until thickened. Remove from heat. Add boiling water to gelatin mixture and stir until gelatin has completely dissolved. Stir gelatin into egg yolk mixture with vanilla. Place in refrigerator until almost set. Beat cream until stiff. Beat egg whites with cream of tartar until stiff, gradually adding remaining ½ cup (125 ml) sugar and continue to beat until very stiff. Combine cream and egg whites and fold into cooled egg yolk mixture with a spatula gently using under and over motion. Pour into prepared crust and refrigerate until set. Decorate with toasted coconut. (To toast coconut, place in a 350°F (180°C) oven for 5-10 minutes until brown).

Chocolate sauce:
½ cup (125 ml) milk
11 oz (330 g) semi-sweet chocolate, chopped
¼ cup (60 ml) cream
2 Tbs (30 ml) unsalted butter
¼ cup (60 ml) sugar

Simmer milk with chocolate, stirring until chocolate is melted. Add cream, butter, sugar, and simmer, stirring until smooth and slightly thickened. Serve warm.

To Serve: Spoon a pool of sauce onto each plate and place a slice of Coconut Bavarian Cream Pie gently in the middle of the plate. Sprinkle with toasted coconut.

CREAM POUND CAKE

Ethel Grayce has made this cake famous in Cincinnati!

Serves 12

6 oz (175 g) butter
½ cup (125 ml) Crisco (vegetable shortening)
3 cups (750 ml) sugar
6 large eggs
3 cups (750 ml) cake flour, rounded
¾ tsp (3 ml) baking powder
1 cup (250 ml) cream
1 tsp (5 ml) vanilla extract

Cream butter, shortening and sugar. Add eggs one by one, beating well in-between. Sift the flour and baking powder together.

Add the flour mixture and cream alternatively to butter mixture, beginning and ending with flour. Add vanilla. Spray a 9" x 13" x 2" (23 x 33 x 5 cms) pan with nonstick spray. Line bottom only with wax paper and spray again. Pour mixture into prepared pan and bake at 350°F (180°C) for 60-70 min. When completely cooled, dust with powdered sugar.

Ethel Grayce
Cincinnati, Ohio

CUSTARD APPLE PIE

Serves 8

½ cup (125 g) butter, at room temperature
⅓ cup (80 ml) sugar
1 cup (250 ml) flour
¼ tsp (2 ml) vanilla

Cream butter and sugar. Add flour and vanilla and blend. Press into bottom and 1" (2.5 cm) up the sides of a greased 9" (23 cm) loose bottom pan.

Blend together in food processor or mixmaster:

8 oz (250 g) cream cheese, at room temperature (Philadelphia)
¼ cup (60 ml) sugar
1 egg
1 tsp (5 ml) vanilla

Spread cream cheese mixture onto pastry.

Slice two Granny Smith apples thinly and combine with juice of 1 lemon and mixture of cinnamon and sugar. Arrange apples decoratively in a circle on cream cheese mixture. Pour remaining juice over apples.

Bake at 450°F (220°C) for 10 minutes and then turn down temperature to 375°F (190°C) and bake for a further 25 minutes.

Best made on day you are serving it.

Penny Kassar
Cincinnati, Ohio

GINGER LEMON-GLAZED CHEESECAKE

Serves 10-12

1 pkg gingersnaps, crushed or 2 cups (500 ml) crushed
4 Tbs (60 ml) butter, melted

Combine and press into a greased 9" (22 cm) springform pan.

12 oz (750 g) cream cheese (Philadelphia style)
12 oz (750 g) ricotta cheese
1 cup (250 ml) sugar
3 eggs
½ cup (125 ml) cream
½ cup (125 ml) sour cream
juice and finely grated rind of 1 lemon

Cream cream cheese, ricotta cheese and sugar until light. Add eggs, one at a time, beating well after each addition. Add remaining ingredients and mix until blended. Pour into prepared pan and bake at 450°F (225°C) for 10 minutes. Reduce oven temperature to 200°F (100°C) and without opening oven, bake for 1 hour. Turn oven off and cool thoroughly in oven.

Spread with lemon glaze and refrigerate until needed.

Lemon glaze topping:
3 egg yolks
⅓-½ cup (80-125 ml) lemon juice
⅓-½ cup (80-125 ml) sugar
½ tsp (3 ml) finely grated lemon rind

Place egg yolks, lemon juice, sugar and rind in glass bowl. Microwave on 50% power for about 5 minutes, whisking every 30 seconds until thickened and smooth or cook in double boiler until thickened, whisking constantly.

Decorate with lemon twists and sprigs of mint.

HALVA CAKE

Serves 10-12

Cake Layers:
½ cup (125 ml) milk — combined
½ cup (125 ml) water
4 oz (125 g) butter
1 cup (250 ml) superfine granulated sugar (castor sugar)
3 eggs, separated
2 cups (500 ml) flour
1 tsp (5 ml) vanilla
2 tsp (10 ml) baking powder

Cream butter and sugar until light and fluffy. Add egg yolks. Sift flour and add alternately with milk and water. Stir in vanilla, fold in baking powder and lastly stiffly beaten egg whites. Spray two 11½" x 17" (27 x 43 cm) pans with nonstick spray. Divide mixture evenly between the two pans and bake in a 375°F (190°C) oven for 7-10 minutes. Cool. Cut the cake in each pan lengthwise into 3 even strips.

Filling:
2 cups (500 ml) cream
12 oz (375 g) dark chocolate, coarsely chopped
6-8 oz (185-250 g) halva, flaked

Heat cream until scalded. Pour over chocolate and stir until smooth. Fold in halva. Spread evenly between the layers of cake.

Glaze:
4 oz (125 g) butter
3 Tbs (45 ml) cocoa
2 egg whites
1 envelope Choc-O-Bake (optional)
3 cups (750 ml) powdered sugar
1 tsp (5 ml) vanilla

Prepare glaze:
Melt butter with cocoa. Mix 2 unbeaten egg whites with Choco-O-Bake (if using) and powdered sugar. Add vanilla. Add to melted butter mixture and cook over low heat until slightly thickened. If glaze gets too thick, heat slightly until required consistency. Pour over cake and allow to drip down sides.

CHOCOLATE CAKE

4 eggs separated
⅔ cup (160 ml) sugar
4 Tbs (60 ml) cocoa
1 tsp (5 ml) vanilla

Grease or spray with nonstick 8" (20 cm) square dish or 8" (20 cm) springform pan. Beat egg whites until stiff and set aside. Beat egg yolks and sugar very well. Add vanilla and fold in sifted cocoa with half the beaten egg whites. Gently fold in remaining egg whites. Pour into prepared pan and bake at 375°F (190°C) for 15-20 minutes. Allow to cool thoroughly.

When cold, cover with the following which have been beaten together.

1 cup (250 ml) cream
2 Tbs (30 ml) sugar
Optional: Sprinkle with nuts or dried cherries or both on top.

Place cake in freezer.

Topping:
8 oz (250 g) bitter-sweet chocolate
2 Tbs (30 ml) milk
2 Tbs (30 ml) oil
1 oz (25 g) butter

Dissolve in double boiler. Pour this mixture over chilled cream. Place in refrigerator. Decorate with chocolate shavings.

Hannah Rosenthal
Johannesburg, South Africa

HILARY'S CARROT CAKE

Serves 12

Mix together:
4 eggs
3 jars [1½ cups (375 ml)] strained carrots (baby food)
1 cup (250 ml) golden raisins (sultanas)
1 large can crushed pineapple, drained

Add:
1½ cups (375 ml) sugar
1 cup (250 ml) oil
1 tsp (5 ml) vanilla
1 cup (250 ml) walnuts, chopped

Sift together:
2 cups (500 ml) flour
2 tsp (10 ml) baking soda (bicarb)
1 tsp (5 ml) salt
2 tsp (10 ml) cinnamon

Combine dry ingredients with wet ingredients just until blended. Bake in ungreased 9" x 13" (22 x 32.5 cm) dish in a 325°F (160°C) oven for 50 minutes.

Frost with cream cheese frosting or orange frosting.

Cream cheese frosting:
See Italian Cream Cake on page 276.

Orange frosting:
3 cups (750 ml) powdered sugar (icing sugar)
2 oz (50 g) soft butter
orange juice to form spreading consistency. Mix all together well.

Hilary Isakow
Michigan

HONEY CAKE

Serves 12

3 tsp (15 ml) ground ginger
¼ tsp (2 ml) ground cloves
½ tsp (3 ml) ground cinnamon
½ tsp (3 ml) nutmeg
3 cups (750 ml) flour
¾ cup (180 ml) sugar

1 tsp (5 ml) baking powder
1 cup (250 ml) oil
1 cup (250 ml) honey
1 cup (250 ml) warm tea or coffee
3 eggs, well beaten
2 tsp (10 ml) baking soda

Sift ginger, cloves, cinnamon, nutmeg, flour, sugar and baking powder into bowl of food mixer. Make a well and mix in the oil, honey, warm tea or coffee, beaten eggs, and lastly, the baking soda which has been dissolved in a little warm water. Beat on low speed for 8 minutes.

Bake in greased bundt pan at 350°F (180°C) for 55-60 minutes. Alternatively, bake at 300°F (150°C) in sheet cake pan for approximately 45 minutes.

ISRAELI APPLE TART

Serves 8-10

3 lbs (1½ kg) apples—Granny Smith, Winesap, Jonathan

Peel and slice. Place in saucepan with ⅓ cup (80 ml) sugar and ½ cup (125 ml) water and ⅛ sliced lemon. Cover and cook on low for 10 minutes. Drain and discard lemon slices and cool thoroughly.

Dough:
4 oz (125 g) butter or margarine
2 Tbs (30 ml) sugar
1 egg
2 Tbs (30 ml) oil
2 cups (500 ml) flour
2 tsp (10 ml) baking powder

Cream butter and sugar. Add egg and oil and beat in. Add flour and baking powder and make into dough.

Press three-quarters of dough into 9" (23 cm) springform pan and halfway up sides. Spoon apples over and sprinkle with 1 Tbs (15 ml) cinnamon and sugar and grate remaining dough on top. Sprinkle with an additional 1 Tbs (15 ml) sugar and dot with butter or margarine. Bake at 350°F (180°C) 50-60 minutes.

Dust top quite thickly with powdered sugar before serving.

ITALIAN CREAM CAKE

Serves 10-12

4 oz (125 g) butter
½ cup (125 ml) oil
1½ cups (375 ml) sugar
5 eggs, separated
1 cup (250 ml) buttermilk
1 tsp (5 ml) baking soda
2 cups (500 ml) flour
1 tsp (5 ml) vanilla
1 cup (250 ml) shredded coconut
½ cup (125 ml) nuts, chopped

Frosting:
8 oz (250 g) cream cheese (Philadelphia style)
4 oz (125 g) butter
1 tsp (5 ml) vanilla
15 oz (450 g) powdered sugar
1 cup (250 ml) chopped nuts

Cream butter, oil, and sugar. Add egg yolks, one at a time. Stir baking soda into buttermilk. Add sifted flour alternatively with buttermilk. Add vanilla, coconut, and chopped nuts. Beat egg whites until stiff and fold into mixture. Pour into 2 greased and floured 9" (23 cm) pans. Bake at 325°F (160°C) for 45 minutes.

When cool, ice with the frosting:

Beat cream cheese and butter. Add vanilla, powdered sugar, and nuts. Beat until spreading consistency.

Keep cake refrigerated. Serve at room temperature.

LEMON ALMOND TORTE

A new twist to an old favorite.

Serves 10-12

Torte:
4 oz (125 g) butter
1 cup (250 ml) sugar
1 cup (250 ml) sliced almonds, toasted (in oven or microwave 2-3 minutes)
2 cups (500 ml) flour
1 tsp (5 ml) baking powder
pinch salt
1 egg
1 tsp (5 ml) grated lemon rind

Lemon curd:
¾ cup (200 ml) sugar
½ cup (125 ml) cornstarch (cornflour)
pinch salt
1 cup (250 ml) milk
3 egg yolks

4 Tbs (60 ml) butter
1 tsp (5 ml) grated lemon rind
¼ cup (60 ml) lemon juice
1 cup (250 ml) sour cream

Meringue:
3 egg whites
¼ tsp (2 ml) cream of tartar

⅓ cup (80 ml) sugar

Preheat oven to 375°F (190°C).

Torte: Cream butter and sugar. Chop almonds in a food processor, using a metal blade. Add flour, baking powder, and salt and process a little longer until blended. Add egg and lemon rind to creamed butter and then add flour mixture and blend into dough. Press into bottom and sides of a 9" (23 cm) loose bottomed pan. The mixture will be a lot of dough but this is more like a cake than cookie crust. Cover with waxed paper, weigh down with dried butter beans and bake in oven for 15-20 minutes; remove paper and beans and return to oven so that the bottom can bake for a further 15 minutes. Reduce oven temperature to 350°F (180°C).

Lemon curd: Place sugar, cornstarch, and salt in top of double boiler. Gradually add milk and cook stirring constantly until thickened. Beat egg yolks until pale. Gradually stir about ½ of hot mixture into yolks; add to remaining hot mixture. Continue to cook in double boiler, stirring constantly until thickened. Remove from heat; stir in butter until melted; add rind and lemon juice. Chill in refrigerator and when cold, fold in sour cream. Pour this mixture into torte shell. Place in 350°F (180°C) oven for 15 minutes.

Meringue: Beat egg whites and cream of tartar until stiff; gradually beat in sugar; spread over hot filling, making sure to seal edges. Sprinkle a ring of sliced almonds around edge of torte and return to oven for 15-20 minutes or until meringue is golden brown.

Serve at room temperature.

LEMON MERINGUE CHEESECAKE

Serves 10-12

Marie biscuit or graham cracker crust:
2 cups (500 ml) crushed biscuits (cookies)
4 oz (125 g) melted butter

Combine and press into a 10" (25 cm) springform pan on the bottom and 2½" (7.5 cm) up the sides.

Cheese filling:
1½ lbs (750 g) cream cheese softened, (Philadelphia style)
1 cup (250 ml) sugar
3 eggs
pinch of salt
1 cup (250 ml) sour cream
1 tsp (5 ml) vanilla
1 Tbs (15 ml) custard powder (dessert mix)
1 Tbs (15 ml) cornstarch (cornflour)

Beat cream cheese and sugar very well. Add eggs one at a time, beating after each addition. Add remaining ingredients and beat just until blended.

Lemon filling:
1 can condensed milk
2 egg yolks
½ cup (125 ml) lemon juice
1 tsp (5 ml) finely grated lemon rind

Combine ingredients until blended.

Spoon half cheese mixture into crust, spoon lemon mixture in middle and top with remaining cheese mixture. Bake in a 350°F (180°C) oven for 20 minutes. Turn oven off and leave in oven for another hour or until cool.

Meringue topping:
4 egg whites
pinch of cream of tartar
4 Tbs (60 ml) sugar

Beat egg whites with cream of tartar until stiff. Continue to beat adding sugar gradually until very stiff. Pile over cooled filling and place in a 375°F (190°C) oven for 5-10 minutes or until golden brown, turn oven off and leave until cool.

This cake can be frozen without the meringue. When required, defrost, top with meringue and bake as directed.

LOW FAT SOUR CREAM CAKE

Serves 10-12

8 oz (250 g) margarine
2 cups (500 ml) sugar
1 Tbs (15 ml) vanilla
1 container Egg Beaters (4 oz:118 ml): equivalent of 2 eggs
16 oz (435 g) container fat free sour cream
1 Tbs (15 ml) baking powder
2¼ cups (560 ml) cake flour

Filling:
¼ cup (60 ml) sugar
3 Tbs (45 ml) cocoa
2 tsp (10 ml) cinnamon
¼ cup (60 ml) brown sugar

Cream margarine and sugar until light and fluffy. Add vanilla and Egg Beaters. Add sour cream and blend well. Sift flour and baking powder together. Fold into margarine and sugar mixture. Sift filling ingredients.

Pour half the batter into greased bundt pan. Sprinkle with half of filling. Add rest of batter and using a knife, cover evenly. Sprinkle remainder of filling onto batter and press in with the back of a spoon.

Bake at 350°F (180°C) for 60-70 minutes or until tester comes out clean. Turn out of pan after 20 minutes. When cool, sprinkle with confectioners sugar.

Delicious—hard to believe it's low fat!

Lynda Tucker
Cincinnati, Ohio

MANGO ROULADE WITH PASSION FRUIT GLAZE

Serves 10-12

5 eggs
1 cup (250 ml) sugar
1 cup (250 ml) plus 2 Tbs (30 ml) flour
½ cup (125 ml) cornstarch
2 oz (50 g) butter
⅓ cup (80 ml) water and milk mixed
2 tsp (10 ml) baking powder

Beat eggs and sugar until light and creamy. Add sifted dry ingredients except baking powder. Add boiled milk and butter and lastly fold in baking powder. Pour into a greased and floured jelly roll pan 15" x 10" x 1" (39 x 26 x 2 cm) and bake in a 400°F (200°C) oven for 8-10 minutes. Turn onto a damp cloth, roll up and allow to cool.

Filling:
1 lb (500 g) cream cheese, softened (Philadelphia style)
1 cup (250 ml) powdered (icing) sugar
2 mangoes, cubed

Beat cream cheese and sugar until combined. Stir in mangoes. Unroll cooled cake. Spread filling over it and roll up carefully. Dust with powdered sugar or pour over the following glaze.

Passion fruit glaze:
2 cups (500 ml) powdered sugar
Passion fruit pulp

Combine to make a nice pouring consistency.

MARISA'S SOUR CREAM APPLE PIE

Marisa Schwartz tasted this pie at a restaurant and asked us to re-create it when we catered for her Batmitzvah.

Serves 10-12

½ cup (125 g) butter, at room temperature
⅓ cup (80 ml) sugar
1 cup (250 ml) plus 2 Tbs (30 ml) flour
¼ tsp (1 ml) vanilla
6 Granny Smith apples, peeled, cored and thinly sliced
5 Tbs (75 ml) sugar
5 tsp (25 ml) cinnamon
1 cup (250 ml) sour cream combined with 2 Tbs (30 ml) sugar

Cream butter and sugar. Add 1 cup (250 ml) flour and vanilla and blend. Press into bottom and sides of a greased 9" (23 cm) springform pan. Toss apples with combined sugar and cinnamon and 2 Tbs (30 ml) flour. Layer sliced apples, spreading a thin layer of sour cream mixture between layers, ending with apples.

Crumble the following mixture on final layer of apples.

¼ cup (60 ml) flour
¼ cup (60 ml) sugar
1½ oz (35 g) butter

Bake apple pie at 450°F (225°C) for 10 minutes and then reduce heat to 375°F (190°C) and bake a further 30 minutes.

To obtain thin uniformly sliced apples, an "apple peeler corer slicer" available in kitchen stores is a must.

MILLIONAIRES NUT TART

Serves 12

Crust:
5 oz (150 g) butter
½ cup (125 ml) sugar
1 Tbs (15 ml) oil
1 egg
2¾ cups (680 ml) flour
1 tsp (5 ml) baking powder

Filling:
1 cup (250 ml) cream
1 cup (250 ml) sugar
⅓ cup (80 ml) light corn syrup or honey
½ cup (125 ml) each walnuts, almonds, pecans, brazil nuts, cashews, pine nuts, macadamias and pistachios

Crust:
Cream butter and sugar. Add oil and beat another minute or two. Add egg and beat in. Lastly, add sifted flour and baking powder. The mixture will be crumbly. Press into a greased 10" (25 cm) springform pan—1" (2.5 cm) up the sides as well. Prick all over. Bake in 350°F (180°C) oven for 15 minutes or until lightly browned.

Filling:
Combine cream, sugar, syrup or honey over low heat. Stir until dissolved and bring to the boil. Allow to boil on medium heat without stirring until mixture thickens and changes to a light caramel color—10-12 minutes. Remove from heat and allow to cool. Stir in nuts.

Pour into par-baked shell and return to oven for another 30-35 minutes or until filling is hot and bubbly.

This tart can also be baked in 2" x 8" (20 cm) loose bottom pans.

PLUM TART

Serves 8

1 egg
⅓ cup (60 ml) sugar
1 cup (250 ml) flour
2 tsp (10 ml) baking powder
2 Tbs (30 ml) butter
½ cup (125 ml) milk
1 tsp (5 ml) vanilla
2 cans plums, apricots or apples, drained
1 cup (250 ml) cream
1 cup (250 ml) sugar

Beat egg and sugar well. Sift flour and baking powder.

Melt butter in milk and add vanilla. Add to eggs and sugar mixture with sifted dry ingredients and beat until smooth. Pour mixture into greased 9" (23 cm) pie dish. Place fruit over mixture. Bake at 350°F (180°C) for 1/2-3/4 hour.

Combine cream and sugar in a saucepan. Bring to the boil, stirring constantly until sugar has dissolved. Pour over cake after removing from oven.

SACHER TORTE

Serves 10-12

6 oz (175 g) butter
¾ cup (180 ml) sugar
6 eggs, separated
1 tsp (5 ml) vanilla
6 oz (175 g) dark chocolate, melted and cooled
1¼ cups (310 ml) flour

Glaze:
¾ cup (180 ml) apricot jam or orange marmalade
3 Tbs (45 ml) Van der Hum liqueur

Chocolate Glaze:
2 oz (50 g) butter
1 cup (250 ml) cream
1 cup (250 ml) sugar
4 oz (125 g) dark chocolate

Chocolate Decoration:
3 oz (75 g) dark chocolate

Prepare Cake: Cream butter and half the sugar. Add egg yolks, vanilla and cooled melted chocolate and continue to beat until fluffy. Beat egg whites until stiff, then gradually beat in remaining sugar. Add sifted flour to the butter/egg yolk mixture and lastly fold in ⅓ of the stiffly beaten egg whites and when that has been incorporated, fold in the rest of the egg whites.

Pour into an 8" (20 cm) loose bottom pan which has been sprayed well with nonstick and bake in a 350°F (180°C) oven for 60 minutes or until a skewer inserted in the center of the cake comes out clean.

Cool in pan on cooling rack for 10 minutes then loosen edges and remove outer ring. Allow to cool thoroughly.

Prepare Glaze: Bring apricot preserves or orange marmalade to the boil and then strain to remove solids. Stir in liquor.

If necessary, trim cake to level top. Cut in half horizontally by marking around the sides with a sharp knife and then use cotton thread to saw through evenly.

Brush top of cake with some of the apricot/marmalade glaze, place 2nd layer on top cut side down. Place on cooling rack and pour over remaining glaze to cover top and sides.

Chill in refrigerator for 1 hour. In the meantime prepare chocolate glaze.

Place butter, sugar and cream in a large nonstick pan and bring to the boil, stirring constantly with a wooden spoon until sugar has dissolved. Allow to boil undisturbed over medium heat 2-3 minutes. Remove from heat, stir in chocolate. Return to medium heat and cook stirring constantly for another 4-5 minutes. Pour over cake on rack, allowing the glaze to cover top and sides, using a metal spatula to smooth. Allow to set in refrigerator for 1 hour.

Decorate with chocolate lines, using melted chocolate or write the word "Sacher" on top with the melted chocolate.

In the photograph, this cake is topped with a white chocolate rose, as described in chocolate decorations (foil petal method).

VAN DER HUM CAKE

Serves 12

Cake:
8 oz (250 g) butter
1¼ (300 ml) sugar
4 eggs
1 tsp (5 ml) vanilla
3 cups (750 ml) flour
1 tsp (5 ml) baking powder
¾ tsp (4 ml) bicarbonate of soda (baking soda)
pinch salt
1 cup (250 ml) buttermilk

Van der Hum sauce:
1 cup (250 ml) sugar
4 oz (125 g) butter
¼ cup (60 ml) water
½ cup (125 ml) KWV Van der Hum Liqueur

Boil sugar, butter and water together for 5 minutes. Add liqueur.

Preheat oven to 350°F (180°C).

Cream butter and sugar until light and creamy. Add eggs, one at a time, beating well after each addition. Add vanilla. Sift together flour, baking powder, and baking soda (bicarb) and salt. Add alternatively to creamed mixture with buttermilk.

Pour into greased and floured 10" (25 cm) bundt (chiffon) pan and bake for 1 hour or until skewer inserted comes out clean. Remove from oven. Cool cake in pan for 15 minutes and then prick surface of cake. Pour sauce over and allow to cool completely and invert onto serving plate.

WHITE CHOCOLATE CHEESECAKE

Serves 10-12

Crust:
2 cups (500 ml) Oreo cookie crumbs, chocolate wafer crumbs for topping number 1, or vanilla crumbs if using topping number 2.
3 oz (90 g) melted butter

Combine cookie crumbs and melted butter. Press into 9" (22 cm) greased springform pan.

Filling:
1½ lbs (750 g) Philadelphia style cream cheese at room temperature
¾ cup (175 ml) sugar
3 eggs
12 oz (360 g) coarsely chopped white chocolate
½ cup (125 ml) cream
1 cup (250 ml) sour cream

Beat cream cheese and sugar until creamy. Add eggs one at a time, beating well after each addition. Melt chocolate, stir in cream and stir until smooth. Add to cheese with sour cream and mix in thoroughly.

Pour into crust and bake at 350°F (180°C) for ½ hour. Turn off oven and leave in oven until completely cool. Top with one of the following toppings.

Topping number 1—Raspberry:
1½ cups (375 ml) raspberries
2 cups (500 ml) sugar
1 Tbs (15 ml) lemon juice
additional raspberries

Combine raspberries, sugar and lemon juice in saucepan and cook over medium heat. Bring to boil, stirring frequently. Reduce heat and simmer until mixture coats the back of a wooden spoon, approximately 15-20 minutes. Remove from heat and strain mixture. Cool.

Spread over cooled cheesecake. Top with additional raspberries.

The cake, without the topping, may be frozen. It should be glazed with topping 1 day before serving.

Topping number 2—White Chocolate Ganache:
½ cup (125 ml) cream
2 Tbs (30 ml) Van der Hum liqueur
11 oz (325 g) white chocolate

Scald cream with liqueur. Remove from heat, add chocolate and mix until smooth.

Cool and pour over cake.

Myrna made the fabulous roses on the white chocolate cheesecake as photographed using two chocolate clays—a peach and a white chocolate, as follows:

Mix 1 cup (250 ml) of white melted chocolate with 2 Tbs (30 ml) corn syrup and mix thoroughly until it makes a clay. Wrap in wax paper and allow to set a couple of hours or overnight. Repeat this process with the peach chocolate or coating. Pinch off small balls of the white and peach chocolate and roll together to form 1 ball the size of a hazelnut (filbert). Place this ball between layers of cling wrap and roll out very thinly with a rolling pin in both directions. Remove top layer of cling wrap carefully as these petals are very delicate and mold these petals (starting with the bud in the center) and layering the petals around to form a rose, pinching the bottom together to secure the rose as you add each petal. Prop up in a egg-cup lined with cling wrap to dry.

UNSWEETENED FLAKY PIE CRUST

This pastry may be used for any savory or sweet tart.

1⅓ cups (320 ml) flour
pinch salt
4 oz (125 g) butter
3 Tbs (45 ml) buttermilk

In food processor, place dry ingredients; add butter and process until resembles coarse meal. Add buttermilk and blend until forms dough.

Refrigerate for 15 minutes before using or wrap in plastic and freeze until required.

Cookies and Small Cakes

COOKIES AND SMALL CAKES

ALMOND CRESCENTS

½ lb (250 g) soft butter
⅓ cup (80 ml) sugar
⅔ cup (160 ml) ground almonds
1 tsp (5 ml) vanilla
2 cups (500 ml) flour
pinch salt

Mix together by hand, softened butter, sugar, ground almonds and vanilla. Sift together flour and salt and knead into mixture. If dough is too soft to handle, chill for a while. Roll into a pencil-thin sausage 1½"-2" (7.5-10 cm) in length. Form into crescents on ungreased baking sheet. Bake at 325°F (160°C) oven just until set. Do not allow to brown.

Remove from oven and while hot, roll in vanilla sugar.

Vanilla sugar:
Granulated sugar stored in a jar with a vanilla bean long enough to impart that delicious vanilla flavor.

AUSTRALIAN CARAMEL LOGS

Shortbread:
2 cups (500 ml) flour
pinch salt
1 Tbs (15 ml) cornstarch
½ lb (250 g) butter
⅓ cup (80 ml) superfine sugar (castor sugar)

Combine and sift flour, salt and cornstarch. Cream butter and sugar. Add sifted ingredients. Roll out and cut into rounds [2½" (6 cm)]. Prick all over with fork and bake on a lightly greased cookie sheet 350°F (180°C) until golden brown. Cool.

Caramel:
14 oz (420 g) caramel chews
½ cup (125 ml) evaporated milk

In heavy saucepan, combine caramels and evaporated milk. Stir occasionally over low heat until melted. Allow to cool and harden.

Sandwich cookie rounds with caramel.

Optional: Roll caramel logs in toasted coconut. To toast coconut, place on flat baking sheet in 300°F (150°C) oven until brown. Watch carefully as it burns easily.

CHINESE CHEWS

8 pieces stem ginger
8-10 maraschino cherries
1 cup (250 ml) sugar
2½ cups (675 ml) flour
1 heaped tsp (5 ml) baking powder
1 Tbs (15 ml) ground ginger
pinch salt
½ lb (250 g) butter
1 egg, lightly beaten
2 Tbs (30 ml) ginger syrup, from stem ginger, or Karo light syrup

Cut ginger and cherries into small pieces. Sift dry ingredients. Add melted butter mixed with ginger, syrup, beaten egg and fruit. Press into an ungreased 13" x 9" (32 x 22 cm) baking pan and bake in a 350°F (180°C) oven for approximately ½ hour or until done. Cover with lemon icing and cut into squares while hot. Remove from pan when cool.

Lemon icing:
1½ cups (375 ml) powdered sugar and enough freshly squeezed lemon juice to make a smooth running consistency.

CREAM TARTLETS

6 oz (180 g) butter
2 cups (500 ml) flour
1 egg yolk mixed with iced water

Rub or grate butter into flour. Mix into dough with egg yolk and water. (This may be done in food processor). Line greased muffin pans with pastry. Prick well. Spoon a little apricot jam on the bottom of each.

Fill with the following:
2 eggs
⅓ cup (80 ml) superfine (castor) sugar
1 cup (250 ml) crushed amaretto cookies
1 tsp (5 ml) vanilla essence
almond halves

Beat eggs and sugar. Add amaretto cookies and vanilla. Spoon filling into crust. Top with almond halves and bake in a 375°F (180°C) oven for 15 minutes. Sprinkle with powdered sugar when cool.

Ethel Grayce
Cincinnati, Ohio

DESIREE ROSEN'S CHOCOLATE CREAM TRUFFLES

½ lb (250 g) high quality chocolate
1 cup (250 ml) cream
Or use nondairy creamer whipped topping for kosher requirements.

Melt chocolate in microwave on lower level 3 to 5 minutes or in double boiler. Heat cream to take off chill (should be warm, not hot). Mix together until smooth and shiny. Flavor with Van der Hum or liquor of your choice (optional). Mix until smooth.

Allow to set in refrigerator. Roll into small balls when firm. Roll in cocoa, chocolate vermicelli (sprinkles), grated white chocolate or chopped nuts or coat in melted chocolate and allow to set in refrigerator.

ETHEL'S ALMOND COFFEE TARTLETS

Shell:
¼ lb (125 g) butter
½ cup (125 ml) sugar
⅔ cup (160 ml) chopped almonds with skin

1 store bought pound cake or cream pound cake on Pg. 269.

Filling:
1 cup (250 ml) cream
1 tsp (5 ml) instant coffee
1 tsp (5 ml) cocoa
2-3 Tbs (30-45 ml) powdered sugar (icing sugar)

Beat all filling ingredients together until thick.

Cream butter and sugar. Add chopped almonds. Line small muffin pans with foil. Pour a little mixture into each pan and shape into shell. Bake 15 minutes and cool completely. Peel off foil.

Put 1 tsp (5 ml) of filling into shell. Cut pound cake slice to size of shell and put on top of filling. Put more filling on top. Put another shell on top of filling.

Ethel Grayce
Cincinnati, Ohio

FAT FREE FRUIT AND NUT CRUNCHIES

6 egg whites
1 cup (250 ml) sugar
2 heaped cups (500 ml) flour
1½ cups (375 ml) nuts—almonds, pecans, walnuts
1 cup (250 ml) mixed dried fruit—raisins, apricots, cherries, ginger, pineapple

Grease a 4½" x 8½" (11 x 21 cms) loaf pan. Cover base with paper and grease paper (or use nonstick spray). Beat egg whites until stiff. Gradually add sugar and continue to beat until very stiff and sugar has dissolved. Sift flour and combine with fruit and nuts. Fold this mixture into beaten whites. Turn into prepared pan and bake in a 350°F (180°C) oven for 40-50 minutes or until lightly browned.

Turn onto cooling rack. When thoroughly cooled (not necessarily the same day) cut into very thin slices using a serrated or electric knife. Place flat onto greased cookie sheets and bake again in a 350°F (180°C) oven until lightly browned, approximately 15 minutes.

These biscuits (cookies) are very crisp and crunchy.

FUDGE COOKIES

1½ cups (375 ml) flour
2 Tbs (30 ml) powdered sugar (icing sugar)
4 oz (125 g) butter

Filling:
1x14 oz (396 g) can condensed milk
½ cup (125 ml) tightly packed soft brown sugar
2 Tbs (30 ml) golden syrup or honey
4 oz (125 g) butter, cut into pieces
1 tsp (5 ml) vanilla

Topping:
½ cup (125 ml) semi-sweet chocolate chips

Method:
Place flour, sugar, and butter in food processor and blend to a crumbly dough. Press onto the bottom only of a 9" (22 cm) square nonstick pan. Prick dough and bake in a 350°F (180°C) oven until nicely browned—about 20-25 minutes. Remove from oven and cool thoroughly.

Prepare filling:
Place all filling ingredients, excluding vanilla, in a microwave-safe bowl. Cook on high (100% power) for 6 minutes, stirring every 2 minutes. Reduce to 50% power (power level 5) and cook another 5 minutes, stirring every minute. Cool slightly and add vanilla. Pour over cooled crust and allow to set.

Topping:
Melt chocolate in microwave-safe bowl on 30% power for 5-7 minutes. Spread over set fudge. Cut into squares when cold. This is easier to do if you wipe off the knife and dip in boiling water between each slice.

Peanut butter fudge cookies:
Stir 1 cup (250 ml) crunchy peanut butter into fudge filling immediately after cooking.

GRANNY ZELDA'S COOKIES

½ lb (250 g) butter
3 cups (750 ml) flour
2 tsp (10 ml) baking powder
⅔ cup (150 ml) sugar
2 eggs

2 Tbs (30 ml) vegetable oil
apricot jam
nuts and raisins
beaten egg

Rub butter into dry ingredients. Combine beaten eggs and oil. Mix to form a dough. (This may be done in the food processor.) Divide dough into 3 equal portions. Roll each portion into a rectangle shape approximately ¼" (1 cm) thick. Spread with apricot jam. Sprinkle nuts and raisins on top. Roll up, jelly roll fashion, and place on greased baking sheet. Brush with beaten egg and sprinkle cinnamon and sugar on top. Bake at 350°F (180°C) until golden brown for 20-25 minutes. Cut into slices when cool.

Jean Tobias
Cincinnati, Ohio

LILY'S RUMANIAN TOFFEES

9 oz (275 g) sugar
2 oz (60 g) cocoa
3 oz (75 g) honey
½ pt (300 ml) cream

In heavy saucepan, boil together all ingredients until soft ball stage. Pour into lined dish and allow to harden.

Dip knife in hot water to cut.

Jenny Weintraub
East London, South Africa

MERCIA'S EASY MERINGUES

Put the following ingredients in mixing bowl all together and beat until stiff:

2 egg whites
4 tsp (20 ml) vinegar
4 Tbs (60 ml) boiling water
1¾ cups (450 ml) superfine sugar (castor)

When stiff, using two spoons, form meringues onto a greased baking sheet and bake at 200°F (100°C) for ½ hour. Turn off oven and leave in oven to dry out.

NO BAKE FLORENTINES

Yield: 30

4 ozs (125 g) dark chocolate, melted
½ lb (250 g) marie biscuits or vanilla wafers, coarsely broken
2 Tbs (30 ml) KWV VSOP Brandy or Paarl Pale Dry Sherry
4 ozs (125 g) butter
½ cup (125 ml) sugar
½ lb (250 g) fruit mix (raisins, golden raisins, currants)
1 egg beaten
½ cup (125 ml) sliced almonds or pine nuts
½ cup (125 ml) red maraschino cherries, coarsely diced
coconut for sprinkling

Line a 9" (22 cm) square pan with foil. Spread the foil with melted chocolate. Press half the cookies onto the chocolate. Sprinkle with sherry or brandy and allow to set in refrigerator.

In a medium saucepan, place butter, sugar, fruit and egg and stir over medium health until mixture boils. Remove from heat. Stir in remaining cookies, nuts and cherries. Spread over refrigerated mixture. Sprinkle with coconut and return to refrigerator to set. Cut into squares when set and peel foil off bottom.

ORANGE DATE SLICES

2¼ cups (560 ml) flour
½ cup (125 ml) sugar
2 tsp (10 ml) ground ginger
¼ tsp (2 ml) mixed spice
grated rind of 1 orange
¼ lb (125 g) butter
2 eggs
2 Tbs (30 ml) golden syrup or Karo light syrup
1 tsp (5 ml) baking soda
1½ tsp (7 ml) warm water
½ lb (250 g) pitted dates
½ cup (125 ml) orange juice
egg white for glaze
sugar for sprinkling

Combine flour, sugar, ginger, mixed spice, and orange rind. Grate in butter. Add beaten eggs and warmed syrup. Add baking soda which has been dissolved in warm water. Form into dough.

Simmer dates with orange juice until soft, then mash them. Divide dough into three parts. Roll each into a long narrow strip. Spread with date mixture and roll up. Alternatively, you can spread with a mixture of apricot preserves, raisins, currants and golden raisins. Brush with egg white and sprinkle with sugar. Bake at 350°F (180°C) (one shelf above middle shelf) for approximately 25-30 minutes, or until golden brown. Cut into slices when cool.

Always plump your fruit by pouring boiling water over it. Rinse and pat dry or leave on absorbent paper overnight.

PECAN NUT COOKIES

1 cup (250 ml) ground pecan nuts (pecan meal)
¼ lb (125 g) butter, softened
2 Tbs (30 ml) sugar
1 cup (250 ml) flour
1 tsp (5 ml) vanilla

Combine all above ingredients. Roll into balls about the size of a walnut. Bake on a greased tray in a 325°F (160°C) oven for approximately 20 minutes. Dip in icing sugar (powdered sugar) while warm.

Before serving, you may wish to dip them again in icing sugar.

Shirley Levy
Cincinnati, Ohio

RUGELACH

Dough:
½ lb (250 g) butter
½ lb (250 g) cream cheese
2 cups (500 ml) flour
½ tsp (3 ml) salt

Cream butter and cream cheese together. Add flour and salt and combine to form dough. Wrap in paper and chill overnight.

Filling:
½ cup (125 ml) sugar
1 Tbs (15 ml) cinnamon
1 cup (250 ml) chopped walnuts
1 cup (250 ml) mixed raisins (golden raisins and currants)

Combine above ingredients.

Roll dough out thinly. Brush with melted butter and sprinkle with filling. Cut into 3" (7.5 cm) squares and roll up diagonally. Place on baking sheet sprayed with nonstick and bake in 350°F (180°C) oven for 15-20 minutes. Sprinkle thickly with powdered (icing) sugar when cool.

SHORTBREAD JAM COOKIES

1 lb (500 g) butter
1 cup (250 ml) sugar
4 cups (440 g) flour
apricot jam
confectioners' sugar

Cream butter and sugar and add flour to make a soft dough.

Roll out into small balls and press down slightly with fork.

Bake at 350°F (180°C) on an ungreased baking sheet until light brown.

While hot, using a small round cookie cutter, press over rounds to trim and make edges neat. Make a small hole in the center of half the cookies, using a smaller cookie cutter.

Sandwich together with apricot jam—dust with confectioners' sugar (icing sugar) and then fill hole with a small amount of additional jam.

Ethel Grayce
Cincinnati, Ohio

STEPH'S RUGELACH

Yield: 8 dozen

Dough:
½ lb (250 g) butter
1 cup (250 ml) sour cream
3¼ cups (800 ml) flour
½ tsp (3 ml) salt

Filling:
⅔ cup (160 ml) cinnamon and sugar
golden raisins
apricot jam
chopped walnuts

Cream butter and sour cream. Add flour and salt and blend well. Wrap in waxed paper and refrigerate 24 hours.

Roll dough into circles, spread with jam, sprinkle with cinnamon and sugar, chopped nuts and raisins. Cut circle into eighths, roll up from wide side first. Bake in 350°F (180°C) oven for 20 minutes.

Freezes well.

Stephanie Gilinsky
Cincinnati, Ohio

STICKY CINNAMON ROLLS

2 pkgs dry yeast
1 cup (250 ml) warm water
2 Tbs (30 ml) sugar
3-oz pkg (90 g) vanilla instant pudding
4 oz (125 g) butter, melted
2 cups (500 ml) milk
½ cup (125 ml) oil
2 eggs—jumbo
8 cups (1 kg) flour
1 tsp (5 ml) salt
additional melted butter
brown sugar
3 Tbs (45 ml) cinnamon

Combine yeast, warm water and sugar. Set aside.

Beat together vanilla pudding, melted butter, milk, oil and eggs. Mix flour and salt and make a well in the middle and add yeast and pudding mixture. Beat in with mixer until smooth. Cover and allow to rise overnight or until double in bulk.

Roll out, spread with melted butter, brown sugar (not too thick) and cinnamon. Roll up like a jelly roll and cut into 3" (8 cm) slices and place cut side up in greased patty pans (muffin pan). Allow to rise again for about ½ hour.

Bake at 350°F (180°C) for 15 minutes. Remove from oven and glaze with the following glaze:

1 lb (500 g) Philadelphia cream cheese mixed with ½ cup (125 ml) powdered sugar and a dash of vanilla essence. Add a little water if necessary.

TRIPLE CHOCOLATE WEDGES

Dough:
6 oz (175 g) butter
¾ cup (200 ml) sugar
1 egg
1 tsp (5 ml) vanilla
1 Tbs (15 ml) oil

1¼ cups (310 ml) flour
2 Tbs (30 ml) cocoa
pinch salt
1 tsp (5 ml) baking powder

Filling:
8 oz (250 g) dark chocolate, coarsely chopped
8 oz (250 g) milk chocolate, coarsely chopped
4 oz (125 g) butter
6 egg yolks and 1 whole egg
½ cup (125 ml) sugar
¼ cup (60 ml) KWV Van der Hum Liqueur
white chocolate for decoration

Cream butter and sugar. Add egg, vanilla, and oil and beat a little longer. Add sifted dry ingredients and blend into a dough. Roll into a 12" (30 cm) round; carefully roll the dough around the rolling pin and transfer to a nonstick (25 cm) round fluted tart pan with loose bottom, or if you prefer, merely press dough into pan. Press down gently against the sides of the pan; trim off excess; prick bottom with a fork and bake the shell in a 375°F (190°C) oven for 15-20 minutes. Allow to cool while preparing the filling.

Place dark chocolate, milk chocolate, and butter in a microwave safe dish and melt on power level 3 for 5-7 minutes. Stir until smooth. Whisk egg yolks and egg in a food mixer with sugar until light and creamy. Add liqueur and chocolate/butter mixture and whisk just until combined. Pour into cooled shell and return to 350°F (180°C) oven for 30 minutes or until set around the edges and slightly moist in the center. Cool and then refrigerate. Cut into wedges using a knife dipped in boiling water, wiping the knife off after each wedge.

Make chocolate ganache as follows:
2 cups (500 ml) cream
12 oz (300 g) dark chocolate, coarsely chopped

Heat cream until boiling; pour over chocolate and stir until melted. Cool until desired pouring consistency is required.

Place wedges on a cooling tray with a cookie sheet beneath. Pour ganache over each wedge, covering completely. Use ganache collected on cookie sheet again as needed. Allow to cool in refrigerator.

Place white chocolate in plastic bag and place in a bowl of boiling water to melt or melt in microwave on defrost. Snip just a tiny bit off one corner of the plastic bag with a sharp scissors and drizzle design over wedges.

TRUFFLE BROWNIES

4 oz (125 g) dark semi-sweet chocolate
½ lb (250 g) butter
1½ cups (375 ml) sugar
1¼ cups (310 ml) flour
½ tsp (2 ml) baking powder
4 eggs
1 tsp (5 ml) vanilla

Topping:
12 oz (375 g) semi-sweet chocolate
1 cup (250 ml) cream

Preheat oven to 350°F (180°C).

Melt chocolate and butter together over gentle heat, stirring constantly until smooth, or melt together in microwave on 50% power. Pour into large bowl and allow to cool.

Add eggs, sugar, sifted flour, baking powder and vanilla to chocolate/butter mixture and whisk all together just until well blended.

Grease and flour or spray with nonstick cooking spray, a 9" (23 cm) square baking pan. Pour mixture into pan and bake 45 minutes or until a skewer inserted in the center comes out clean. Remove from oven, place on cooling tray and allow to cool completely in pan.

Spread with topping; cut into squares; remove carefully from pan.

Topping:
Chop chocolate coarsely and place in bowl. Heat cream to boiling point. Pour over chocolate and stir until chocolate has melted completely. Refrigerate until thick. If it does not thicken sufficiently, beat until required consistency is reached.

WHITE CHOCOLATE CASHEW BROWNIES

4 oz (125 g) butter
2 cups (500 ml) brown sugar
2 eggs, slightly beaten
1 tsp (5 ml) vanilla
1¼ cups (300 ml) flour
2 tsp (10 ml) baking powder
1 cup (250 ml) high quality white chocolate pieces
1 cup (250 ml) toasted cashews, coarsely chopped

Preheat oven to 350°F (180°C). Lightly grease a 9" x 12" (22 x 27 cm) pan. In microwave, on medium heat, melt butter (2-3 minutes). Stir in brown sugar and allow to cool.

Add eggs, vanilla, sifted flour and baking powder and blend thoroughly. Fold in white chocolate and nuts. Spoon into prepared pan and bake 25-30 minutes or until a crust forms on top. Cool in pan 20 minutes. Cut into bars.

Melt additional white chocolate (microwave, power level 3, for 3-5 minutes); drop a tsp (5 ml) on top of each bar and top with additional toasted cashews (optional).